Tapestry of Memory

Tapestry of Memory

Evidence and Testimony in Life-Story Narratives

Nanci Adler
Selma Leydesdorff

editors

Transaction Publishers
New Brunswick (U.S.A.) and London (U.K.)

Copyright © 2013 by Transaction Publishers, New Brunswick, New Jersey.

All rights reserved under International and Pan-American Copyright Conventions. No part of this book may be reproduced or transmitted in any form or by any means, electronic or mechanical, including photocopy, recording, or any information storage and retrieval system, without prior permission in writing from the publisher. All inquiries should be addressed to Transaction Publishers, Rutgers—The State University of New Jersey, 35 Berrue Circle, Piscataway, New Jersey 08854-8042. www.transactionpub.com

This book is printed on acid-free paper that meets the American National Standard for Permanence of Paper for Printed Library Materials.

Library of Congress Catalog Number: 2012032344
ISBN: 978-1-4128-5165-7
Printed in the United States of America

Library of Congress Cataloging-in-Publication Data

Tapestry of memory : evidence and testimony in life-story narratives / Nanci Adler and Selma Leydesdorff, editors.
    p. cm.
 Includes bibliographical references and index.
 ISBN 978-1-4128-5165-7 (alk. paper)
 1. Historiography--Methodology--Case studies. 2. Memory--Case studies. 3. Collective memory--Case studies. I. Adler, Nanci. II. Leydesdorff, Selma.
 D16.T228 2013
 907.2--dc23

2012032344

Contents

Acknowledgments   vii

Introduction: On the Evidence Value of Personal Testimony   ix
Selma Leydesdorff and Nanci Adler

I   Official Testimony and Other "Facts and Evidence"

1   Historicizing Hate: Testimonies and Photos about the Holocaust Trauma during the Hungarian Post-WWII Trials   3
Andrea Pető

2   The Legacies of the Stalinist Repression: Narratives of the Children of Loyalist "Enemies of the People"   19
Nanci Adler

3   "You Don't Believe Me?": Truth and Testimony in Cypriot Refugee Narratives   37
Helen Taylor

4   Between Social and Individual Memory: Being a Polish Woman in a Stalinist Prison   55
Anna Muller

II   The Creation of a New History and the Integration of Collective Memory in the Story of One's Self

5   "They Didn't Rape Me": Traces of Gendered Violence and Sexual Injury in the Testimonies of Spanish Republican Women Survivors of the Franco Dictatorship   77
Gina Herrmann

6	On Testimony: The Pain of Speaking and the Speaking of Pain *Srila Roy*	97
7	Memories of Argentina's Past over Time: The Memories of Tacuara *María Valeria Galván*	111
8	History, Memory, Narrative: Expressions of Collective Memory in the Northern Cheyenne Testimony *Sachiko Kawaura*	133
9	Voices behind the Mic: Sports Broadcasters, Autobiography, and Competing Narratives of the Past *Richard Haynes*	153
III	**Claims Based on Narratives versus Official History**	
10	The "Book of Us": Will and Community in South African Land Restitution *Christiaan Beyers*	177
11	"What May or May Not Have Happened in the Past": Truth, Lies, and the Refusal to Witness Indigenous Australian Testimony *Kelly Butler*	199
12	Individual Desire or Social Duty? The Role of Testimony in a Restitution Procedure: An Inquiry into Social Practice *Nicole L. Immler*	219
List of Contributors		237
Index		241

Acknowledgments

This volume was made possible by the devoted work of a number of individuals to whom we would like to take this opportunity to acknowledge gratitude. In the first place, we would like to thank the contributing authors for their diligence, willingness to engage with our critical comments, patience, and conscientiousness, but mostly for the original work they have done and described here. We hope the questions they raise will be just the beginning of a discussion. The Oral History and Life Stories Network sessions of the European Social Science History Conference in Ghent in 2010 provided an excellent venue to develop many of the ideas that came to fruition in these chapters. New authors with new chapters were added at the conference of the International Oral History Association in 2010 in Prague. We are also thankful to Andrew McIntosh and the editorial team at Transaction Publishers for their great efficiency, Sara Mulder and Lotte van Helvoort for their technical help in Amsterdam, and Peter Froehlich of Indiana University Press for readily providing permissions. The NIOD Institute for War, Holocaust and Genocide Studies and the Department of Arts, Religion, and Culture of the University of Amsterdam facilitated time and space for us to work on what became a major project. Finally, and perhaps most important, we would like to thank our subjects for allowing us to listen to them and record their stories; we hope they find themselves faithfully represented in our narratives.

Introduction: On the Evidence Value of Personal Testimony

Selma Leydesdorff and Nanci Adler

Tapestries are made up of warps and wefts, intertwined threads that run parallel to the length and width of the loom. These cloths are woven together in complex and systematic ways that leave warp (length) threads hidden. What, we may ask, does this have to do with memory? The simple answer is that memory—in all its complexity—can be much like tapestry, weaving together, selecting, and shaping experience; memory's warps are the events it conceals under its surface. If we recognize memory's relationship to tapestry, then we can better understand the benefit of being able to probe with the tool of oral history of witnesses to events. We hope the present volume amply elucidates this argument, as we explore the warps and wefts of memory that analysis of a broad range of life stories has revealed.

Victims' testimonies and memoirs can be invaluable sources for filling in the blanks of official history and for directing us to new questions. They can teach us a number of things—for example, the fact that autobiographical accounts are not necessarily what happened but rather perceptions of what happened. They allow us to reconstruct a story, but no matter how true, each story is an edited version of the personal truth. Therefore, the storyteller must be placed in the proper sociohistorical context because life will always be more chaotic than the stories we construct to make sense of it. It is thus critical to researching autobiographies to recognize the narrative's constitutional incapacity to be lifelike, as philosopher Louis Mink has eloquently observed:

> stories are not lived but told. Life has no beginnings, middles, end . . . [they belong to] the story we tell ourselves later. There are hopes, plans, battles, and ideas, but only in retrospective stories are hopes unfulfilled, plans miscarried, battles decisive, and ideas seminal.[1]

One event could be described by different people who experienced it in entirely different ways. And at different times, stories are different, so we sometimes find a disjunction of narratives, even from the same individual. However, if we can ascertain common elements in the narratives of several individuals, testimony can be transformed into evidence, upon which we can draw substantiated conclusions. Important issues are the degree of accuracy of the teller's memory, how much of the experience is unique to the individual and how much is typical of such experiences, how current events might have influenced the memory, and what such influence might reveal about the past and the present. Further, before a narrative account is stamped as "true," it has to be accepted within the framework in which present-day vocabularies integrate the past and mediate the future. Accordingly, what is considered "truth" or "true" is not static but is influenced by various factors, which include memory, politics, and ideology.

An account not perceived as true in the past can become true at a different moment in history. For instance, if a woman raped by her husband filed a complaint to the police four decades ago, she might simply have been dismissed; rape was not considered to exist within marriage, and there was not even a label for her accusation. However, thinking about human rights has evolved, and the idea that a woman can be raped by her husband is now recognized. What happened to the woman is the same, her pain and shame might be the same, but the ways of describing it have dramatically changed.

Narratives also serve as a means through which subjects can express how they consider their lives to be interwoven with others. When the narrative is told to a responsive listener, this expression is part of a seemingly shared world, with shared frames of reference, where people agree on what is true or not true. Whether the narrative is official or personal, it organizes experience into a sequence of events and gives it meaning. Essentially, it tells us, "This is what happened," "This is what it meant," and "This is how we deal with it."[2] Narratives reconstruct reality by selecting what to attend to, what is important and unimportant, what is good and bad, and how events are causally linked to each other.[3]

Sometimes, in the case of spoken narratives or interviews, the narrative itself becomes an arena for exploring what is acceptable, transferable, and comprehensible. In this volume we offer a closer look at changing vocabularies and the way they influence the perception and framing of the past. The editors are historians, but through the interdisciplinary nature of the volume we seek to show how the same problem manifests itself in the broader field of cultural studies, sociology, and other forms of narrative studies.

Working with the volatile corpus of narrated personal accounts, we have become accustomed to being questioned about the evidence and truth value of our findings. But such questions are seldom discussed in terms of why and how vocabularies change, and how these changes recontextualize memory cultures.[4] We hope that this volume of wide-ranging case studies serves to fuel this debate. Our motivation stems from both of our fields of research: Nanci Adler has witnessed the rise or re-emergence in post-Soviet society of certain frameworks for remembering the past, and Selma Leydesdorff is keenly aware of how much the Holocaust has been reinterpreted since the countries of the former Soviet empire started to generate new stories and argue for new categories of victims. Consequently, the language to describe and interpret atrocities in Europe has changed dramatically.

The Reconstruction of Experience

Despite acknowledging that there is a changeable truth, outside academia—mostly in journalism—the search for an absolute truth is still dominant. Some traditions in the social sciences also seek an absolute truth, whereby representativeness is crucial to the sample. While the dichotomy of acceptance and rejection of the biographical turn[5]— qualitative research based on narratives[6]— has existed for decades, this volume aims first to engage with and then to move beyond the discussion by concentrating on the next steps that can be made.

We take for granted that researchers working with historical interviews recognize the malleability of memory and the subjective and changeable nature of narratives of the past, along with their vulnerability to self-censure. The latter is a particular challenge inherent to working with such subjective data. Oral historians have regularly defended themselves even before questions were raised, because of the fact that any personal narrative is just one reconstruction of what happened, and its utility is often constrained by the empirical limitations of generalizing from small subsets. Nevertheless, as noted above, support for the typicality of even a subset of one can be provided by confirming evidence from other personal narratives that converge on similar events.

We resolved to bring these themes together in a single volume to illuminate how "truth" and "evidence" form part of a much wider debate on the representation of history. It is our great pleasure to be able to add this contribution to the series *Memory and Narrative*, in which historical memories are not seen as primarily, or solely, resulting from proof or "hard facts." From this perspective, stories can serve as tools to facilitate our understanding of the changes in historical consciousness.[7]

Research on historical memories has followed changing and shifting trends. Some decades ago the "false memory debate" and the role of memories in lawsuits and trials overshadowed and obstructed a reasonable discussion about the historiographical value of memories.[8] Today the discussion is dominated by the debates in cognitive psychology and grand samples about forgetting,[9] as well as studies on the ways in which the brain stores memories.[10] Some researchers, who still question the quality or veracity of testimonies and consider eyewitness accounts and memory unreliable, garner support from studies of the brain and present-day neuroscientific advances. A plethora of conferences feature psychological studies showing how memory can be manipulated. However, one could argue that these investigations are concerned with the present rather than the past, and their conclusions should not be transferred to historians' and cultural scientists' objectives. It appears that we have now reached a crossroad of developments in the field, an auspicious moment to take a step back to reflect upon and a step forward to evaluate the value of narrative accounts of the past.

During the last three decades historians were not alone in acknowledging the crucial role memory plays in the reconstruction of the past. Elie Wiesel aptly named the modern age the "Age of Testimony." Leading scholars make use of memories, autobiographies, and other "changeable and subjective sources." Especially in the study of mass atrocity in the modern era, it has become the norm to use memories. Written and spoken narratives of the lived experience of events have offered a wider narrative than the data from traditional approaches, but only recently have the spoken narratives also been studied as *oral* sources. Using the text of a transcript is no longer sufficient because any spoken narrative about the past is the result of the context in which that story is told.

Today many memory communities have created their own collection of testimonies, or aim to do so. Their constituencies of survivors talk and testify about collective trauma as a result of natural disasters (for example, Hurricane Katrina), and about the memories of atrocities such as 9/11.[11] Sometimes document and video archives are created, and sometimes the voices of the protagonists are captured on film, as was the case in *Journey from the Fall*, in which Vietnamese refugees tell about their escapes and their horrendous lives under Vietnamese communism.[12] The victims' need to speak about what they endured can bring about acknowledgment and also empowerment in the repositioning of their self.[13] Psychologist D'Ann R. Penner has shown this function of speaking out in her oral history of Hurricane Katrina, wherein she describes how creating a monument brought with it unanticipated accusations about racism in the relief effort that followed the disaster.[14]

Personal narratives add the visceral immediacy of lived experience to the scholarly discourse of history. Because these experiences only become history as they are gleaned, contextualized, and disseminated, the history they become should be informed by their cultural, social, and historical provenance, along with their credibility and a consideration of how they may have been changed by the gleaning process.[15] As noted, challenges to their credibility include the failures and distortions of memory with the passage of time, sometimes made worse by traumatic stress.[16] Added to these is the unavoidable bias of their interpretive frame: all stories combine a description of what happened with an argument (often implicit) regarding how events should be construed. Political censorship prevents some stories from being told, and an overlapping self-censorship prevents some from even being conceived.[17]

Memory and Testimony

The distinction between memory and testimony is crucial to the theme of this volume. Memory is selective, but it can offer proof for the legal truth. The aim of testimony is to provide an audience with facts that can be transformed into evidence of what was seen or experienced.[18] As the German memory theorist Aleida Assmann has noted, modern historians are less concerned with the events "than the experience and aftermath of the events in the lives of those who experienced them and those who decide to remember them, together with the problem of how to represent them."[19] According to Assmann, history and memory are no longer rivals, as posited in the mid-1980s in Pierre Nora's magnum opus *Places of Memory*.[20] The increased valorization of testimony in court, especially international courts, is a major explanation for this shift. As a result of the increased legal use of testimony since the 1980s, a legal framework in which factual information is crucial to discerning truth has dominated and constrained testimony. The ensuing court narrative has not significantly served to advance the work of those who seriously study memory, because such approaches overly focus on the chronology, coherence of the story, and the consistency of the argument rather than the historian's concern for understanding the perception of history in an individual life. As Jan Gross, historian of the Holocaust, has cogently argued:

> It takes a moment (which sometimes may stretch into years or decades), and a *prise de conscience*, to realize that the vocabulary we employ—"victim," "testimony," "witness"—puts a deceptive courtroom frame on the story.[21]

In the early years of oral history, researchers were mostly seeking a new kind of truth—"other histories," considered to be perhaps more democratic or more valid as they addressed a wider range of social and political issues that were considered neglected by more traditional historiography. Lynn Abrams[22] has termed this process "recovery history." These historians aspired to present a different and valid image of the past, in which less privileged groups—or less accepted issues—became more visible. They argued that historians have always used testimonies and accounts of the past, and doubts about the generalizations that could be made from these sources have always existed. The collection and dissemination of such data gave certain groups of people a place in history. The argument that oral sources create new ways of looking at history, and through them we find, or sometimes reconstruct, new histories, is still valid and regularly validated.

It is apparent from, among other sources, the many stories published in our series and the research of both editors of this volume, that there are many gaps in our knowledge that interviews can fill. After years of listening to and recording the narratives of the survivors of Srebrenica, Selma Leydesdorff observed in her project with the last survivors of Sobibor that at the end of their lives, some of them revealed new information about their experience of this killing site.[23] And Nanci Adler conducted interviews, first to decipher the long-silenced story of return from the Gulag, and later to understand why some returnees—or their children—still or again believed in communism.[24] Indeed, those who interview will trace new facts, uncover new evidence, and perhaps most of all, be informed enough to assign new meanings to the past.

Developments in the Field

Over the decades, attention has shifted from the recovery history of the early period of oral history to new interpretations inspired by memory studies[25] and psychoanalysis, where the study of memory and—as a counterpoint—forgetting are central. Indeed, as noted above, memories are selective, and our greatest current challenge is the questions surrounding the relationship between the social aspects of memory, our personal desire sometimes to forget, our motivations for not disclosing or discussing certain subjects, and lastly, how we neurobiologically process what we see, feel, and experience.[26]

Studying memory is no longer only the historian's task. During the last forty years, research has moved beyond examining what happened to examining why it happened, how the story is told, and why it may change. These questions have led to new crossroads across disciplines. The various editions of the canonical text *The Voice of the Past*,[27] by Paul Thompson, and the history of the major edited textbooks for the field of oral history, trace this seminal change. While Thompson's early (1968) volume was primarily concerned with community history and the force of alternative histories, his 1988 volume contained a chapter called "Memory and the Self," in which he related his fascination with what had not been told, with dreams, fears, and fantasies, inner desires, and anxieties.[28] Thompson called for researchers to uncover "the sources of bias, rather than pretend they can be nullified,"[29] and he defended himself against the attack from sociologists who are satisfied only if they extrapolate from a random sample. Thompson reasoned thus:

> The historian starts with a difficulty not shared by the sociologists. If old people alive today were themselves a balanced cross-section of their generation in the past, in principle we should only need to draw a random sample from a list of their names ... But we can be certain that such a "random sample," although providing the most certain form of present representation, would distort the past. The historian can only create a frame which is, at least in some of its key dimensions, reliable.[30]

In Thompson's 2000 edition, the question of why something is told in a particular way took precedence over the former sociological evidence; the book reflects how the field underwent a tremendous development and was dominated by questions about (inter)subjectivity and interaction in the process of interviewing. It has become commonly accepted that narratives about the past change over time; they are always part of particular genres. Ron Grele, the former director of the distinguished Columbia Center for Oral History, stated in 1975, "Interviewees are selected, not because they present some abstract statistical norm, but because they typify historical processes."[31] This approach rests on the assumption that every individual experience represents a class of experiences. Thus, generalizations regarding that class can be inferred if we can accurately place the specific experience within its appropriate context.

Indeed we have come a long way from the early questions on representativeness and evidence, a development to which Italian oral historians Luisa Passerini and Alessandro Portelli fundamentally contributed.

Passerini opened the debate on what was *not* told during an interview. In her pathbreaking article in the *History Workshop Journal* on the apparent consensus during Italian fascism, she described the silenced story of dissent traceable in the propaganda, persistently targeting major strata of the population in a desperate effort to attract support.[32] Alessandro Portelli, in his turn, described how oral sources create a specific kind of knowledge,[33] while showing that conceptions of events could be collectively changed. For him, the "orality" of the interview about the past was most important. Portelli described oral sources as a narrative in which the boundary between what takes place outside the narrator and what happens inside, between what concerns the individual and what concerns the group, may become more elusive than in established written genres, such that personal "truth" may coincide with shared imagination.[34] His book, *The Order Has Been Carried Out,* describes the various meanings assigned to a massacre during the Second World War in Rome and the different lenses through which the stories of this mass murder are viewed.[35] From analyzing the distortion of data by memory, Portelli ventured on to confront historical consciousness and the assignment of meaning.

The last decades of the twentieth century marked the launch of several major international projects, especially on the Second World War, as the ranks of surviving witnesses began to dwindle. Examples are the Mauthausen Documantation Project[36] in Austria and the German Forced Labour Project.[37] Historians crossed paths in these projects with the many therapists who had been treating survivors suffering from the psychological difficulty of negotiating their trauma and (re)integrating into everyday life. The rapprochement also came from the side of psychology. Much earlier, in 1979, psychoanalyst Dori Laub and others started the renowned Fortunoff collection at the Yale University library. Most of its researchers were not historians.[38] The enormous collection of the Shoah Visual Foundation, which Steven Spielberg established in 1994 with a different purpose, is yet another example of the trend of gathering life-story interviews.[39] Because the interviews for the latter project were conducted on such a large scale, and because they were videotaped, this collection gave a major impetus to the use of new technologies, even if it failed to make a significant intellectual and theoretical contribution to the debate on (difficult) memories.

In the former communist world, from the moment survivors broke their silence, life stories have been collected,[40] and there are ongoing initiatives in Latin America (especially Argentina), Cambodia, Indonesia, and Africa, to name just a few of the vast range of societies embracing this approach to chronicling experience in the aftermath of repression.[41] Most recently, a major collection on memories of September 11 has been added to the Columbia Center for Oral History. The quantity is so large and diverse that it is as yet unpredictable how these archives may be used in the future.[42] And this is but a sampling of the many collections that exist today.

Memory and Oral History

For three decades our series *Memory and Narrative* and its predecessors have studied the various mediations of the past in memory. As we became increasingly interested in the mediation of memory, we have consistently tried to map out the next steps for thinking about oral history. We have worked in shifting interdisciplinary groups and with several different publishers. Our major focus has been how memory is transmitted, mediated, and transformed. We have also published work on how speaking about the past is interwoven into existing genres, and the editors of the volume *Narrative and Genre*[43] expanded on Elisabeth Tonkin's pioneering book *Narrating Our Pasts*.[44] In that work, Tonkin argued that all stories of our pasts—even speaking up informally—are part of genres. In the volumes *Contested Pasts* and *Regimes of Memory*, Susannah Radstone and Kate Hodgkin analyzed the ways in which stories disappear from our perceptions of memory, often as a result of social and political forces.[45]

Memory and oral history are, more than anything else, personal interpretations of the past that assign meaning to events. What is remembered is in part the result of an interaction between the public and the collective, between the teller and the audience. Consequently, research has also been carried out on the ways in which the public can shape memory,[46] following Maurice Halbwach's work on collective memory.[47] Some stories are well received and believed to be "true." These stories may reflect how people want to look at history and events at a particular moment. A validating audience can make a difficult story easier to tell. The proceedings of the South African Truth Commission (TRC), for example, not only revealed the participants' experiences but also contributed to forging an inclusive national history, because the TRC facilitated a dialogue between official and personal narratives.

It is well known that memories of the past and the process of remembrance are discursive fields that can vary tremendously. They are continuously subject to transformation in the context of the strong interaction between individual and collective memories. This relationship between the collective and the individual has given rise to a rich debate among historians and scholars from other disciplines such as cognitive sciences, neurosciences, cultural studies, anthropology, transitional justice, and many others interested in the past. In the process of storing events in the personal memory, the social environment is crucial to the selection of memories and to the ways they are glued together to constitute the identity of the person who remembers. Inevitably, the present as well as expectations for the future influence this process. Memory not only stores the past but restructures, mediates, and adapts it to the semantic frames and needs of a given society. The memory of personal experience is therefore embedded in and voiced within the historical frames, genres, and grand narratives that enable individuals to make sense of their experiences and to have a credible voice in their societies. Other moments of the creation of facts will pose the same historiographic problems described above.

The Pursuit of Evidence

In the aforementioned context, the ties between testimony (and many oral histories bear profound resemblance to testimony), history, and the law have always been very close. Judicial testimony, as implied above, generally does not attend to other histories. The courts cannot deal with, nor are they mandated to specifically address, such matters as despair, imagination, and that which is not obvious. Courts seek testimony, but they do not want life stories. By and large, judges do not bear witness to the whole trauma.[48] Nevertheless, the law and its languages are relevant influences on the way historians have to argue. Only by solid argumentation can a historian's work persuasively reconstruct reality and create an image of what is assumed to be true.

The production of evidence is indeed an integral part of the discipline of history, and we should bear in mind that the historical tradition is originally rooted in the juridical. The interaction between the two fields has focused historians' attention on events, but the trend of studying attitudes and mentalities has enabled historians to explore the less obvious. The venue of the courtroom has shown us that different actors hold widely varied—even conflicting—versions of the same events. In his brilliant article "Judging History," Richard Wilson demonstrated how in the case of modern international courts, the judges write history,[49] or at least a certain narrative of how and why events transpired. As an example, some Yugoslavia Tribunal judgments have contributed to the pursuit of historical accuracy regarding the causes of the conflict, yet contending parties often enter and leave the courtroom with their own "truths" still intact.[50] Not surprisingly, many of the detailed histories of destruction in the former

Yugoslavia are based on thousands of testimonies. The Eichmann trial set the precedent for the massive use of victims' testimonies.[51] However, we should not forget that the fabrication of spurious evidence was also a mechanism of Communist persecution.

The foregoing reflects on the types of gaps and the multitude of advances in the field of oral history and narrative study with regard to how to evaluate personal testimony. This discussion was partly inspired by and partly a response to the questions our contributors addressed. When we received the reactions to our call for papers on the creation of evidence, many writers suggested articles dealing with testimony in stories involving lawsuits and legal claims—with a focus on how it was being used, what was being told, and what was not being told. From the rich number of submissions, we have selected a sample of essays in which the construction of evidence is central, but we have not limited ourselves to testimony. Many of our contributing authors have offered fresh approaches to this question.

Part I: Official Testimony and Other "Facts and Evidence"

Since the theme of this volume is truth and evidence, we have also included several pieces that are based not solely on oral history but on narratives in documents, testimonies and eyewitness accounts. We surmise that these also inform us about ways to deal with the changing nature of testimony. We open this volume with an article by Andrea Pető, who describes how early tribunals of Nazi criminals in Hungary were venues where victims spoke up and showed their emotions. But gradually these emotions were channeled into "normalization," as she characterizes the trials, over the course of which the emotions of victims became more and more absent. Communist language replaced the cries, whispers, and mourning of survivors. A photograph informed Pető of the way in which the trials were slowly transformed so as to become part of mainstream history, while in the public arena they became less emotionally laden. People gradually learned how to testify and speak about their experiences, and the hate toward Jews and desire for revenge on perpetrators were replaced by the construction of a legal truth.

In its turn, this legal truth led to a dominant anti-fascist rhetoric during the Cold War, which was less and less connected to the emotions of suffering. By purporting to offer a venue to speak up and to inscribe victims' stories into the mainstream historical narrative, the tribunals became successful anti-fascist courts, making political use of what had happened. This theater of the People's Courts was one of the first forums in Europe in which the horrors of Nazism were publicly told. Only later did the Nuremberg trials follow. Despite their moving testimonies during that period, Pető describes how the deep emotions felt by those who testified became publicly lost and forgotten.

Nanci Adler describes the ways in which children of Communist inmates of the Gulag had internalized a particular vision of history and how that narrative enabled them to accept or adapt to what had happened to their parents and to go on with their lives. Of all the articles offered here, her discussion challenges us the most to consider the coexistence of separate "truths" and the veracity, even validity, of counterintuitive accounts. The children of executed or imprisoned parents were often raised in orphanages, where attempts were regularly made to indoctrinate them into believing that their parents were "enemies of the people." With regard to discerning their own sentiments toward the Party that victimized their parents, Adler writes that "the narrators are often so guarded that it is difficult to distinguish between their accommodation *to* the immutable and their assimilation *of* the immutable—probably even for them." She cites a variety of examples of belief in stories and/or adaptation to them, starting with a mother who remained loyal to Communism despite her ordeal in the camps. Others rejected the Party because of its repressive policies.

Some of the subjects were interviewed in the post-Soviet era, and some of the narrative memoir accounts emerged from the Gorbachev era. All were engaged in the process of revisiting their belief in Communism, understanding the nature of the repression, and reconsidering what had happened to their parents. But a grounded assessment of the past was often difficult because it could devalue the suffering in the camps and the heroism of survival and endurance. Some of these children of Communist victims appeared to need the protection and security the Communist Party seemed to give them. Their personal story of repression became the true story of repression, and they did not question their interpretation of facts. They had incorporated the Party's narrative into their own and struggled with the post-Soviet revelations. Their moral defeat was averted by the state's positive version of history, and by self-imposed censorship, both of which have outlasted the demise of Communism.

How we can trust that the oral account is really the memory of something? How can we believe there is truth in the stories people do not want to listen to? Helen Taylor tackles this problem in her essay. She argues that since narratives are individual, it is difficult to make generalizations, and since memories are so diverse it is hard to understand patterns. Refugees are often obliged to lie during the process of their application for asylum.

In her research with Turkish and Greek refugees from Cyprus, she experienced moments of her own disbelief, resulting in not following up on narratives that were important for the life story. She learned to recognize that sometimes elements are introduced to make the meaning of the narrative clearer. In the case of her interviews, the weeping Panagia (Virgin Mary) was one such example. She realized that this story had more to do with the narrator's desire to be believed than the need for her losses to be acknowledged. Following Dori Laub, who wrote that prior knowledge should not "hinder or obstruct listening with foregone conclusions and preconceived dismissals," she understood that unexpected information might emerge. She also concluded that it might be useful to give the refugees control over the narrative, and the act of speaking up facilitated the transition from victim to agent.

During the interview, the subjects tried to make sense of their past and a chaotic world. Taylor argues that their stories impelled her to question her own preconceptions and gave her insight into the interaction between the collective and the individual experience. For some, talking about the past and being believed was empowering; for others speaking was painful. The tension between the desire to bear witness and the desire to forget often brings about conflicting impulses. Based on her observations, Taylor asserts that the complexity of the ensuing silence and pain challenges evidence-based research, because emotional truth is complex and difficult to recover. She concludes that it is exactly that side of the story that can illuminate new realities and experiences.

Another group of contributions to this book deals with how people present themselves during testimony. In the articles of Anna Muller and Gina Herrmann we hear the voices of women who have been victims of violence, resulting in long prison terms. They were victims of criminal laws and were subjected to prolonged periods of lawsuits, punishment, accusations, and torture. They all share their accounts not as mere victims, but as survivors with life stories of pride. Especially in the work of Anna Muller, who interviewed such former inmates in Polish Communist prisons, the women retained their dignity. Her work appears to be partially inspired by Katherine Jolluck's research on Polish female prisoners in the Gulag, in which she shows how women maintained their pride and personalities.[52] What they told had nothing to do with the formal side of life in a camp. Anna Muller tries to demystify the existing images of women who had become role models of resistance. The interviewed women tried to establish their own space to show how different their experience was and how much they did not fit into a standard representation. By listening as carefully as Muller did, she offered them the chance to talk about events that had become important over time.

These women appeared as heroines, strong and unbreakable, and their strength had always been related to the wish for an independent Poland. Their wills, it seemed, would never be broken. But the interviews created room for sorrow, hesitation, and regret. It was possible to show agency under extremely harsh conditions then and during the interviews now. But since the author was looking for what it meant to them to be a woman, she ultimately admits that the traditional model of a Polish woman she describes in her article gives very little space for understanding that.

Part II: The Creation of a New History and the Integration of Collective Memory in the Story of One's Self

Gina Herrmann also conducted interviews on being a victim of political repression in her article on republican women suffering in Spanish Fascist cells. She explicitly wanted to locate stories of sexual violence against women, because the stories that have been told over the years have been smothered by taboo and shame. Herrmann is not describing the acts of violence as such; rather, she is focused on the way in which women narrate, and are evasive about, what actually transpired. There are many ways to hint at sexual violence. The oral testimonial project of these women is fraught with a tension between competing discourses of heroic activism, resistance, and political bravery, on the one hand, and memories of sexualized violence, on the other, Hermann reports. She doubts that we should take traumatic stories as an immediate truth or a representation of reality but rather suggests that we should interpret them as signs of survival and adaptation. These subjects used and still use a changing truth as a way to protect themselves.

Speaking of pain is the theme of Srila Roy's study of the extreme left Naxelbari movement in eastern India. She discusses the priority given by feminist historians to testimony and speaking up. Roy interviewed men and women for periods of three to seven years and then focused on the single case of Latika, who witnessed the torture of her immediate family and took it upon herself to make a case against the police. Interviewing Latika, it became clear that she was too traumatized to record her life story, and too concentrated on precise details. Roy considers her act of speaking up, her telling this story to give truth a material basis, as a performative speech act. It enabled her suffering to become part of the public domain. But, as Roy argues, the act of testimony "forecloses the possibility of listening to and acknowledging individual suffering," while bearing witness for others erases the self. Hence, the survivor's truth becomes less important than the truth of the witness. An artificial, plural "we" stands in contrast to the "I" who suffers.

Valeria Galván explores the memories of the right-wing Tacuara movement in Argentina over time. Although for a long time this movement—which originated in the sixties—was viewed extremely negatively, new examination of the leftist militancy of the seventies made some revisit and rethink their attitudes toward the organization. Gradually attitudes shifted, and the image of the Tacuara became more positive. Originally deemed anti-Semitic, the movement was able to salvage some esteem from the left for their successful de-Nazification efforts within the organization. The fact that they were among the first urban guerilla movements gave them a place in the history of the radical left. Galvan describes the confrontation between the subjective memories of ex-members and the ideological and mental narratives of the past in the public. As it now stands, members of this extremely violent guerilla movement have come to be viewed as idealistic youth, but at the same time the demonized image of them has also persisted for some. These public transformations and fluctuations resound in the interviews Galvan conducted with former members, who were tragic but idealistic figures.

In her study of Cheyenne stories, Sachiko Kawaura traces the collective memory that stands in sharp contrast to the official American narrative. Her focus is on the story of the Exodus from Indian Territory (1878). This story is used to support the tribe's claim to the right of living on the land. When the Northern Cheyenne were forced to live on Indian Territory in the aftermath of the wars of the 1870s, a group of hundreds of people left in 1878 to return to their homeland. After being captured, they refused to go back to the Territory. The Exodus led to the creation of a reservation, and today 99 percent of the reservation land is owned by the tribe or individual tribe members.

Kawaura describes how in the struggle of the tribes, the Exodus story—now framed as a sacrifice—has a constitutive role. In the oral histories she recorded, Kawaura shows how this collective memory is interwoven with personal memories. The interviewees express their connection with the traditions of their community in stories in which they adapt the collective memory of the tribe in order to make sense out of their private experiences. Among these, the story of the Exodus is the most telling, as it is based on the connection to history, land, and cultural practices. The ensuing narrations provide a counter-history to the national history of the United States, offering a new "truth" that we can derive from new interpretations of narrated evidence.

From a vastly different perspective, Richard Haynes explores the linkage between individual and collective narratives of sports broadcasting histories, and discusses how broadcasting engaged with sports and transformed it as a cultural form. Particularly relevant to the current volume is the way in which this essay analyzes the "historical and theoretical usefulness of autobiography in understanding the past." It looks at autobiography as documentary evidence and asks what the autobiography can contribute to the historical record. By combining the autobiographical account with other types of empirical evidence, Haynes argues, we gain access to "more tacit knowledge"—in this case, of how this genre worked, what characterized the people who made it, and how memories are retained.

Haynes explores how autobiographies "reinstate the voices" of practitioners, whose stories differ from the "official," traditional history of broadcasting. Much can be understood about class and gender, for example, if we use these narratives to examine how commentators began their careers. Such social distinctions were important for the BBC. Further, Haynes asserts that autobiography helps us to gain historical perspective on the key social role audiences play in the message delivered. One radio commentator, he tells us, shaped his technique for addressing the audience by having a blind man sitting next to him as he broadcast. Another had a deaf war veteran sit in front of the commentators' box, which impelled him to explain the game clearly, using a conversational mode since he was, in fact, interacting with this "listener." The commentators' accounts of these and other practices offer insight into how the broadcast narrative was framed. Haynes' essay also illustrates how such investigation offers a different history, one focusing on the commentators' biographies rather than the better-known biographies of those they commented on. Some of their autobiographies, Haynes informs us, "topped the non-fiction charts," giving a special voice and audience to those who had not been the protagonists.

Part III: Claims Based on Narratives versus Official History

As Chris Beyers shows, speaking to one another in a group context can create new evidence, which is the product of the dialogue between people. Beyers did field work in South Africa, an exemplary case of spoken testimonies gaining official status, played a major role in the hearings of the Truth and Reconciliation Commission. These testimonies became admissible, even indispensable, evidence for legal claims. Their strength is reinforced when a group of victims shares a narrative and forms a community memory. In his essay, Beyers focuses on the memories of residents of the notorious District Six in Cape Town, from which the old inhabitants had been forcibly removed. Meetings demanding land restitution brought the former residents together for the first time since their displacement. Their restitution claims were based on a collective memory and the creation of a commonality of experience, while they also expressed the claimants' entitlement to the space that had been personally theirs.

By speaking with groups, Chris Beyers gains perspective on their sense of their moral and political rights. In analyzing interviews and group discussions, Beyers finds theoretical support in the work of Mikhail Bakhtin, on the dialogue with others. Using Bakhtin's framework, Beyers seeks to understand how claimants in fact constitute their own moral grounds for truth, regardless of the fact that these may be construed as distorted from within a positivistic or legalistic evidential framework. The individual utterance is viewed as the result of a reaction to a conversation where the self is oriented towards the other in forming an identity.

In her essay on Indigenous Australian testimony, Kelly Butler argues that telling a story involves two parties: one that tells and one that listens—an empathic listener, in Laub's terms. While some non-Indigenous Australians were willing to act as "secondary witnesses" to affirm the truth of the testimony so that it would be better accepted, others—indeed many prominent Australians—refused. The 1997 Report of the Human Rights and Equal Opportunity Commission into the Separation of Aboriginal and Torres Strait Islander Children from their Families, *Bringing Them Home*, was mostly based on oral testimonies. A conservative media backlash fostered skepticism, and the report was accused of being untrue and biased. Butler notes that the Prime Minister was among those who urged Australians to stop "navel gazing" about what "may or may not have happened in the past." The report became a catalyst for the debate on justice, responsibility, and the nation. It split Australian society on the question of how much the non-Indigenous should be compelled to listen and eventually apologize.

The acceptance of intergenerational responsibility by non-Indigenous Australians was replaced by "practical" reconciliation aimed at encouraging Indigenous Australians to improve their lives. This approach denied their right to testify, while testimony was crucial to the process of reconciliation as it had developed over the years. Serious doubts were expressed about testimonies regarding the abduction of children, and those who spoke up were accused of a "false memory syndrome." Their testimony was contested by "real facts"; the spoken word was replaced by the written document. In one case, a mother was found guilty of having consented to the removal of her child from her home. Gradually, all Indigenous testimony came under suspicion, and the vocal minority of secondary witnesses who had supported their stories was marginalized. Indigenous testimony and its vision of history were accused of tainting the colonial past. Butler emphasizes that by not accepting the role of the secondary witnesses, testimony was made impossible, and with it an active and responsible force for change.

In her article on restitution claims, Nicole Immler traces how in the course of the restitution process, Jewish victims of Nazi persecution were gradually allowed to speak up. Originally the proceedings left little space for experiences of everyday life and suffering. Even though this suffering could never be sufficiently compensated, the survivors nevertheless wanted to tell what they felt. They were not trusted, and the authorities asserted that many cases did not constitute a rightful claim. The Eichmann trial of 1961, by including the experience of victims, gave them agency. Despite this change many victims preferred to be silent in a world that would not understand them.

Although at first the petitioners had only been asked to confirm what was in the documents, they gradually came to be considered people who were eyewitnesses to an epoch, who could mediate the past with the help of emotions. Immler carefully tracks the involvement of testimonies in Austria's dealings with compensation. In one case, a woman's petition was turned down; Immler analyzes the traumatic result of the bureaucratic negotiations that followed. Though the claimant wanted to speak up on behalf of her murdered family, she hesitated to entrust herself to an unknown decision-maker and to testify in front of an unknown audience. Immler shows how this case highlights the performative dimension of testifying, which has no fitting place for what the eyewitness really wants to say. In the end, written archival documents and her ability to navigate her way through the formal side of the procedure allowed this survivor to win her case. Immler's investigation offers a cautionary tale for the field of transitional justice. Despite recognition of the importance of testimony, it has also proved to be a source of frustration, because the eyewitnesses are often confronted with an institution that, as Immler argues, "looks for concrete truth and evidence," which is not the same as the need for "a comprehending mind, which means the whole communication process itself, is at least as important as the outcome of the proceedings."

Our hope with *Tapestry of Memory* is to give the debate among interviewers new fuel to revisit and rethink the relationship between their descriptions and their desire to describe a story as closely as possible to what they think is true. Given that much of contemporary history is contested or challenged by other visions and versions, we sincerely believe that questions about representation, generalization, and truth are only limitedly useful. A more overarching, central, and critical theme remains how the interactions between society, the state, legal mechanisms, and the individual change ideas of what constitutes reality and truth, testimony and evidence.

Notes

1. Louis O. Mink, "History and Fiction as Modes of Comprehension," *New Literary History* 1(1969): 557–558.
2. Nanci Adler, *Keeping Faith with the Party: Communist Believers Return from the Gulag* (Bloomington: Indiana University Press), 2012, 70–71.
3. George Gerbner, "Cultural Indicators: The Third Voice," *Communications Technology and Public Policy*, eds. George Gerbner, Larry Gross, Willian H. Melody (New York: John Wiley and Sons, 1973), 555–573.
4. Exceptions are two volumes in our series: Susannah Radstone and Kate Hodgkin, *Memory, History, Nation: Contest Pasts* (New Brunswick: Transaction Publishers, 2005); Susannah Radstone and Kate Hodgkin, *Regimes of Memory* (New Brunswick: Transaction Publishers, 2003).
5. Prue Chamberlain, Joanna Bornat, Tom Wengraf, *The Turn to Biographical Methods in Social Science* (London: Routledge, 2000).
6. Catherine Kohler Riessman, *Narrative Methods for the Human Sciences* (Los Angeles: Sage Publications 2008).
7. See Lynn Abrams, *Oral History Theory* (London: Routledge, 2010).
8. Most important was Elizabeth F. Loftus, *Eyewitness Testimony* (Cambridge: Harvard University Press, 1979).
9. William Hirst, et al. "Long-Term Memory for the Terrorist Attack of September 11: Flashbulb Memories, Event Memories, and the Factors that Influence Their Retention," *Journal of Experimental Psychology* 138, 2 (2009): 161–176; Yves Burnod, *An Adaptive Neural Network: The Cerebral Cortex* (Upper Saddle River, NJ: Prentice Hall, 1991); see also Yifat Gutman, Adam D. Brown, and Amy Sodaro, eds., *Memory and the Future: Transnational Politics, Ethics and Society* (New York: Macmillan, 2010).
10. An exciting example can be found in the "Memorial de Caen," where by inserting sensors in the exhibition, neurologists are finding out what visitors physically experience when they see the mass of objects presented there. They assume that people will mainly remember the objects upon which they had focused or been attracted to.
11. Mary Marshall Clark, "Herodotus Reconsidered: An Oral History of September 11, 2001, in New York City," *Radical History Review*, 111 (Fall 2011): 79–89.
12. Ham Tran, *Journey from the Fall*, DVD, www.geniusproducts, 2007.
13. Erika Apfelbaum, "And Now What, After Such Tribulations? Memory and Dislocation in the Era of Uprooting," *American Psychologist* 55 (2000): 1008–1013; Dori Laub, "Truth and Testimony, The Process and the Struggle" in *Trauma: Explorations in Memory* ed. Cathy Caruth (Baltimore: Johns Hopkins University Press, 1995), 61–76; Paul Gready, *Writing as Resistance: Life Stories of Imprisonment, Exile,*

and *Homecoming from Apartheid South Africa* (Lanham, MD: Lexington Books, 2003).

14. D'Ann R. Penner, "Assault Rifles, Separated Families, and Murder in Their Eyes: Unasked Questions after Hurricane Katrina," *Journal of American Studies* 44 (2010): 573–599; see also D'Ann R. Penner and Keith C. Ferdinand, *Overcoming Katrina: African American Voices from the Crescent City and Beyond* (New York: Palgrave, Macmillan, 2009).
15. Jo Beahrs, "Memory as Power: Who is to Decide?," *Journal of the American Academy of Psychiatry and the Law* 27 (1999): 462–470; Jerome Bruner, "Life as Narrative," *Social Research* 71 (2004): 11–32; Jerome Bruner, "The Narrative Construction of Reality," *Critical Inquiry* 18 (1991): 1–21. See also Thomas D. Albright, Eric R. Kandel, and Michael I. Posner, "Cognitive Neuroscience," *Current Opinion in Neurobiology* 10 (2000): 612–624.
16. Marc D. Feldman and Jacqueline M. Feldman, with Roxanne Smith, *Stranger Than Fiction: When Our Minds Betray Us* (Washington DC: American Psychiatric Press, 1998).
17. See Adler, *Keeping Faith*; Choman Hardi, *Gendered Experiences of Genocide* (London: Ashgate, 2011).
18. In the fascinating production "I Came to Testify," from the PBS series *Women, War, and Peace*, (producer Pam Hogan); sixteen women talk about being raped in Foca during the Bosnian war. These testimonies led to a new interpretation of rape as a crime by ICTY. See http://www.pbs.org/wnet/women-war-and-peace/full-episodes/i-came-to-testify/
19. Aleida Assmann, "History, Memory, and the Genre of Testimony," *Poetics Today*, 27 (2006): 263.
20. The canonical work of Pierre Nora, *Les Lieux de Memoire*, 7 TOMES, (Paris, 1984–86) made a sharp distinction between history and memory. It is part of the weakness of the work.
21. Jan Grosz, "One Line at a Time," *Poetics Today* 27 (2006): 425–429.
22. Abrams, 5.
23. Selma Leydesdorff, *Surviving the Bosnian Genocide: The Women of Srebrenica Speak* (Bloomington: Indiana University Press, 2011).
24. Nanci Adler, *The Gulag Survivor: Beyond the Soviet System* (New Brunswick: Transaction Publishers, 2002); Adler, *Keeping Faith*. . . .
25. Susannah Radstone, Bill Schwarz, *Memory: Histories, Theories, Debates* (New York: Fordham University Press, 2010).
26. Yifat Gutman, Adam D. Brown, and Amy Sodaro, "Introduction: Memory and the Future; Why a Change of Focus is Necessary," in *Memory . . . and the Future . . .*: 1–9.
27. Paul Thompson, *Voice of the Past: Oral History* (New York: Oxford University Press, 1968, 1988, 2000); new edition forthcoming.
28. Paul Thompson, *Voices of the Past: Oral History* second edition (New York: Oxford University Press, 1988), 154.
29. Ibid., 117.
30. Ibid., 125.
31. Ronald J. Grele, "Movement without Aim, Methodological and Theoretical Problems in Oral History," in *The Oral History Reader*, eds. Robert Perks and Alistair Thomson, (London: Routledge, 1998), 41. (Original published in Ronald J. Grele and Studs Terkel, *Envelopes of Sound: The Art of Oral History,* Greenwood Publishing Group, 1985. We have cited from this excellent reader because it is more widely available.)
32. Luisa Passerini, "Work, Ideology and Consensus under Italian Fascism," *History Workshop Journal* 8 (1979): 82–108. See also Passerini, *Fascism in Popular Memory* (New York: Cambridge University Press, 1987).

33. Later reprinted as Alessandro Portelli, "What Makes Oral History Different?" in *The Death of Luigi Trastulli: Form and Meaning in Oral History* (Albany: SUNY Press, 1992), 45–58.
34. Ibid., 49.
35. Alessandro Portelli, *The Order Has Been Carried Out: History, Memory, and Meaning of a Nazi Massacre in Rome* (New York: Palgrave Macmillan, 2003).
36. Gerhard Botz, Alexander Prenninger and Regina Fritz, eds., *Mauthausen überleben und erinnern*. vol. 1: *Wege nach Mauthausen* (Münster and Vienna: LIT Verlag, 2011).
37. Alexander von Plato, Almut Leh, Christoph Thonfeld, eds., *Hitler's Slaves: Life Stories of Forced Laborers in Nazi-occupied Europe* (New York: Berghahn Books, 2010).
38. Dori Laub and Federico Finchelstein, "Memory and History from Past to Future: A Dialogue with Dori Laub on Trauma and Testimony," in Gutman, et al. *Memory...*, 50–66.
39. Henry Greenspan, *On Listening to Holocaust Survivors: Recounting and Life History* (Westport, CT: Praeger, 1998).
40. The organization Memorial (www.memo.ru) has conducted a number of oral history projects since 1988, and there are several such initiatives being carried out throughout the former East bloc.
41. The International Center of Transitional Justice has created a Truth and Memory Program to support initiatives that address these issues throughout the world.
42. Nancy MacKay *Curating Oral Histories: From Interview to Archive* (Walnut Creek, CA: Left Coast Press, 2007). Juliana M. Nykolaiszyn, review of *Curating Oral Histories: From Interview to Archive*, by Nancy MacKay, *Oral History Review* 36 (2009): 302–304.
43. Mary Chamberlain and Paul Thompson, *Narrative and Genre* (New Brunswick: Transaction Publishers, 2004).
44. Elizabeth Tonkin, *Narrating our Pasts: The Social Construction of Oral History* (New York: Cambridge University Press, 1992).
45. Susannah Radstone and Kate Hodgkin, *Memory, History, Nation: Contested Pasts* (New Brunswick: Transaction Publishers, 2005); Susannah Radstone and Kate Hodgkin, *Regimes of Memory* (New Brunswick: Transaction Publishers, 2003).
46. Molly Andrews, *Shaping Histories: Narratives of Political Change* (New York: Cambridge University Press, 2007).
47. Erika Appelbaum, "Halbwachs and the Social Properties of Memory," in Radstone and Schwarz, *Memory...*, 77–93; Maurice Halbwachs, *Les Cadres Sociaux de la Memoire* (Paris: Albin Michel, 1994); Maurice Halbwachs, *La memoire collective* (Paris: Presses Universitaire de France, 1950).
48. Selma Leydesdorff, "How Shall we Remember Srebrenica?: Will the Language of Law Structure Our Memory?" in Gutman, et al. *Memory of the Future*, 121–141.
49. Richard Wilson, "Judging History: The Historical Record of the International Tribunal for the Former Yugoslavia," *Human Rights Quarterly* 27 (2005): 908–942.
50. Andreas Gross, "Draft resolution and report on the use of experience of 'Truth Commissions'," report to the Council of Europe, 4 December 2007, 8.
51. Marianne Hirsch and Leo Spitzer, "The Witness in the Archive: Holocaust Studies/Memory Studies," in *Memory Studies* 2 (2009): 151–170.
52. Katherine R. Jolluck, *Exile and Identity: Polish Women in the Soviet Union during World War II* (Pittsburgh: University of Pittsburgh Press, 2002).

I

Official Testimony and Other "Facts and Evidence"

1

Historicizing Hate: Testimonies and Photos about the Holocaust Trauma during the Hungarian Post-WWII Trials

Andrea Pető

Introduction

The trial of László Endre (1895–1946), the former State Secretary of Home Affairs, was followed by the Hungarian media with keen interest. Endre had overseen—with the assistance of an efficient state apparatus of 200,000 civil servants—the deportation of 400,000 Hungarian Jews over the course of three months in the summer of 1944. On one of the days of the trial, which lasted from 17 December 1945 until 7 January 1946, he was escorted on foot by two policemen to the "People's Courtroom" in Budapest. A photograph, preserved in the archives of the Hungarian National Museum, captured the moment when a middle-aged woman on the street shouted at Endre, while shaking her fist. The accused seems to be smiling smugly at the woman. She could not reach him, as he was protected by the two policemen. The photo was part of a photographic genre; photojournalists documented the post-war lustration process, accompanying the defendants on their journeys from the courtroom to the prison—and sometimes even to the gallows. To my knowledge, this particular photo was never published, unlike others possibly taken on the same day in the courtroom. They show that very same woman, wearing sunglasses and sitting silently in a prominent spot on the public benches.

The photographs are exceptional; they capture the manifestation of the victim's emotions and, at the same time, a moment of communication between her and the perpetrator. There are better-known images of the trial, which were either published in the daily papers or by historians seeking to illustrate their narratives about the history of the "People's Tribunals" and the juridical processes after World War II in Hungary. These photos documented what happened in the courtrooms, with their "talking heads" and silent audiences. The other "public" (that is, published) photograph of Endre and the woman wearing sunglasses was taken in the courtroom; it captured an orchestrated and hierarchical relationship shaped by the legal framework.[1]

These two photos compel us to consider the trials and the entire post-WWII transitional justice period as a space where the full emotional burden of the crimes committed during World War II was manifested. These crimes included the deportation of 600,000 Hungarian Jews, who had been denied their rights by the anti-Jewish legislation that was enacted between 1938 and 1942.[2] Most of the rich international literature focuses on the post-war trials in Germany, especially in the American, British, and French occupational zones, and on the Eichmann trial in Israel. These venues approached witness testimony quite differently, as Shoshana Felman describes: the "Nuremberg prosecution made a decision to shun witnesses and base the case against the Nazi leaders exclusively on documents, whereas the prosecution in the Eichmann trial chose to rely extensively on witnesses as well as documents to substantiate its case," because immediately after the war the prosecution believed in the authentic power of written documents.[3] Since the Hungarian People's Court relied mostly on testimonies and not documents, its proceedings can reveal new, thus far neglected characteristics of the post-war trials. Of all the countries under Soviet occupation only Hungary was allowed to institutionalize people's tribunals of the Soviet type as a legal site for "dealing with the past." Hungary was the only country where the five members were delegated by political parties without any public participation, representing continuity with pre-war times. These trials were held shortly after the end of the war, from 4 February 1945, well before Nuremberg.[4] Thus, there was no considerable, detectable "memory gap"[5] between the lived experience and what later became the impermissibility of speaking about the events. Nor was there a ritualized or standardized narrative frame that could be used to speak about the Holocaust in Hungary. Therefore, in legal procedures, testimonies were initially the primary means of articulating the meaning of the Holocaust. Moreover,

Hungary represents a unique case in terms of the institutionalization of war crimes tribunals.

During the trials the actors of transitional justice were able to speak about emotions, in relation to the events that caused their reactions.[6] By exploring this aspect of their testimonies, this chapter aims to contribute to the extensive literature on emotions, while also investigating the legal documents in two ways.[7] First, the People's Tribunal process was a way to construct "emotional communities."[8] Investigating transcripts of the trials thus helps us to trace how the language of emotions was learned and performed in court.[9] Second, the trials served as a civilized form for the expression of hate and reflected the emotional standards of the period. Whereas "fear is felt," hate can be manifested.[10] After the cataclysm of war, the expression of hate became a form of resistance and agency. As Sara Ahmed pointed out, "hate is involved in the very negotiation of boundaries between selves and others,"[11] and trials were the spaces where this negotiation "between the subject and the imagined other"[12] happened through the ritualized language of the law.

The People's Tribunals were expected to start the process of normalization and to reconstruct social cohesion by determining the meanings of social interactions during World War II. As a part of the post-war normalization they were supposed to transmit moral judgments about emotions and about the acts stemming from them. Their function was also to punish and to serve as a warning to the perpetrators. The legal language of the court served to mediate and express emotions. The court was a highly structured space for communication between criminals, victims, and witnesses.

The Function of People's Tribunals

The People's Tribunal provided a space in which different social conflicts were staged while various parties struggled to define the meaning of the Holocaust and its consequences. Their agency was based on class (the victorious Communist Party of Hungary used these trials to label the previous ruling elite as responsible for class bias) and gender (ten percent of the perpetrators were women, a comparatively high percentage). They all became part of this particular legal discourse when approximately 60,000 cases were heard.[13]

The manifestations of these conflicts in the courtroom determined interpretations of post-WWII social life. Trials were crucial institutions in the post-war normalization because they redefined citizenship as one "set of institutionally embedded political, social, and cultural practices";

their legal practice also served as a site for the "display of certain 'civic emotions' as a marker of a person's inclusion in the political word."[14] For example, the Eichmann trial was instrumental in formulating not only the narrative frame of the Holocaust as seen through the lens of the victim, but it also laid a foundation for an Israeli identity.[15] Historians have tended to neglect those emotions. They often did not see them because emotions do not leave any traces in legal historical sources. To make emotions visible, we need testimonies, such as those in the early People's Court Tribunals, which were dynamic and volatile.

Methodology and Sources

This article is part of a larger research project, based out of Budapest, entitled "The Memory of WWII and Transitional Justice." In the Budapest City Archives, researchers have at their disposal a register containing the names of defendants during the People's Tribunals. Based on this register, I conducted my research, selecting 6,000 female defendants from a list of 70,000 people convicted in Budapest. I examined approximately 200 files of female perpetrators in detail. I also read the contemporary press, interviewed judges, lawyers, children of the convicted, survivors, and witnesses to the People's Tribunals, and I tried to find all possible photographs and newsreels about the People's Tribunals for a larger research project on legal memory of WWII. In this chapter, based on an analysis of these sources, I seek to connect the emotions, cultural meanings, and social organization—the post-WWII People's Tribunals in Hungary—that were expected to "deal with" the emotion of hate from both sides. Their aim was to prevent social explosions, such as lynching, and to "normalize" the post-war situation. In this chapter I would also like to explain the construction of a divided memory and competing narratives about World War II, by showing how the testimonies given at the People's Tribunals served as a space for the articulation of emotions, while shaping the discourses on emotions and on emotional normalization.

The Importance of People's Tribunals: Corrective Justice and Negotiating Emotions

After 1945, the purpose of the court cases conducted throughout Europe was to demonstrate, by educating and enlightening the *populus*, the norms and values of the post-Holocaust world. Ernst Cassirer stated that only those constitutions that were "written into the citizens' mind"[16] could function. The institution itself, the People's Tribunal, was completely unprepared in both institutional and emotional terms for its historical mission. István Bibó (1911–1979), in his seminal 1948 article on the "Jewish question," noted the absence in post-liberation Hungary of lynching and revenge murders, which he referred to as "explosive and disorderly ways of seeking satisfaction."[17] In the immediate aftermath of the war in France, Yugoslavia, Bulgaria, and Italy (where, incidentally, significant resistance and partisan movements had existed), collaborators faced various forms of street justice—none of which had any kind of institutional approval.

In Hungary survivors and victims' relatives awaited liberation, because for them it meant moving on with their life, but also the possibility of corrective justice. The fabric of Hungarian society had been torn apart by World War II; there was no social cohesion. Moreover, there had been neither domestic armed resistance nor a partisan movement in Hungary. Individual cases (the "rescuers" who have received wide publicity in recent years) do not obscure the fact that the Hungarian administrative state system and bureaucracy collapsed. The contradictory operations of the Jewish Council and its (lack of) choices have been examined, analyzed, and illuminated.[18] In Hungary as in many other places in Europe, there was no institution or organization that was ethically beyond reproach—and which could therefore have operated as a cohesive force in the aftermath of the war. This was the political and institutional vacuum that the People's Tribunals were expected to fill.

The verdicts of the People's Tribunal depended on timing and the identity of the accused. When the first cases came up, the west of the country was still a conflict zone. Meticulous legal work was almost impossible. After the liberation of Budapest, the city's Jewish survivors immediately filed their complaints. When the survivors of the death camps began to return to Hungary in mid-1945, a whole series of accusations and complaints were filed. The People's Tribunals were not prepared to examine all these cases because the institution was overwhelmed by their sheer number. In Germany the feeling was that the "lesser murderers" were punished and the "big ones" got off,[19] but in Hungary just the opposite was true. Due to the ideological zeal and political ambitions of the Communist Party, those prosecuted tended to be prominent politicians, government ministers, and military leaders. This zeal was absent when it came to ordinary collaborators, who were so numerous that for practical reasons many of them were never punished.[20]

Snyder and Vinjamuri outlined a typology of international justice: the first type is legalism, where courts are the main institutions of justice;

the second is pragmatism, where deals are made with the participants in the process; and the third is emotionalism, where one may observe "an emotional catharsis in the community of victims and an acceptance of blame by the perpetrators."[21] In the case of Hungary only the legalist approach was present; pragmatism was not politically viable after the Holocaust, and emotionalism was not possible given the lack of consensus on the interpretation of the Holocaust. The legalist approach was not without consequences. Various historians have criticized the political and legal framework in Hungary.[22] As far as criticism of the political framework is concerned, the general point of departure of such analysis is that the People's Tribunals became a tool of the Communist authorities who controlled the Ministry of Justice. They contributed to the development of a new political system through the use of retroactive justice and exceptional courts for punishment. I shall argue that the importance of this legal procedure as a site of communicative memory is related more to the construction of emotions through memory than to direct "conspiratory" political aims of the Communist Party to orchestrate a political takeover; moreover, I will argue that the structure of the People's Tribunals also served as a site of resistance to establishing guilt and responsibility for the Holocaust in Hungary. Instead of denoting the guilty, this forum facilitated the labeling of its participants as victims of Communist oppression.

During the legal process both the victims (and witnesses) and the perpetrators were asked to retell their stories in front of those present. For the victims, the testimonies were acts of re-experiencing and an attempt to normalize past feelings in the present, in front of the perpetrators and other victims. The first testimonies were given in the investigative phase of the trials. The witnesses were expected to answer questions raised by legal professionals. In this way the trials created the legal language of remembering the Holocaust. The legal procedure brought under one roof members of the various groups—including people who had despised each other—in order to construct a narrative version of events by means of the legal rituals of remembering. The genre of the manifestation of emotions was the "confession . . . as a locus of social control and discourse production."[23] This approach raises two questions: What sources can the historian use to trace these expressions of emotion? And how do these emotions shape the meanings assigned to them?

The emotions constructed during this process were a part of a history, and the retelling of their stories had major consequences for those involved. The lengths of trials at the People's Tribunals could vary from a couple of months to one or two years. As I analyzed the documents of the People's Tribunals case by case, I could see how the argumentation and explanations for certain acts changed over time.[24] Between 1945 and 1949, both the legal framework of the People's Tribunals and the political climate changed. Witnesses and defendants found themselves in a continuous process of renegotiating their experiences before the court as they gave their testimonies. The whole juridical process changed after the adoption of Act VII (1946) on the "Criminal Law Protection of the Democratic Order of the State and the Republic," which included a rather broad definition of "anti-democratic statements and actions" as major crimes. This enabled the system to use the exceptional courts for direct political purposes and to eliminate open opposition to Communism.[25] After 1946, the term "Jew" was slowly omitted from the documents; it was replaced by the terms "victims" and "persecuted." The construction of these terms obscured Jewish identity. This process was part of the revival of post-war anti-Semitism that made Jews invisible at the social level. Being a "class enemy" turned out to be more important in that political situation than what actually happened before 1945. Such coded language counteracted the formation of unified identities. In this way the discourses of emotion reinforced status differences as a result of the logic of individualized corrective justice. Still, this *individualized* approach to crime, which did not allow an alternative, did not accord with the larger historical narrative, the normative appraisal of war. Legal loopholes and counterarguments made by the defense and defense witnesses rendered it impossible to pass judgments on individual responsibility without accepting this approach to justice.[26]

The politics of victimhood, constructed through particular discourses, was an attempt to gain political influence and compensation by the survivors. In the Hungarian context this strategy could not work, since victimhood came to be seen as responsible, in a figurative sense, for the establishment of—and instrumental to—the transitional legal system in Hungary. Manifestations of emotion were mostly shaped by language and in the courtroom. The past was mediated through legal language.[27] As Svasek points out, the "social self is constantly reconstituted through perceptual experience."[28] The trials served as a site for the formation of victims' inter-subjectivity. The language of the confession was constrained by the legal milieu from which it stemmed and was influenced by social interaction and its construction of meaning. The court trials also required "disciplined" behavior and a prescribed choreography on the part of the actors. Even though the People's Tribunals were new institutions, they adhered to a criminal code and judicial practice that had been regulated in the nineteenth century. Although the People's Tribunals are portrayed as exceptional courts, they nevertheless represented a continuity of legal tradition in the sense that, in the aftermath of World War I, the Hungarian Soviet Republic was similarly eliminated by transitional legal means that set up exceptional courts.

We have little or no information regarding the emotions that were manifested in the courtroom; they were not recorded in the court documents. (Very few and only the so-called high-profile court cases were recorded by audio or audiovisual means.) The lynching mood of the trials and their disruption, which included whistling and shouting, were all "felt" in the courtroom as a manifestation of emotions. These phenomena can be analyzed through sources that refer to such moments during the trials. Those who violated the norms of good behavior were removed physically from the courtroom, and disruptive onlookers risked becoming the targets of police action.[29]

The trials were institutionalized processes of learning at two levels: the high-profile cases that received much publicity in the media and the so-called minor cases, addressing crimes and conflicts in a localized context. The learning process affected all the actors, because the People's Tribunals represented a public ceremony with a commemorative character. Rituals, such as trials, legitimize and control emotions.[30] The court trials can be interpreted as social dramas or, as Turner defined them, as "units of a harmonic or disharmonic process, arising in conflict situations"[31] with four phases: breaching of the norm, crises, redressive action, and reintegration of the disturbed social group.[32] In the next section I shall analyze the actors in the process and attempt to explain how they influenced the rituals. Here, the People's Court will be viewed as a form of transmitting trauma by means of the testimonies and through judgments and the justifications for such judgments.

Players in the Social Drama

The Legal Professionals

The newly appointed People's professional judges of the tribunals needed an immaculate past—spotless as far as collaboration with the Horthy regime was concerned. Therefore the professional judges were either of Jewish origin or refugees from Hungarian territories that were detached from Hungary after WWI. These jurists had no access to professional networks, and therefore they had no other possibility but to accept appointments in the People's Courts, which had very low prestige in the legal profession.[33] In the course of their work, the judges tried to use the framework provided by the Criminal Code and to apply the provisions of the Criminal Code as well as the special regulations of the People's Tribunal legislation. Their verdicts, which were often quoted verbatim in newspapers, served as judgments not only of the events but also of the acts at a general political level.

Five other nonprofessional civil judges were appointed by the five coalition parties, the Communist Party being only one of them. They did not have any legal background, so they needed to be trained during the trials. These nonprofessional judges "learned" how to react to certain situations but mostly followed the instructions they received from their parties—if they received any. They did not intervene in the trials as far as we can reconstruct such intervention from the documents, but we can see where they had different opinions on wording, that is, in classifying the crime during the appeal process.

The court did not ask for emotions but for specific memories of actual events. This, of course, raises the question of whether, and to what extent, people can remember traumatic events. As we know, traumatic experiences tend to shatter cognitive and perceptual capacities. The rhetoric of the testimony changed from weighty description to those codes that the court was able to decipher easily by means of the newly established legal framework.[34]

Perpetrators

As far as the perpetrators were concerned, it was a matter of life and death to know, and possibly influence, the classification of their wartime actions when they testified, thereby gaining a chance to secure an acquittal. Lughod has argued that the "discourses of emotion and emotional discourses can serve . . . for the relatively powerless as loci of resistance and idioms of rebellion."[35] In this case, however, these "emotional discourses" served to empower the perpetrators, because the legal discourses constructed around the crimes of the Holocaust provided a site of resistance to "old Hungary." The legal and political criticism of the process of the People's Courts undermined the justice of war. In view of the controversial character of the process,[36] there was some space to establish a parallel moral value system of superiority for those who were judged by the trial, regardless of their crimes.[37] In this context the powerless were the perpetrators, who tried to insist upon the application of the letter of the law while questioning the justice of the war and the legitimacy of the law. The counter-narratives were constructed in the same way as during the Auschwitz trials: the perpetrators were presented as individuals, with "no necessary relationship to anything but their own moral choices."[38] This approach, which was combined with criticism of retroactive justice, created a sentimental bond among those who considered themselves to be victims of "Stalinist justizmord," the Sovietization of the Hungarian criminal system. It both diminished the importance of the crimes they had committed and ignored social and structural dimensions.

Victims

A key figure in this process was the plaintiff, who had suffered and survived the violation.[39] For therapeutic and other reasons, rituals were needed to provide justice to those who had suffered. The court cases were mixed: in some cases, the state—in the form of an attorney—took over the role of the plaintiff, because the victims had been killed; even their bodies were missing. In all the cases, some of the witnesses were Holocaust survivors.[40] The mixed character of the narration—attorneys speaking for the dead and the living, witnesses testifying for themselves and for those they missed—shaped the narrative space available for the articulation of emotions in the form of answers to the questions.

Addressing the issue of loss, LaCapra differentiates between absence at a transhistorical level and loss at the historical level. He writes: "When absence is converted into loss, one increases the likelihood of misplaced nostalgia and utopian politics in quest of a new totality or fully unified community."[41] The social space where emotions were mediated and where loss was expected to be converted into absence was the tribunal. I argue here that one of the reasons why this mediation or conversion process failed in post-war Hungary was the unified and essentialized construction of emotion as a form of "coping with" the post-war crises. The essentialized concept of "hate" exhibited by anti-Semites towards Jews, and a hunger for revenge on the part of surviving Jews, were expected to be mediated by the newly constructed institutions of the People's Tribunals.

These court trials were designed in the framework of reconstructing the truth, but we need to ask whether that was the proper place to reconstruct objective truth. The court trials used various types of evidence. When high-profile former politicians were the accused, their speeches, interviews, and published articles were used as evidence. At first, attorneys used press material as proof.[42] The problem was that the atrocities were mostly undocumented; moreover, they were committed in the hope that the witnesses would be killed and never return from the camps. When survivors did return or come out of hiding, they gave testimonies.

Audience and Language

The bodily interaction, perceptual experience, and construction of meaning happened in the same space of the court but with a very different outcome.[43] On the public benches, relatives of perpetrators and victims sat next to each other. Reviewing the photographs taken at the trials, we can see that 90 percent of the people in the public gallery were women. In the dark, privately owned amateur photos, we see crowded rooms and people sitting in their winter coats because there was no heat.[44] Some of them showed open sympathy toward former members of the Arrow Cross Party (Hungarian Nazi Party), offering them food parcels; others wanted to lynch them. For example, on August 24, 1948, a protest broke out at the trial of the defendants who had been based at the Arrow Cross headquarters in the Fifth District of Budapest. Many in the audience of the courtroom confessed that they were "going to the trials out of curiosity."[45] In the next hearing it was obvious that those disrupting the courtroom were the perpetrators' relatives, while the counter-protests came from relatives of the victims, who wanted to prevent the former from handing over parcels of food to the accused. This was an extraordinary case of loss of control in the midst of Communist dictatorship. The trial had to be canceled because of these events.

All of this can be read in the minutes of the trial, but historians are not always so lucky when it comes to finding sources. The court hearings, and subsequent discussions of events among those who had attended the hearings, contributed to the formation of a common narrative, based on the different versions of the story told by the survivors and on behalf of the survivors. The story of the events was constructed as a canonized language of the tribunal. During the court process a hegemonic memory of events was constructed from the various individual testimonies, and this version was recorded in the court documents and repeated in the verdict.[46]

The victims formed, learned, and mastered the language of the People's Tribunal which was to offer them justice. Although all the daily newspapers published reports on the People's Tribunals, press coverage would not have been sufficient in itself to prepare victims for what they could expect in the court. Therefore victims and witnesses went to the tribunals not only to see justice take place but also to learn how to formulate and speak about their experiences with a view to achieving their goals in the courtroom. In the case of Uncle A.,[47] during his frequent visits to the trials he managed not only to identify the woman who was responsible for the mass murder committed in his house—which had taken the lives of his son, wife, mother, and father—but also to learn the language of the courtroom. We see this in the various documents he submitted to the attorney's office describing the events of October 15, 1944, in a manner that reflected the legal language of the People's attorneys.[48] The public benches represented the space where individual opinions could be expressed as a part of the public ritual. The February–March 1946 trial of Szálasi, who was the leader of the fascist Arrow Cross Party and the head of the Hungarian Quisling government, was overseen by the notorious Judge Péter Jankó. It was broadcast by Hungarian Radio, and some parts were also shown in newsreels at movie theaters. Listeners were surprised by the public expressions of dissatisfaction as Szálasi made his statements; Judge Jankó made no attempt to silence the public. Before and after the trials, discussions among the audience and the interaction between the audience and the court gave a meaning and words to experiences of suffering during the war.

Truth in Testimonies

Peter Brooks has pointed to the religious roots of testimonies at courts and the consequences of this for the kind of truth revealed during such procedures. The truth is not an issue, because what counts is the therapeutic value and explanatory force of the testimony. Brooks, following Freud, differentiates between "material truth" and "psychic truth" in psychoanalysis, which is "that truth of mind and emotions that offers a coherent and therapeutic life narrative . . . and is not wholly dependent on referential truth or correspondence to a set of facts."[49] I am arguing here that during the People's Tribunals, parts of the "material truth" were revealed without the "psychic truth," and this contributed to the controversial construction of emotionality.

Following the typology of Campbell, four types of memories were presented in the court: the testimonial memories of witnesses, the prosecutor's model of memory in the paradigm of truth and error, the defense concept of mentality, and the judge's evidential memories evaluating the material of the court as evidence.[50] Each of them understand memory in a different way, and this, in turn, influenced how the emotions were shaped. Applying

Campbell's analysis to the People's Court trials, the built-in discrepancies relating to the construction of meaning during the trial caused the most dissatisfaction with the activity of the court among the various parties involved. Moreover all parties returned home with a belief that they were "right." However, in the case of the witnesses, "memory functions both as a description of the traumatic injury and as a claim of a wrong."[51] The testimony is not an individual activity; it is constructed to impress the audience and to appeal to the community. The defense defines memory as a mentality, and questions not only its content but also its reliability. In the case of the People's Tribunals, this also called into question the legitimacy of the procedure. The prosecutor was expected to check the relationship between the event and the recollection of the event. I know of no cases of witnesses or perpetrators changing their testimonies after being cross-examined by the prosecutor. If there was a change, it always resulted from the intervention of prosecutors who were "professionally" and politically convinced that the accused was guilty. Especially in the initial trials in the first half of 1945, the tribunal did not assess the accuracy of the facts presented by witnesses or the legal framework in which these acts were judged. Therefore the defendants and their lawyers tended to apply "cognitivist, empirical epistemology,"[52] and this enabled them to successfully challenge the verdicts—particularly in the low-profile cases. The consequence was that cases heard by the People's Tribunals lasted for years. Because of the sheer numbers, many defendants were out on bail until the verdicts were pronounced, very often living in the same house where the crimes had been committed—together with survivors of these crimes. This did not contribute to a process of reconciliation in post-war Hungary.

Conclusion

Actors on both sides entered the legal process trusting in a fair trial. Such trust was risky, and in this case everyone was left disappointed, not only because of the ways in which the People's Tribunals operated but also because of the manner in which individual corrective justice functioned. Brooks points out that in confessions "truth is an inter-subjective, transactional, transferential kind of truth," and this contributed to the mixed reception of the results of the trials at the People's Tribunals.[53]

Reading the recollections of the perpetrators and talking to their children, one gets the impression that the People's Tribunals were passionate and violent venues for revenge. On the other hand, talking to the victims and witnesses one gets an impression of fear and dissatisfaction. The members of the legal apparatus talked about the activity of the People's Tribunals in technical terms, as a process for the in-group professionals who were, of course, aware of the technical deficiencies of the institution but whose profession—and defense of the interests of their clients—was independent of both the political regime and the courts.

Renate Rosaldo viewed emotions as moral forces that control and shape political and social actions.[54] The emotions manifested in the People's Tribunals left all parties dissatisfied. Bourdieu's term "emotional capital"[55] is also an instrumentalization of sentiments and feelings as a form of agency. This "emotional capital" also informs the competing versions of victimhood and suffering in all participants of the judicial process. To express an opinion is to gain power over the narrative and the constructing agency. In the Cold War context, criticizing the process was a contribution to undermining the dominant anti-fascist historical narrative frame. This chapter has been an attempt to illustrate the consequences, in a particular historical situation, of the failure of the courts—the only possible means of remedy—to give the impression and "feeling" of a "fair" trial, and to reconcile feelings of hate.

Notes

1. Andrea Pető, "Death and the Picture: Representation of War Criminals and Construction of Divided Memory about WWII in Hungary," in *Faces of Death. Visualising History* eds. Andrea Pető, Klaertje Schrijvers (Pisa: Edizioni Plus, Pisa University Press, 2009), 39–57.
2. On the post-war trials in Hungary see László Karsai, "The People's Courts and Revolutionary Justice in Hungary, 1945–46," in *The Second World War and its Aftermath* eds. István Deák, Jan T. Gross, Tony Judt, (New York: Columbia University Press, 2000), 137–51.
3. Shoshana Felman, *The Juridical Unconscious: Trials and Traumas in the Twentieth Century* (Harvard University Press, 2002), 132.
4. For an analysis of war crime trials in Germany see Donald Bloxham, *Genocide on Trial. War Crimes Trials and the Formation of Holocaust History and Memory* (New York: Oxford University Press, 2001).
5. Grünfeld quoted in Ronit Lentin, "Expected to Live: Women Shoah Survivors' Testimonial Silence," *Women's Studies International Forum* 23 (2001): 691.
6. For an overview of how emotions came to be at the center of interdisciplinary scholarly attention see William M. Reddy, *The Navigation of Feeling: A Framework for the History of Emotions* (Cape Town: Dock House, 2001); Catharine Lutz and Geoffrey M. White, "The Anthropology of Emotions," *Annual Review of Anthropology* 15 (1986): 405–36.
7. Felman, *The Juridicial Unconscious*.
8. Barbara Rosenwein, "Worrying about Emotions in History," *American Historical Review* 107 (2002): 842.
9. Sheila Fitzpatrick, "Happiness and 'Toska': An Essay in the History of Emotions in Pre-war Soviet Russia," *Australian Journal of Politics and History* 50 (2004): 357.

10. Joanna Bourke, "Fear and Anxiety: Writing about Emotions in Modern History," *History Workshop Journal* 55 (2003): 123.
11. Sara Ahmed, "The Organization of Hate," *Law and Critique* 12 (2001): 353.
12. Ibid., 351.
13. For a critique of the legal discourse see, among others, Felman, *The Juridical Unconscious*, and Devin O. Pendas, *The Frankfurt Auschwitz Trial, 1963–1965: Genocide, History, and the Limits of the Law* (New York: Cambridge University Press, 2006).
14. Sergii Yekelchyk, "The Civic Duty of Hate: Stalinist Citizenship as Political Practice and Civic Emotion (Kiev, 1943–53)," in *Kritika: Explorations in Russian and Eurasian History* 3 (2006): 529.
15. Felman, *The Juridicial Unconscious*; Pendas, *The Frankfurt Auschwitz Trial.*
16. Vivian Grosswald Curran, "Racism's Past and Law's Future," *Vermont Law Review* 1 (2004): 1.
17. István Bibó, *Democracy, Revolution, Self-Determination: Selected Writings.* ed. Nagy Károly, trans. András Boros-Kazai, Social Science Monographs, (New York: Columbia University Press 1991), 290. Work was published in Boulder, CO.
18. Mária Schmidt, *Kollaboráció vagy kooperáció? A budapesti Zsidó Tanács* [Collaboration or Cooperation? The Jewish Council in Budapest] (Budapest: Minerva, 1990).
19. Pendas, *The Frankfurt Auschwitz Trial,* 290.
20. For one example, see Andrea Pető, "About the Narratives of a Blood Libel Case in Post-Shoah Hungary," in *Comparative Central European Holocaust Studies* eds. Louise Vasvari and Steven Totosy de Zepetnek (West Lafayette, IN: Purdue University Press, 2009), 240–53.
21. Jack Snyder, Leslie Vinjamuri, "Trials and Errors: Principle and Pragmatism in Strategies of International Justice," *International Security* 28 (2003–2004): 15.
22. For more on this see Andrea Pető, "Problems of Transitional Justice in Hungary: An Analysis of the People's Tribunals in Post-War Hungary and the Treatment of Female Perpetrators,"*Zeitgeschichte* 34 (2007): 335–49.
23. Lila Abu-Lughod and Catherine A. Lutz, "Introduction: Emotion, Discourse, and the Politics of Everyday Life," in *Language and Politics of Emotions* eds. Lila Abu-Lughod and Catherine A. Lutz (Paris, Cambridge: Maison des Sciences de l'Homme, Cambridge University Press 1990), 6.
24. Andrea Pető, "Conflicting Narratives about a Post Shoah Blood Libel Case in Budapest in 1946," in *Die „ Wahrheit" der Erinnerung—Jüdische Lebensgeschichten* eds. Elenore Lappin, Albert Lichtblau, (Salzburg: Institut für Geschichte der Juden in Österreich, Zentrum für jüdische Kulturgeschichte der Universität Salzburg, 2008), 24–35.
25. For more on this see Pető, "Problems of Transitional Justice in Hungary."
26. See Pendas, *The Frankfurt Auschwitz Trial.*
27. Selma Leydesdorff, "How shall we remember Srebrenica? Will the Language of Law Structure our Memory?" in *Memory and the Future, Transnational Politics, Ethics, and Society* eds. Yifat Gutman, Adam D. Brown, and Amy Sodaro (London, New York: Palgrave, 2010), 121–141.
28. Maruska Svasek, "Introduction," in *Postsocialism: Politics and Emotions in Central and Eastern Europe* ed. Maruska Svasek (New York: Berghahn Books, 2006) 13.
29. See the trial at Budapest City Archive 22519/49.
30. Paul Sant Cassia, "When Intuitive Knowledge Fails: Emotion, Art and Resolution," in *Mixed Emotions? Anthropological Studies of Feeling* eds. Kay Milton and Maruska Svasek (New York, Oxford: Berg, 2005), 112.
31. Victor Turner, *Dramas, Field, and Metaphors: Symbolic Action in Human Society* (Ithaca: Cornell University Press, 1974), 37.

32. Turner, *Dramas, Fields, and Metaphors*, 38–41.
33. Interview with a judge (2005) and Hungarian National Archives Section of People's Tribunals XIX-E-1-l 1.
34. Felman, *The Juridicial Unconscious*.
35. Lughod and Lutz, "Introduction," 15.
36. Pető, *Problems of Transitional Justice*.
37. Abu Lughod and Lutz, "Introduction," 15.
38. Pendas, *The Frankfurt Auschwitz Trial*, 293.
39. For more see Felman, *The Juridicial Unconscious*, esp. 131–169.
40. About the impossibility of providing witnesses see Felman, Shoshana, "The Return of the Voice: Claude Lanzman's Shoah," in *Testimony: Crises of Wittnessing on Literature, Psychoanalysis and History* eds. Shoshana Felman and Dori Laub, (New York: Routledge, 1992), 80.
41. Dominick LaCapra, "Trauma, Absence, Loss," *Critical Inquiry* 25 (1999): 700.
42. See my interview with a judge (2005) and a detective (2007) of the People's Tribunals.
43. Maruska Svasek, "The Politics of Chosen Trauma: Expellee Memories, Emotions and Identities," in *Mixed Emotions? Anthropological Studies of Feeling* eds. Kay Milton and Maruska Svasek (New York, Oxford: Berg, 2005), 211.
44. These privately owned photos made their way into public collections. Photo Archive of the Hungarian Museum of Crime.
45. Budapest City Archive 22519/49: 14.
46. Pető Andrea, "About the Narratives of a Blood Libel Case in Post Shoah Hungary," *Comparative Central European Holocaust Studies* eds. Louise Vasvari, Steven Totosy de Zepetnek (West Lafayette, IN: Purdue University Press, 2009), 240–253; and Andrea Pető, "Privatized Memory?: The Story of Erecting the first Holocaust Memorial in Budapest" in *Memories of Mass Repression: Narrating Life Stories in the Aftermath of Atrocity* eds. Nanci Adler Selma Leydersdorff, Mary Chamberlain, and Leyla Neyzi (New Brunswick: Transaction Publishers, 2009), 157–75.
47. I am researching his story for my next book.
48. Pető, "Privatized Memory?"
49. Peter Brooks, *Troubling Confessions: Speaking Guilt in Law and Literature* (Chicago: University of Chicago Press, 2000), 118.
50. Kristen Campbell, "Legal Memories: Sexual Assault, Memory, and International Humanitarian Law," *Signs* 28 (2002), 165.
51. Ibid.
52. Ibid., 168.
53. Brooks, *Troubling Confessions*, 128.
54. Renato I. Rosaldo, "Grief and a Headhunter's Rage: On the Cultural Force of Emotions," in *Text, Play, and Story: Construction and Reconstruction of Self and Society* ed. Edward. M. Bruner (Long Grove, IL: Waveland Press, 1984), 178–95.
55. Maruska Svasek, "Introduction," in *Postsocialism: Politics and Emotions in Central and Eastern Europe* ed. Maruska Svasek (New York: Berghahn Books, 2006), 18.

2

The Legacies of the Stalinist Repression: Narratives of the Children of Loyalist "Enemies of the People"

Nanci Adler

The dissolution of the Soviet Union and the demise of the Communist Party had not been foreseen by either Communists or non-Communists. But the Party faithful were particularly ill-prepared to make sense of the disappearance of an empire, much less the political institution that had successfully conflated itself with "the people" and patriotism. Where, now, was meaning to be found, especially for the children of executed or incarcerated parents, who were raised in Soviet orphanages, where the policy was to indoctrinate them to believe that their parents' detention was justified by a now defunct Party which their parents had supported? Their narratives are testimony to the effects of decades of living in a closed, repressive system. They describe an amalgam of idealism and alienation, as well as an intermingling of open and clandestine rejections of Communism. But the narrators are often so guarded that it is difficult to distinguish between their accommodation *to* the immutable and their assimilation *of* the immutable—probably even for the narrators themselves.

As the orphaned and displaced "heirs of the Gulag," the children of executed or imprisoned Communist loyalists bore unique political and

---

* Parts of this chapter were excerpted from Nanci Adler, *Keeping Faith With the Party: Communist Believers Return from the Gulag* (Bloomington: Indiana University Press, 2012).

psychological burdens. But all the "heirs of Stalin" (those whose parents were victimized in the 1930s, 1940s, and 1950s) had to find a way of adapting to Stalin's immediate and long-term influence after the dictator's demise in 1953. Some were infected by the repression and became carriers of the repression. Their authentic, sometimes positive views on the Party, despite ample evidence of the victimizations, reflect the persistence of coexisting "truths,"[1] the absence of public discussions of the repression, and the influence of national narratives that valorize the Communist past. Their perspectives give us insight into the different ways of negotiating historical evidence. Others became resistors of repression and tried to spread resistance. This chapter will explore some of the questions that confronted the second generation (the children of repressed Communist loyalists), and look at how their accounts reflect the short- and long-term legacies of decades of repression. This research is part of a larger study on Gulag returnees, based on interviews, published and unpublished memoirs, and archival documentation. Here we will also consider how this past is mediated by memory in a society where there is a persistent trend of repressing the memory of repression.

The Children of the Repressed

When the Soviet Union collapsed, so also did the meaning it had created for its citizens. The first generation of Party loyalists had to salvage meaning from the failure of their dedicated efforts. Their children bore their own set of issues, different from the first generation, but equally complex. They had to look for meaning in their own and their country's past, and in the sacrifices of their parents.[2]

The enormity and the suddenness of the collapse made it seem incredible, especially to Party loyalists. Following the dissolution of the Soviet Union, the conflict between old and new politics was displayed on the first day of the 1992 hearing on the constitutionality of banning the Communist Party. The arguments of the Party's defenders were acidly described in the daily *Izvestiia*. For example, one defender challenged the justification of banning the most "massive Party in the country," the very Party that had "rallied many millions of countrymen and served their interests" and led them to victory in the "Great Patriotic War, for which three million Communists sacrificed their lives."[3]

Also on display was the personal and political legacy bequeathed by the first generation of Communists to their children. People's Deputy D. Stepanov, a man whose father had been arrested in 1940 and died in the Gulag, delivered an impassioned defense of the Party. In response, an *Izvestiia* journalist, Iurii Feofanov, reflected the viewpoint of many skeptics, but also revealed an inability to comprehend the emotional appeal of the Communist Party. He wrote:

> Here was this son defending with sincere pathos that same Party that had killed his father. It's some phenomenon, this Communist conviction in the righteousness of a cause so soaked in bitterness, tears, and blood.[4]

Feofanov had no difficulty understanding the allegiance of ordinary Party functionaries who were at risk of losing the perks and power they had accumulated; these were material and practical losses. But he gave insufficient weight to the immaterial, emotional component of Party membership—the intrinsic satisfaction of union with an ideologically inspired community. Such satisfactions may have been counterintuitive to nonbelievers but were powerfully compelling to adherents like "People's Deputy" Stepanov. He was grateful to the Party that had permitted him to overcome an unpromising beginning. Despite his family's tainted history, he had worked his way up to a political position of some standing, and this rise was abetted by an attitude consistent with what was expected of a Party member in his position.

Early in their lives, Stepanov and many others in his generation lost their parents to the terror, and grew up in orphanages that stigmatized their "criminal" parents, while indoctrinating them in the socially redeeming legitimacy of the terror. They responded with a wide range of adaptations. Some, following their parents' example, became active, dedicated Party members.[5] Others—in fact the majority—were apolitical or felt antipathy toward the Party that had persecuted their parents, according to Roy Medvedev, a dissident historian whose father had fallen victim to the terror. As "children of enemies of the people," moreover, most had few opportunities for Party careers, or for that matter, any careers. They were often denied access to higher education, government-run institutes, and merited advancement.

Medvedev himself did not seek a Party career because he was certain that the blemish of his father's tragic fate would have barred his acceptance.[6] Instead, he became a respected pedagogue and a scholar. In 1971, he published *Let History Judge* abroad; this was a pioneering work that was instrumental in exposing the crimes of the Stalinist apparatus. It supported the Leninist line, deplored Stalinism, and denounced Stalin and other Party officials, but it shielded the system by attributing culpability to individual miscreants.

While the political sentiments of a group are predictable, the sentiments of any single member are not. Stepanov, Medvedev, and a host of dissidents emerged from the personal, familial, and political trauma of losing a parent with different attitudes toward the Party. How did they account for this?

Nadezhda Ioffe

If the parents did survive, they were often able to exert influence on their children's perceptions of the Gulag experience or the Soviet system. Some parents, such as Nadezhda Ioffe, daughter of the well-known revolutionary Adolf Ioffe, withheld their negative views of the Party from their children. In a 1997 interview, Nadezhda confessed her deep regret, on one of the occasions that she was being sent back to the Gulag, that she had not told her daughter Natasha the things she had experienced in the Gulag, and the things she knew about the terror:

> Why didn't I tell her why they shot her father? Why didn't I tell her the truth about collectivization and industrialization? That the country was being destroyed. That the peasantry was being physically wiped out . . .[7]

She accounted for this concealment by saying she had wanted Natasha to be able to retain the support offered by the ideology of Communism. Natasha was an active Komsomol (Communist Youth League) member, head of her organization, and "she believed in all of it—in socialism, in Communism, that the Soviet regime was the best in the world. That we were an example to the world's proletariat."[8] However, protecting her daughter from the psychological stress of cognitive dissonance[9] and the political risks of disclosure could also have justified withholding this information from Natasha. It was during Stalin's time that Nadezhda's three imprisonments took place, and children were encouraged to place Party loyalty over family loyalty.[10]

Nataliia Rappaport

There were also survivors' children, like Nataliia Rappaport, who rejected the Party that their formerly repressed parents continued to support. Nataliia's father, Iakov Rappaport, had been a Party member since World War II, and was a prominent physician when he was swept up in 1953 by the so-called "Doctors' Plot," Stalin's last wave of terror. At the time of his arrest on false charges of plotting to kill the Kremlin leadership, Nataliia was fourteen years old. She and her sister were both members of the Komsomol. Nataliia recalled how terrified she was during the anti-Semitic campaign prior to her father's arrest, when she overheard her schoolmates debating whether the executions of these "killer doctors" would be public.

When her father was taken to the notorious Lefortovo prison in Moscow, her mother was required to leave their home to witness a search of their dacha. Upon her return the next morning, she found Nataliia huddled in the corner where she had fearfully spent the night, despairing of ever seeing her mother again. As for Iakov Rappaport, he was initially subjected to "conveyor-belt" interrogations of sleep deprivation for days on end, then unexpectedly released in April of 1953. His life had been saved by Stalin's death. He waited twenty years before recording his experiences in the 1970s, but did not publish the memoirs until 1988, at age ninety.

The doctors were the first to be rehabilitated—cleared of criminal charges—and additionally Rappaport was reinstated in the Party.[11] He claimed to have had his doubts about the Party but hoped that "someday common sense would triumph."[12] When he heard Mikhail Gorbachev's reference to the "Doctors' Plot" in his November 1987 Revolution Day speech, he was gratified that he had lived to see that day. However, Nataliia had been stigmatized as an outcast as a result of her father's arrest, and she spent decades resenting the Party that had mistreated her family. Yet, she revealed in a 1988 interview that if she were to be asked anew to join, now in the Gorbachev era, she probably would have done so.[13] Nataliia, like her father, was receptive to returning to the hope that had originally imbued their past, in the new beginning promised by Gorbachev.

Evgeniia Vladimirovna Smirnova

Almost twenty years after the fall of the Soviet Union, I interviewed or re-interviewed survivors of the Stalinist repressions. One of them was Evgeniia Vladimirovna Smirnova, whose mother entered and exited the Gulag a fanatic loyalist while Evgeniia herself joined the anti-Stalinist organization Memorial. Her story describes a gradual, informed departure from the beliefs of her parents, all the while recognizing that what worked for them did not work for her. Both parents were veteran Party members. Her father, Vladimir Solomonovich Markovich, a Party member since 1920, was an engineer who had directed an institute on rail modernization of the People's Commissariat of Transportation. He was expelled from the Party and the Institute in 1936, arrested in 1937 as a Trotskyite and a German spy, and executed in June of 1939. Her mother, Evgeniia Aleksandrovna Shtern, had joined the Party in 1919 and worked as a censor in a Moscow publishing house. She was arrested for "counter-revolutionary activities" in 1937 and sentenced to five years in prison. She spent the first two years of her incarceration in the dreaded Iaroslavl political isolator, and was then transferred to Kolyma. She was released in 1944, but re-arrested in 1949 and sentenced to "perpetual exile" (essentially prison without walls[14]) in Kolyma.[15] At that time, Evgeniia, their daughter, had just managed to get a job in Moscow—no small feat for a child of repressed parents. Evgeniia's superiors cautioned her to avoid contact with her mother, and she did.[16]

Evgeniia's mother, however, sent letters to her daughter from Kolyma. She wrote with seeming pride, "We are working in Kolyma, trying to fulfil the norms, we almost always succeed."[17] Evgeniia's mother sometimes even over-fulfilled the norms. She was a tough and driven woman who, already at age sixteen, had served on the front in the Civil War. Yet Evgeniia thought about her mother's petite stature and shuddered at what a strain such heavy labor might impose on her health.

Even as a child, Evgeniia's mother had been an ardent Communist, deeply influenced by an older sister, who envisioned a fulfilling struggle toward a "bright future." She embraced the reforms instituted by Khrushchev at the XX Party Congress (where the Secret Speech was read) as evidence that the Party was returning to its right path. Her values affirmed, Evgeniia's mother returned to active Party work. In the seventies she worked hard to promote Communism, even gathering materials for a museum on the history of the Komsomol.

Evgeniia, however, had a different reaction to the unfolding course of events in the country and in her family. She had been raised as a Leninist, a Pioneer (Communist Girl or Boy Scouts) and Komsomol member, and with such an idealistic view of Communism that at the beginning of the war with the Nazis she could not understand why the proletariat of one country would fight another: "from my youth, I always considered that the proletariat of all countries should unite."[18] But even though many of her values had been "internalized," as she described them, she "parted with her illusions" in response to the realities of the repression. Unlike her mother, Evgeniia did not want to become a Party member. Although she stopped short of actively joining the human rights movement of the sixties, she "did what she could" by providing a hiding place for samizdat manuscripts (underground journals of human rights activities) in her apartment—a location considered above suspicion. Of course, she never told her mother. In this act, she was taking a legal risk, justified by a political shift, based on an earlier ideological shift. In our interview,

I asked whether this had been a big step for her. She explained that it was already clear by then that this was the right thing to do. She had been raised to do the "right thing," but, in contrast to her mother, she had lost faith in the Party's rectitude.

Evgeniia's mother died in 1987 but lived to witness the beginning of Gorbachev's liberalizing perestroika, which they both hailed as an "improvement of the Party," rather than a move against it. Two years after her mother's death, Evgeniia joined the organization Memorial, a victims' organization and human rights watchdog aimed at research and dissemination of material on Stalinism. With their help, she was able to uncover the true story of her father's victimization, since the information on his death certificate had been falsified. She learned that he had been imprisoned for two years, in Sverdlovsk and then in Moscow. It was claimed that he had confessed, but there was also a petition he had sent to the court in which he denied his confession—the type of legal "Catch-22" that could take rehabilitation commissions decades to decipher. This is how it read:

> I understand that under the current circumstances the Party cannot believe anyone's words and should carefully check every individual. But they checked me, and did not find anything criminal. And now I request that my case be closed and that I be given the opportunity to work as a Soviet engineer, and contribute my efforts and knowledge to benefit the Motherland.[19]

Evgeniia participated with Memorial in publicizing the plight of victims of the terror. She began her efforts by delivering a speech in her father's former institute, at an event held in honor of her father. She worked with Memorial, going to Gulag returnees' houses with questionnaires that were used to establish an accessible archive of the victims of the terror. In so doing, Evgeniia met the victims—most of them ordinary citizens, non-Party members, who had been subjected to extraordinary terror. Unlike her mother, Evgeniia found no redeeming value in the repression. This is her account of one interview:

> One of the people I went to see had been incarcerated in Svobodny [camp in the Far East]. He had a lovely wife, when I went to him we talked for two days. His children were already grown. He told me that he had a wonderful family, but that I was the first person to whom he had told this story of his camp history. He has since died. He said at that time that if he had not been in camp, he would have gladly volunteered to be at the front. He said that he knew he would have died there but that it would have been better than what happened to him.[20]

Other victims, even in 1989, would not talk to her at all about their camp experience. As Evgeniia gathered stories of victims, she struggled to understand how her ideologically principled mother and her similarly principled comrades in arms could have remained devoted to a system that had victimized them, along with millions of others. She recognized that her mother's devotion to Communism provided her life with an enduring sense of meaning, such that even the labor camp could be a satisfying labor of love, but Evgeniia found it painful to think about how different and devoid of meaning the incarceration must have been for the majority of the victims. She lamented,

> Look at who is listed in [Memorial's publication] *Rasstrel'nye spiski* (*Execution Lists*).[21] People with a low education, accused of anti-Soviet agitation. It's just horrible . . . These poor souls did nothing, they had no relationship to the system whatsoever . . . they didn't bother anyone . . .[22]

Evgeniia wondered why her mother and her mother's peers had retained their ideological beliefs during and after the Gulag, when the political outcome seemed so different from what they had originally expected. She contrasted this with her own outcome-dependent assessment of the Communist Party—and that of others: "There are people who, when faced with new circumstances, change their opinion." She attributed her mother's changeless convictions to her "internal constitution." In context, this could be interpreted as a combination of rigidity and a steadfast commitment to a more far-reaching ideological vision. Evgeniia also recognized that her mother and many of her dedicated comrades in arms had framed the Gulag experience as a meaningful, redeeming ideological journey destined to achieve the goals of Communism. So viewed, her mother's steadfast dedication was a rational, outcome-dependent assessment. Retaining their beliefs may have helped loyalists survive the camp and post-camp experiences, and so their enduring allegiance was, at the very least, a matter of self-preservation.

Mariia Il'inichna Kuznetsova

Like Evgeniia, Mariia Il'inichna Kuznetsova was a daughter of Communist parents who had been repressed, but she retained a much more positive view of the Party and the system. Mariia's view endured her father's execution and her mother's incarceration because it was guided by her mother's enduring belief. But there was a downside. While Mariia's positive attitude toward Communism had facilitated her adaptation to the repression, it hindered her adaptation to the Gorbachev era disclosures about the repression.

Mariia's father, Il'ia L'vovich Il'in, had been a prominent Communist Party official who served as the Secretary of the Kiev Provincial Party Committee and then as the Secretary of the Astrakhan City Party Committee. He was arrested in July of 1937, executed in November of that year in Moscow, then buried in the notorious Donskoi Cemetery on the outskirts of Moscow. Her mother, Mariia Markovna Il'ina, was the director of a silk combine in Kiev when she was arrested in 1937 as the "family member of an enemy of the people." She was incarcerated in the Pot'ma camp and then sent on to a Gulag location in the Komi Autonomous Republic until her release in 1948. Camp records show that she was an *udarnik* (shock worker—i.e., she excelled) in the camp. After liberation she lived in Cherkassy until her rehabilitation in 1956.

Upon their parents' arrest, Mariia and her two brothers, Feliks and Vladimir, were sent to orphanages, as were most children of the repressed.[23] Vladimir had turned sixteen shortly after his arrival at the children's home, so he was soon dispatched to a camp in the Far East. Mariia's mother had managed to keep track of her children's whereabouts even from camp, and begged the authorities to take her son out of the Gulag and send him to the front so that he could die an honorable death. But the authorities paid little heed to the requests of families of "enemies of the people." Her plea was not granted, and Vladimir died in the camp.[24] Despite all the hardships her family had experienced, Mariia's attitude toward life was that "the world is not without good people."

After eleven years, Mariia was able to reunite with her mother, and in 1948, after her mother was liberated, she took Mariia out of the orphanage and put her into a school. There, she excelled, and the teachers treated her well. They even added her name to a list of children of war victims so that she would not suffer the discrimination so regularly heaped on a child whose father had been an "enemy of the people." Unimpeded by such customary obstructions to social advancement, Mariia became a Pioneer and a Komsomol member and even served as secretary of her Komsomol organization.

In spite of her mother's encouragement, Mariia chose not to join the Party—but not because of any ideological objections. By the time she had reached the age when she could join, Mariia was already married to a Party member who wanted her to stay home and take care of the family. For him, "one Communist in the family was enough," so she deferred to his wishes.

Mariia and her husband each viewed Party membership differently. Mariia was an idealist who was inspired by the Party. Her husband was a pragmatist who had joined the Party to advance his career. Mariia and her mother maintained an idealized vision of the Party even after their experience of repression. As Mariia explained, her mother found a way to look past what had happened to her own family, and focus, instead, on the goal:

> She knew there were enemies. She believed in the progress of the socialist system . . . She believed in the victory of the Revolution. She just figured there were mistakes, and there were chips. You know the expression "when you cut wood, chips fly"; she was a chip . . . [She resolutely expected that] a just, wonderful Communist society would be built.[25]

Although many wives of "enemies of the people" maintained that their own husbands had been unjustifiably arrested, they justified the expediency of such measures because "there were enemies."[26] At least, according to Mariia, this is "what they said." She recognized that they might have thought otherwise but were voicing explanations provided and permitted by the Party. However she had little doubt regarding her mother's attitude toward such challenging issues. Nor did her mother; when in doubt she would simply pick up a Soviet-speak instruction manual entitled "One Hundred Questions, One Hundred Answers,"[27] and that settled the issue by dictating the politically correct response. Mariia sometimes wondered if her mother was so positive for Mariia's sake, to spare her the conflict of growing up with discordant beliefs, but she concluded that her mother's sentiments had to have been genuine.[28]

Shortly after the XX Party Congress, Mariia's mother was reinstated, and she immediately resumed her Party work. This entailed bolstering the Party's image—for example, by speaking at Pioneer gatherings about the Party's victories. The subject of the camps was not on the agenda at these meetings. She seemed to take it personally when Mariia chose not to join the Party. Disappointed, her mother scoffed, "If you don't need the Party, the Party doesn't need you." But Mariia had a more nuanced response. She did not need to be a card-carrying Party member to be a devoted Communist. She proudly raised her two children as Pioneers and Komsomols, with the ideals that had informed her own upbringing—the conviction that the cause of Communism was just and would triumph. Even so, there was a generational shift. Mariia's daughter wanted little to do with this cause.

In 2008, as Mariia reflected on her mother's life, she tried to understand how her mother had dealt with the personal and material losses of the repression. In brief, she concluded that those losses were bearable because they were not what her mother most valued in life. "My mother was very bright, she found happiness not in material things, but in spiritual things. Spiritual was not God, but the Party—you give your life in service and sacrifice."[29] Having found this spiritual connectedness to the Communist ideology in the same way that others find it in religious faith, Mariia's mother could sustain her loyalty to Communism, despite disappointments in the behavior of some Communists.

Many, including Mariia's mother, could have no ideological quarrel with the Party because they relied on the Party as the authority that provided the correct interpretation of Communism. Mariia's mother's faith in Communism was not challenged for her as it would later be for Mariia. Her mother died in 1964, still believing that the repression was a harsh but high-minded necessity for creating a just Communist society. Unlike Mariia, she did not have her faith challenged by the post-Khrushchev fluctuations in the Party's approach to the past, including the Brezhnev era re-Stalinization and the Gorbachev era disclosures on repression under Lenin. Mariia said that she and her husband did not support the dissident movement (1960s–1980s), but they felt generally positive about it. The Party had changed, and the dissidents, according to Mariia, were against the Party at that time, not the old Party. Mariia concurred with the dissidents' disapproval of how the Party functioned under Brezhnev, but affirmed her enduring belief in the ideals represented by the Party. Regarding the Gorbachev era, Mariia experienced it as unsettling. She liked him, but questioned his priorities—she thought it was a mistake to have opened the archives.[30]

Early on, Mariia's response to the revelations about the Stalinist past emphasized their damaging effects to the public image of the Soviet Union. She objected that these disclosures had gone too far because they seemed to nullify everything that the Soviet Union had achieved. She explained, "we became disheartened by what we heard." Moreover, though Mariia approved of modernization, change, and improvement, she maintained that a basis of socialism could still have been retained.

However, the increasing public attention to the repression was having an unanticipated influence on Mariia. By a process that was confusing even to her, Mariia found it harder to maintain her belief in Communism after the information from the archives became public. This challenge to her faith in Communism was confusing because the archives should not have revealed much more than she already knew from personal experience. What was different now was an audience that brought a different interpretive frame. A new meaning to old events was now reflected back to Mariia through the response of a different audience. Until Gorbachev lifted the censorship on public discussions of the terror and exposed it to the scrutiny of public discourse, Mariia had been able to maintain a limited view of the chronology and scope of the repression. Now she was forced to revisit and critically assess the old, mutually validating interpretations of the repression that she had learned from her mother and her cohorts. Now she was forced to realize that the use of physical coercion to promote the Communist ideology was also practiced under Lenin. She admitted, "I was the last of everyone I knew to really understand that so much of the system of repression started with Lenin; we always wrote everything off to Stalin."[31] Mariia would have preferred to remain oblivious to this because it undermined so much that was foundational to her understanding of her family and her country.

Confronted with dissonant facts, Mariia had to change her cognitions and search anew for meaning. She explained, "it was very hard, you lose the ground beneath your feet because you don't understand what the truth is."[32] She might more aptly have said that she now recognizes other "truths." From this, she wondered whether, perhaps, her father had died in vain and her mother had labored in vain. In activating these latent issues, seemingly settled but still unsettling, she reluctantly acknowledged, "I guess what they did wasn't right, but they were fighting for the good of the people, sincerely fighting. It was not for themselves."[33] As we talked, it became clear that the part that "wasn't right" presumably referred to her father's work in Kiev.

Mariia acknowledged being "very upset" by the fact that her father had occupied a high position—Secretary of the Provincial Committee in Kiev—at the time of the 1932–33 post-collectivization famine in Ukraine. She could not understand how he could have overseen the Party's murderous policies of confiscating grain from starving peasants. She claimed that her mother had been unaware of this, though they had all been living there at the time. I asked Mariia whether, perhaps, her mother knew what was happening but had considered it too risky to discuss the famine with Mariia unless she could buttress the mass starvation with an ideological justification.[34] There would have been risk at two levels: for one, it might have diminished the Party's standing in Mariia's eyes; for another, any balanced discussion of Party policy could have been interpreted as an expression of anti-Soviet sentiments. Mariia conceded that these would be plausible grounds for her mother's censorship.

Fortuitously, the very archives that Mariia had dreaded to read provided her with a potentially positive view of her father. This is another rich example of the Catch-22 legal/ethical conundrum that still stymies the rehabilitation process. When Mariia was finally able to read her father's case file, she discovered that he had been accused of disagreeing with the Party's policies in the villages. If this was really true, rather than fabricated charges trumped up to justify executing him for other reasons, then she could valorize her father as a "hero." However, the materials necessary to corroborate her speculation were not accessible. And though she was aware that most of the charges in these files were fabricated, she was comforted by the hope that her father was nobly guilty as charged.

Nearly two decades after the collapse of the Soviet Union, Mariia felt some ambivalence about the Party, but her feelings were primarily favorable. Like her mother, Mariia was able to look past negative events to find support for such positive feelings. She claimed to have an unfavorable attitude toward the "KGB-FSB . . . it started with the opening of the archives. When I understood their role [in the country's history of repression], I understood that they were capable of anything." She was shocked at the election of Putin, a former member of the FSB. And though she had revered Lenin—and, perhaps, still did—she wanted to see his body removed from the mausoleum and buried. For decades Mariia had believed that those who made the revolution had "mostly clean hearts and hands."[35] She needed to believe this. But, when contradictory facts entered the public discourse, she reluctantly conceded that even Lenin did "horrible things" and was "cruel." Even so, her overall favorable assessment of the Party in her life-story narrative is testimony to the triumph of what she would prefer to feel over what she knows; it was arguably faith-based rather than evidence-based.

Looking back on the trajectory of Communism and the end of the Soviet experience, some voiced regrets, their own and perhaps those of their parents who had left their families nearly a century earlier to join the Revolution. Their dream was never realized, a political derailment they sometimes blamed on Gorbachev and perestroika. As one interviewee lamented:

> I think we made a terrible mistake. Gorbachev, Iakovlev, and other perestroika figures could have chosen a more Chinese variant . . . People believed in the equality of nations and ideals. Gorbachev is responsible for ruining everything.[36]

Such survivors would have preferred to see a version of modernization and reform that retained the socialist basis and ideals in which they had believed, and for which they had paid a price.

The View from Within

This chapter merely begins to delve into the under-researched issues attendant to the second generation of Gulag survivors—many of whom were not the "builders of socialism" or card-carrying Party members. However, even such a limited sample of children of repressed Party loyalists, who do not speak for their entire cohort, permits us to draw some conclusions. Their reflections direct us to larger questions, relevant to testimony and repressed people. The power of a system to control the individual's appraisal of events is attested to by the convictions the loyalists had incorporated into their personal experience narratives.

While recognizing the arbitrary hardships imposed on them, in their life stories few loyalists blamed the Party or the system. To the extent that we respect the sincerity of our narrators, we recognize that they are the arbiters of their needs, and their appraisal of events may be assumed to fit their needs. A critical reappraisal of what had happened to them and their Party could be wrenching and potentially destabilizing because it would risk devaluing the meaning of their suffering in the camps, their redemptive martyrdom, and the triumph of survival.

With varying degrees of emphasis on one or another need, these stories describe the struggle of the children of repressed parents to satisfy three basic needs: for safety, community, and meaning. In the absence of a protective family and an institutionalized religion (which was forbidden in the Soviet Union), the Communist Party was often the only organization that could provide for these needs.

After People's Deputy Stepanov lost his father and his political security to the repression, he was able to repair his political security by adapting to the Party that he was now defending in the Duma. Roy Medvedev was able to find community in the dissident movement, and had the courage to risk his safety by criticizing Stalin at a time when the Party was trying to partially rehabilitate him. They found enduring meaning in what the Party had meant for their fathers. Natasha Ioffe's mother, Nadezhda, shielded her from the knowledge that Natasha's father had been executed as an "enemy of the people." Nor did Nadezhda reveal the criminal behavior she had witnessed in the Gulag, in order to help Natasha live more comfortably in a world controlled by the Communist Party. Nataliia Rappaport could find no such comfort in the Communist Party because after her father's arrest in 1953 for the "Doctors' Plot," she was alienated by and from the rampant state-sponsored anti-Semitism. As an adult, she would conceivably have been open to joining the Party in the Gorbachev era.

Neither Evgeniia Smirnova nor Mariia Kuznetsova reported any sense of indignation or even surprise at their mothers' enduring loyalty to the Party—even after losing their husbands and being incarcerated in the Gulag. The loyalty that had survived in the returnee parents had also, to some extent, survived them—in their children. Two decades after the end of the Soviet Union, even in hindsight, these daughters of repressed parents had questions, but they did not condemn the Party; in fact they praised the sincerity of the efforts that had been made to build Communism. These efforts were ultimately unsuccessful, but the system that had been built, encouraged, and at times brutally enforced, over the course of decades, remained for some a source of safety, community, and meaning. The ambivalence in these narratives attests to the difficulty of assessing the past on an individual level. On a national level such a task is even more complicated.

Conclusion

In 1962, acclaimed Russian poet Evgenii Evtushenko's "The Heirs to Stalin," published in *Pravda,* celebrated the removal of Stalin's body from the Lenin Mausoleum, but asked how Stalin was to be removed from Stalin's heirs. A fundamental reason why this discussion—and "Stalin's ghost"—could rise again and again is because all of the official attempts to reckon with the Stalinist past were inconsistent. They were born of ambivalence, an ambivalence that resonated both from the "top down" and from the "bottom up," as attested by many of the survivors' narratives.

In closed societies, political systems are rarely subjected to critical public scrutiny, nor are they accountable to their citizens. Rather, the burden is on the citizens to accommodate to the system or assimilate it in order to survive. Since Stalin's death in 1953, the view of the Stalinist past has been adjusted to fit individual and national needs. Efforts by organizations such as Memorial, to bring the repression into the arena of public discourse, often were and are not officially encouraged. In the Soviet era, there was a fairly consistent recognition that a fuller history of the repression could undermine the legitimacy of the regime, and in the post-Soviet era, the past was promoted as a rallying point for patriotism and national pride. Consequently, the Party and many loyalist survivors defended *their* history of the repression as *the* history of the repression by claiming authority over the "facts" as well as the interpretation of the facts. The political system shaped its citizens' cognitive appraisals by supplying narratives of events that justified its methods of governance, and the Party narrative was sometimes incorporated into the individual's narrative.

How might we further understand this merging of the personal and political narrative, as evidenced by many of the accounts above? Whether a narrative is the official history of a Party or the personal experience of an individual, it performs the essential function of organizing experience into a sequence of events and giving it meaning. In operation, the narrative tells us: "this is what happened," "this is what it meant," and "this is how we deal with it." [37] To the majority of prisoners, their persecution was unexpected and uncontrollable, but they tried to regain some control over events by the story they told themselves, each other, and imagined others. In this way, the meaning of what happened could be influenced by how they dealt with it.[38]

There was no "happy ending" to the story of Soviet Communism. The system represented by the Party ended up murdering millions of its own citizens, including those who supported and built it. For several reasons, it also ended up collapsing,[39] leaving most citizens with conflicting memories of the Soviet experience. Instead of constructively gleaning lessons from its failure—an exercise that could perhaps achieve a politically different "happy ending"—there has been a conscious effort to turn the defeat into victory through a careful selection of what should be remembered and which elements of the past should not be attended to. The personal and political narratives that have emerged reflect this selection in a legacy of censorship and self-censorship that has long outlived the demise of the system.

Notes

1. See Erin Daly, "Truth Skepticism: An Inquiry into the Value of Truth in Times of Transition," *The International Journal of Transitional Justice* 2 (2008): 23–41.
2. For more on the experiences of this group, see the richly documented volume by Cathy A. Frierson and Semyon S. Vilensky *Children of the Gulag* (New Haven: Yale University Press, 2010).
3. Iurii Feofanov, "XXX S'ezd KPSS v zale konstitutionnogo suda," *Izvestiia*, 8 July 1992.
4. Ibid.
5. For more on children of special settlers, see Oxana Klimkova, "Special Settlements in Soviet Russia," *Kritika* 8 (2007): 128–138. See also Figes, 349, 352.
6. Roy Medvedev, interview with author at his Moscow dacha, June 19, 2005.
7. Nadezhda Ioffe, transcript of interview with Professor Albert Leong, November 17, 1997, 24.
8. Ibid.
9. See Leon A. Festinger, *A Theory of Cognitive Dissonance* (Stanford: Stanford University Press, 1957); Eddie Harmon-Jones and Judson Mills, *Cognitive Dissonance:*

Progress on a Pivotal Theory in Social Psychology, (Washington: American Psychological Association, 1997), Chapter 1.
10. See also Nadezhda A. Joffe, *Back in Time: My Life, My Fate, My Epoch*, trans. Frederick S. Choate (Oak Park, MI: Labor Publications, Inc., 1995).
11. His Party membership may have been returned at the same time as he was rehabilitated.
12. Felicity Barringer, "Soviet Survivor Relives 'Doctors' Plot'," *New York Times*, 13 May 1988. Nataliia's memoirs were also published in journal form, see Rapoport, Nataliia, "Pamiat'—eto tozhe meditsina," in *Sputnik*, 10–11 (May 16), 10 (May 23), 1988.
13. Barringer.
14. See Nanci Adler, *The Gulag Survivor: Beyond the Soviet System* (New Brunswick: Transaction Publishers, 2002), Chapter 2.
15. Orlando Figes, The Family Histories, www.orlandofiges.com, accessed 10 March 2008.
16. Evgeniia Vladimirovna Smirnova, interview with author, Moscow, March 18, 2008.
17. Ibid.
18. Ibid.
19. Evgeniia Smirnova, transcript of interview with Alena Kozlova, October 2004, 58–59.
20. Smirnova, interview with author, Moscow, March 18, 2009.
21. Valentina Tikhanova, ed. *Rasstrel'nye spiski*, Vypusk 1 Donskoe kladbishche, 1934–40 (Moscow: NIPTs Memorial, 1993). This work encompasses the short biographies of 670 of the Moscow victims of execution on political charges, whose ashes are buried at the Donskoi crematory. The list contains only the victims whose fates had been ascertained as of January 1, 1993.
22. Smirnova, interview with author, March 18, 2008.
23. Figes, The Family Histories, www.orlandofiges.com, accessed 10 March 2008.
24. Mariia Il'inichna Kuznetsova, interview with author, Moscow, March 15, 2008.
25. Ibid.
26. Kuznetsova, transcript of interview with Irina Ostrovskaia, 39.
27. Ibid. Mariia's husband served as an economic advisor to the Ministry of Trade. They were stationed in Nepal and Libya, where Mariia had inevitable contact with foreigners. She referred to this manual up until 1985.
28. Kuznetsova, interview with author, Moscow, March 15, 2008.
29. Ibid.
30. Ibid.
31. Ibid.
32. Ibid.
33. Ibid.
34. Such discussion was, of course, unlikely because of the secrecy surrounding these policies.
35. Kuznetsova, interview with author, March 15, 2008.
36. Gerta Evgen'evna Chuprun, interview with author, Moscow, March 20, 2008.
37. See Jerome Bruner, *Actual Minds, Possible Worlds* (Cambridge: Harvard University Press, 1986).
38. On the purpose of the normative personal experience narrative, see Kenneth J. Gergen, Mary G. Gergen, "Narratives of the Self," in Theodore R. Sarbin, Karl E. Scheibe, eds., *Studies in Social Identity* (New York: Praeger, 1983), 254–273.
39. See Stephen F. Cohen, *Soviet Fate and Lost Alternatives* (New York: Columbia University Press, 2009), Chapter 5.

3

"You Don't Believe Me?": Truth and Testimony in Cypriot Refugee Narratives

Helen Taylor

All lives are stories waiting to be told, but the life experiences of refugees are destined to be narrated. In some cases these narratives are a matter of survival, as the refugee is compelled to produce stories of persecution in order to gain asylum. During exile, stories offer the refugee a way to keep the lost home alive and pass on memories to subsequent generations. Meanwhile, in some situations, accounts of war and flight are used as testimony to past injustices, in order to seek reparation or return home in the future. Some refugee narratives reach a wider audience through compelling autobiographies of exile, which offer insight into the experience of displacement.[1] Similarly, oral and community historians have long recorded narratives of migration, which help to build a collective picture of exile. Academic research, on the other hand, has been slower to recognize the value of refugees' stories as the focus of study rather than as supporting material. However, the narrative turn in refugee studies in recent years has shone light onto the experience of forced migration. Indeed, such stories have provided access to new and important knowledge that would not have been gained elsewhere. By using narrative methods, however, forced-migration researchers have been forced to engage with some of the ongoing debates about evidence and truth in life stories. In addition, these issues have to be considered in the context of the hostile climate currently facing refugees in many regions of the world, making researchers doubly aware of the importance of trusting, rather than challenging, refugee narratives.

Some refugees see testimony as a way of taking back control in such disempowering circumstances, and for them the research context can be an opportunity to make known the injustices they have experienced. For others, the testimonial impulse is tempered by the desire to bury troublesome memories of the past and remain silent. In both cases there are methodological challenges that must be engaged with. This chapter will explore some of these issues, with particular reference to primary narrative research into the meaning of home for Greek Cypriot and Turkish Cypriot refugees living in protracted exile in London.

The research in question, conducted in 2004, comprised in-depth interviews with twenty-two first-generation Cypriots who became refugees as a result either of the intercommunal violence and marginalization of Turkish Cypriots during the 1960s, or the Greek coup and Turkish invasion of 1974, which caused about 250,000 Cypriots to lose their homes when the island was divided into the Turkish Cypriot north and Greek Cypriot south. Some of these individuals made their way to Britain, where many Cypriots already lived as a result of the country's former colonial relationship with the island. The use of narrative methodology, in the form of unstructured interviews, gave those involved in the research space to talk about their experiences at length, and the resulting stories revealed some profound truths about displacement.[2] The research journey was also instructive in the importance of not pre-judging outcomes, and of placing trust in the narratives themselves.

The Constructed Narrative

The narrative form allows for complexity and contradiction, for idiosyncrasies and the emergence of seemingly insignificant details that can take research in a different direction. It is well suited, therefore, to the difficult task of understanding the chaos of war and the challenges of exile, as well as the sometimes conflicting desires to build a new life while keeping alive memories of the lost home. As Julia Powles argues, in an article on the usefulness of life history and personal narrative as a basis for research with refugees, some issues "can only really be communicated through narrative since they are not readily amenable to generalization."[3] In spite of popular media portrayals of faceless huddled masses of refugees, each exile has their own individual story. The experience of forced migration is not the same for all refugees, and the search for generalizations will not reveal the best understanding of exile. In contrast, narratives demonstrate the lack of homogeneity among refugees and, in doing so, challenge unhelpful stereotypes.[4] This, however, leads to one of the criticisms of narratives in the academic context.

The difficulty of reaching generalizable conclusions from diverse individual narratives has been seen as a drawback by those who prefer more conventional forms of data collection. But here I agree with Mark Freeman, who argues in a paper on the shortcomings of scientific investigation when exploring the human subject, that narrative enquiry is in fact "more *authentically* scientific" than "systematic, precise, quantitatively-grounded empirical enterprises," in that it displays greater fidelity to the phenomena under investigation—namely "the living, loving, suffering, dying human being."[5] Individual refugee narratives will have far more to teach us about the lived experience of exile than more formulaic data-collection exercises.

The suspicion of narrative as a basis for research arises from the fact—widely accepted among narrative researchers—that narratives are constructed representations of the self at a particular moment, as memory selects aspects of the past that best serve the needs of the present. This suggests that narratives arise out of a process of construction over time, meaning that alternative versions would have been possible in different circumstances. So how can stories be trusted when they cannot be relied upon to stay the same over time? This mutability is celebrated in the transmission of folktales and myths, which are passed down through generations and elaborated over time, but when the narratives in question deal with life events that are being examined in a research context, doubts often arise. How do we know that the version we are being told is the "correct" one? How can we analyze "data" that may deviate from "fact"? How do we generalize from individual, possibly conflicting, narratives? How can events from the past be remembered accurately in the present? Where is the "truth" to be found?

In response to such doubts, Freeman also criticizes elsewhere what he sees as "the fetishisation of accuracy," stating that it is precisely the distance from the short-sightedness of the past that allows narrative to develop a clearer picture, "to see and describe things *anew*, from a vantage point that will hopefully be superior."[6] This is true in the case of refugee stories, which are influenced by individual and collective memories, family accounts, media reports, public history, and recent events and, as a result, are rich sources of information. Rather than casting doubt on the veracity of individual narratives, the ongoing process of collaborative construction provides greater insight into the larger social context of exile, telling us about events that happened in the past and how those events are now viewed by individuals and the community. As Catherine Riessman asserts, in work looking at the analysis of personal narratives in the research context, narratives concerning past events "are of interest precisely because narrators interpret the past in stories rather than reproduce the past as it was."[7] While we may not be accessing historical, factual truth (if indeed it is ever possible to access this), we are witnessing a far more illuminating emotional truth.

Alessandro Portelli has discussed these matters at length, in particular in his exploration of the death of Italian steelworker Luigi Trastulli. Trastulli died in a clash with police in March 1949, in the Umbrian town of Terni, during a demonstration against the signing of the NATO treaty. However, in collective memory, the death has commonly been transposed to the street battles that occurred when a large number of steelworkers were laid off in 1953, an event which had a greater significance for workers and political activists in the town.[8] In assessing this collective inaccuracy, Portelli explains that the oral sources he uses "are not always fully reliable in point of fact. Rather than this being a weakness, this is however, their strength: errors, inventions, and myths lead us through and beyond facts to their meanings."[9] What matters is why popular memory has misremembered the incident and what this tells us about the political and social context under investigation. In this instance, the errors occurred because of the collective need to place Trastulli's death in a more appropriate and fitting political context.

The wider personal and political context of a narrative may indeed influence its adherence to historical accuracy, so that testimonies of trauma, such as those of the Holocaust, are often altered by the enormity of the events being described. In an exploration of the challenges of recording Holocaust testimonies on video, psychiatrist Dori Laub writes of the account of a survivor from Auschwitz who recalls seeing four chimneys exploding during the Auschwitz uprising, when only one was actually destroyed.[10] The inaccuracy caused her account to be discounted by historians, but Laub argues that the woman was "testifying not simply to empirical historical facts, but to the very secret of survival" and to the fact that she had seen the "unimaginable taking place . . . this bursting open of the very frame of Auschwitz."[11] The factual inaccuracies of her testimony do not make it doubtful but rather tell us about the prolonged and profound impact of such terrible and extreme events.

Trusting Refugees

Debates about the nature of truth in narrative must also be examined in the context of the suspicion with which refugees' stories are often received in the asylum system. Philip Marfleet, who explores the global picture of forced migration in a historical and political context, refers to an "official culture of scepticism" within the immigration offices of North America and Western Europe, quoting a former British immigration officer working in an Asian capital, who said, "Our starting point was that refugees are economic migrants . . . Once you believe that the vast majority of applicants have false stories everyone is under suspicion."[12] Certainly, for many refugees, telling stories in the context of the asylum interview is an experience with potentially disastrous consequences. If their story is not believed, asylum may be refused, and they could be returned to a situation of grave danger or compelled to a life in limbo awaiting the outcome of repeated asylum appeals. It is not enough that refugees simply tell the truth; the information they give must also satisfy the current quotas and standards of the asylum system they are appealing to.[13] Marfleet illustrates this with reference to a Sudanese refugee who walked all the way to Cairo only to be disbelieved by an immigration official: "He laughed and said that nobody could walk that far and this story would not help me."[14] Although the refugee was telling his true life story, his narrative was taken as a work of fiction and was not believed.

Another consequence of the vagaries of the asylum system is that some refugees are compelled to give an altered version of events because they have been forced to flee without the correct papers or have had to buy false papers in order to leave their country or enter another. Some withhold information in order to protect others back home, while others know they have to tell officials what they think they want to hear in order to gain asylum. It is into this situation of suspicion and mistrust on both sides that a researcher hoping to collect refugee narratives emerges. For those conducting research in refugee camps or with newly arrived refugees still immersed in the asylum process, the potential problems are writ large. Refugees who have been questioned repeatedly by immigration officials, relief workers, and police may have an understandable reluctance to tell their story to a researcher, as John Chr. Knudsen explains, in a volume exploring the perpetuation of mistrust of and by refugees in a hostile political climate. "Why should the refugee trust the researcher," he asks, "a person whose questions and, even more dangerously, whose interpretations may represent a threat to their future?"[15] The challenge for the researcher, therefore, is to avoid replicating the role of the immigration official, excavating facts and cross-examining the refugee about their reasons for flight. Rather, the researcher must start from a position of trust, allowing the refugee the space to tell their narrative so that truths about the nature of exile can be revealed and meaningful knowledge gained. For refugees living in protracted exile with rights of residency, the implications of telling their story are not quite so loaded. Nonetheless, the researcher must still be aware that war, flight, and exile have repercussions over years and down generations and, as a result, refugee narratives should always be treated with sensitivity and respect.

My own research with Greek Cypriot and Turkish Cypriot refugees in London involved individuals who had been in exile for thirty to forty years and had established lives in Britain. They were not, therefore, in the most vulnerable category of refugees. However, the effects of exile were still very much present in their daily lives, as was their need for their stories to be heard and believed. Their narratives told me a lot about their personal experiences, as well as the collective experience of exile, and during the process of listening to and writing about their stories, I was forced to question my own preconceptions.

Weeping Statues and the Danger of Doubt

One woman who generously shared her life story with me was Adrienne, a Greek Cypriot woman in her forties, who had been a teenager when she became a refugee in 1974, after the second wave of Turkish military action on the island.[16] When her village near the northern town of Famagusta was invaded, villagers were taken to a nearby village where they were held by Turkish troops for three months, before the Red Cross escorted them to the south of the island. A number of men from the village, including Adrienne's uncle, were taken hostage and went "missing."[17] Her family lived in the southern town of Limassol for five years before Adrienne came to England for an arranged marriage to a British-born Greek Cypriot, who had died of cancer a year before our interview.

Adrienne's narrative was lively, humorous, and rich with detail about her experience in the immediate aftermath of the war, as well as her life in London and her difficulties since her husband died. Indeed, there was so much of interest to me as a researcher that I was conscious of selecting which topics to follow up as the interview progressed and time ran out. As a result, I discounted one particular incident—Adrienne's account of a statue of the Virgin Mary, the Panagia, weeping—as not relevant to my research about the meaning of home for Cypriot refugees. However, my main reason for not following up the episode was, quite simply, that I did not believe it. This section of the narrative is quoted here in full, including my questions as well as the interjections of Adrienne's British-born brother-in-law and cousin, who were present at the interview:

> Adrienne: I remember something before 1974 and it stays in my memory and it's going to stay forever. Panagia, it was a special day and we went to this monastery and [it was the] saint's day and [the icon] was crying. I'm not joking, she was crying.
>
> Brother-in-law [To HT]: This Panagia is Mary. It's Mary.
>
> Adrienne: Yeah, she was crying. And tears they were coming from [her eyes]. They would go there and they go away, constantly.
>
> HT: On the statue?
>
> Adrienne: Yeah, I'm not joking. And people I told, they said: "Don't be so crazy, they've done something in there on the icon and it's crying." And after a few days it was the war in Cyprus and people were saying because something was going to happen she was crying. It's something I saw with my own eyes. [To brother-in-law] You don't believe me?
>
> Brother-in-law: I don't believe, no, no.
>
> Adrienne: Honestly.
>
> HT: So you'd gone to the monastery for a special day?
>
> Adrienne: Special day, it was Panagia, yeah.
>
> Brother-in-law [To HT]: It was Panagia.
>
> Adrienne: Panagia yes.
>
> Brother-in-law [To HT]: It's a saint's day.
>
> Cousin: The tenth. Between the tenth and—
>
> Adrienne: No it wasn't. It was before, before. It was another day. It was another.
>
> Cousin: Yeah, because that was August wasn't it and it must have been in July.
>
> Adrienne: July was—
>
> Cousin: July was the—

Brother-in-law: July was when they invaded.

Adrienne: Yeah and people in there were really surprised seeing an icon cry and it—

Brother-in-law: Did anyone else see it?

Adrienne: —was so real.

Brother-in-law: Did anyone else see it?

Adrienne: Everybody saw it, yeah. But I don't really discuss with anybody and I don't really see a lot of people. But some of the people they were saying I was a crazy and they done something. Probably put something in the back [of the icon].

HT: So then what happened? Had there been trouble before the invasion? Did you know that something was going to happen?

Adrienne's brother-in-law makes it clear that he doubts the veracity of this event (although in all other aspects he showed great sensitivity and respect for Adrienne during the interview). He tells her clearly, "I don't believe, no, no," asking her twice: "Did anyone else see it?" My slightly incredulous question, "On the statue?" suggests that I don't believe her either, as does the fact that I move on quickly to another issue at the end of the episode. The confusion over dates casts further doubt on the account, even though Adrienne says it "stays in my memory and it's going to stay forever." The most important saint's day for Mary is the festival of the Assumption of the Virgin Mary on 15 August, yet Turkey's initial military action lasted from 20 to 30 July 1974 and was resumed on 14 August. If the weeping icon was believed to have been an omen for the Turkish invasion, it couldn't have happened after the soldiers arrived. It could be that Adrienne is thinking of another saint's day, or that the two events were not concurrent but have become so in her mind because of her need to unite them. Just as political activists in Portelli's account of Luigi Trastulli's death transferred the worker's murder to a more relevant time, so Adrienne may have shifted the saint's day to sit more fittingly in her memory as an omen of the invasion. Adrienne seems frustrated by her relatives' attempts to establish the exact date of the incident and turns the conversation back to the weeping icon. Both they and I were clearly missing the point.

The Panagia is believed to fulfill a role as protector of the Greek nation, as well as being the link between the human family and the divine family.[18]

There is also a long tradition of weeping icons in Orthodox Christianity, which are generally believed to be an omen of bad events.[19] More recent reports of similar events in Cyprus include a 400-year-old icon of the Virgin Mary and Jesus seen to be weeping at Kykko Monastery in 1997, sixty miles southwest of Nicosia. More than 20,000 Greek Cypriot pilgrims visited the "miracle," which was seen as an ominous sign for the island's future.[20] In keeping with this convention, Adrienne's weeping icon is inextricably linked in her memory to the Turkish military action and her consequent exile. On reflection, it is clearly not important whether the dates are wrong, whether the icon did in fact weep, or whether it was witnessed by anyone else. The truth of the narrative can be found in the fact that, for Adrienne, the war and becoming a refugee were calamitous life events, for which the crying Panagia was a fitting omen. It is the emotional truth, not the factual accuracy, that is of interest here, on both a human and a research level.

By connecting the refugees' traumatic experience of war and exile to the weeping icon, Adrienne may have been expressing hope that her suffering would be recognized. Yet the disbelief of her brother-in-law, as well as her statement that people "were saying I was crazy," imply that Adrienne does not think her account of the war would have been taken seriously. Adrienne says about the story of the icon, "I don't really discuss with anybody and I don't really see a lot of people." She then later added, after talking freely for nearly three hours, that she had never before told anyone in detail about her wartime experiences—neither her late husband nor her two adult sons. Her brother-in-law concurred, saying to her after the interview, "A lot of people, me included, don't really know the truth. Listening to what you've said tonight, it's really quite moving." Erica Apfelbaum has spoken of how survivors of unfathomable events, such as the Holocaust or the Armenian genocide, sometimes remain silent if they feel that others won't understand or don't share their experience. "Those who survive exist in a no-person's land of silence in which the experiences of the past receive no legitimation," she says.[21] This may also be the case for refugees who have witnessed the splitting apart of their homes and their social worlds.

This seems to suggest further that the incident with the Panagia has less to do with the veracity of the religious miracle and more with Adrienne's need to be believed and have her losses acknowledged. Whether the narrated event is factually accurate or not, there is certainly a great deal of truth in the narrative, which casts light on the experience of forced displacement. It is also a reminder that as researchers we need to listen for the truth in incidents we may initially discount because of our own preconceptions. As a researcher, starting from a position of trust in refugee narratives, I was nonetheless tripped up by my own cultural bias. Having no religious faith myself, I was unable to see beyond my inability to believe that an icon could cry. Subconsciously judging the account to be untrue, I almost discarded this section of the narrative and overlooked the emotional truth that was staring me in the face. I am chastened by Dori Laub's guidance to those listening to testimony, that their prior knowledge should not "hinder or obstruct listening with foregone conclusions and preconceived dismissals, should not be an obstacle or a foreclosure to new, diverging, unexpected information."[22] Not only is it bad manners to listen to an individual's narrative with too many preconceptions, it also makes for bad research.

Testimony and Taking Control

The testimonial function of narrative after war, exile, or other injustice has been examined previously, illustrating the importance of speaking out for those who have been wronged or suffered trauma.[23] For refugees, bearing witness to the events of the past, either as individuals or as part of a political movement demanding reparation or return, can be empowering. For example, in the Sanctuary movement in the United States, William Westerman explains, Guatemalan and El Salvadorean refugees used testimony so that individual stories heard alongside each other would put pressure on the US government of the time.[24] In addition, he says, the act of giving testimony for these and other refugees symbolizes the transition from victim to actor, so that "history no longer makes them. They make it, write it, speak it."[25] Similarly, in his illuminating work on the politics of narrative, Michael Jackson stresses the importance of storytelling in giving refugees a sense of agency when confronted with disempowering life events, so that even though they are unable to change what has happened to them they can nonetheless define the meaning of such events.[26] For the refugee, he explains, "constructing, relating and sharing stories is basic to this reclamation of [their] humanity—of turning object into subject, givenness into choice, what into who."[27] Indeed, the awareness that one is telling a story that is of interest to others and is worth listening to, recording, and in some cases studying, can be empowering. Adrienne, who had not talked publicly about her experience of war, asked me halfway through our meeting how many refugees I had spoken to, before stating cheerfully, "I'm the best one, so far!" Her confidence in the value of her story grew, so that by the end of the interview she told me, "'I'm going to write my story . . . I'm going to write a little book. It's not going to be a bestseller but it's going to be something. We could make a movie, you know that. I'm not joking." By defining the meaning of her own experiences she has, as Westerman states, made history rather than being made by it.

Many refugees, including the Cypriot refugees I spoke to, use stories as a way of making sense of the past, present and future, in order to render exile manageable and life livable. As Norman Denzin states, explaining the centrality of narrative to all our lives, the "stories we tell help us to wrestle with the chaos around us, helping us to make sense of the world when things go wrong."[28] The refugee's need to make sense of forced displacement may give rise to a testimonial impulse, which has benefits and drawbacks for the researcher. Firstly, it means that there are often articulate and willing representatives of refugee communities who are eager to share their story, as part of an ongoing project to make public the events that led to their exile. Indeed, such community leaders and spokespeople are often the first individuals that the researcher encounters and may lead to other interviewees. The stories they tell will have been told many times before, in public and more intimate settings, and as a result will have been altered and embellished as other members of the family and community have added their version of events. Far from this diminishing their value, however, the resulting collectively constructed narratives offer the researcher access to both individual and collective experience. In addition, these individuals are often able to speak at length about issues that they have given much consideration.

One of the perceived downsides of conducting research with those eager to testify is that their political project might obscure the pure "data" by influencing their account. However, once again, it is important to return to the principle of trust in the integrity of the narrative. For example, during my research I interviewed Dimitris, a Greek Cypriot, and Salih, a Turkish Cypriot, both of whom were leaders of their village committees in exile. Both men were explicit about their desire to further their political campaigns for reparations and saw my research as a potential platform for airing their opinions. Salih, whose village had been razed to the ground in 1964, set up a village association in 2003 to campaign for an apology from the Greek Cypriot government and the rebuilding of his village. Meanwhile, Dimitris fled his village during the Turkish military action of 1974 and is the *muhtar* (mayor) of his village in exile. While both men spoke at length about their personal experiences in Cyprus and

Britain, their longing for their lost homes, and their feelings about what had happened to them, they also shared their views on the politics of Cyprus and their hopes for the future of the island.

It would be naïve to expect politically active individuals like Salih and Dimitris to hold back on their views about the larger political picture and only talk about events personal to them. Indeed, due to the highly charged circumstances that lead to exile, there can be few refugees without firm political opinions, and most will feel strongly about the events that changed the course of their lives. It is also misguided to try to separate personal stories from the social context that surrounds them. Historian E. H. Carr noted that "society and the individual are inseparable, they are necessary and complementary to each other," going on to say that "history is a social process, in which individuals are engaged as social beings."[29] This makes the study of individual lives not simply an alternative approach to the study of society but an essential part of it. Indeed, I agree with Andrews et al., when they state that narrative research is able to "challenge the conventional dualism between individual and society" as "material social conditions, discourses and practices interweave with subjectively experienced desires and identities."[30]

Collecting narratives from those keen to bear witness to past events gives the researcher insight, not just into the personal experience of the refugee, but also into the political currents among the exile community. By collecting a number of these narratives together, the researcher is able to build a picture of the experience of exile within a community and attitudes toward the current political situation. For example, while I was conducting research with Cypriots in London, border restrictions separating the north and south of the island were relaxed in Cyprus, making return visits to their lost homes a possibility for these refugees for the first time in thirty years. As a result the political and personal implications of making such journeys were hotly debated. Each of my narrators expressed their personal opinions and feelings about their homes, the war, and the country they had left behind, but collectively the narratives also revealed political undercurrents in the diaspora and Cyprus, as well as differences in attitudes toward return among Greek Cypriots and Turkish Cypriots.

Exploring the usefulness of individual narratives as a social research tool, Samuel Schrager describes each story as grounded in the social world from which it arises.[31] Personal narratives emerging from a group with an experience in common—such as migration—will bear the marks of community interaction and the collective elaboration of stories over time. Far from devaluing the individual life story, identifying the convergences and divergences between such accounts enables the researcher to build up a picture of a group or event, the resulting "patterning of sentiments" indicating the structure of feelings within a society.[32] Although inherently valuable in themselves, when gathered together these accounts tell us something about society—both the society that led to these individuals becoming refugees and the society in which they now live.

The Burden of Remembering

Alongside those refugees who find the act of giving testimony empowering, there are those for whom speaking about the past is painful and difficult, and some who choose to remain silent altogether. Newly arrived refugees may be reluctant to talk if they believe that they or their family are still in danger, or if they are concerned that information they provide will be used to their detriment by immigration services. These situations may be challenging for the researcher, and in certain circumstances research will not be appropriate. In other cases the researcher must become adept at making the most out of minimal information. Research with refugees living in protracted exile is different in nature, but there will still be occasions when memories are difficult to revisit. Adrienne revealed that she had never spoken about her wartime experiences to her family; this may have been because she was unsure whether she would be believed, but she also implied that she found certain episodes painful to remember. At the end of our interview she said to me, "All night tonight, I mean I agreed for you to come, but I'm living there now. I see everything come back and I'm not sure how I'm going to feel tomorrow."[33]

The extensive literature on Holocaust testimony points to the survivor's struggle between the desire to bear witness and the desire to forget the terrible events of the past. Geoffrey H. Hartman, for example, refers to Holocaust testimonies as a "burdened retrieval . . . caught between a morbid and necessary remembrance."[34] While the narratives of Cypriot refugees are told from a very different context, they too bear the marks of a painful past, which produces the conflicting impulses to remember and to forget. Maroulla, an energetic and committed campaigner for the rights of Greek Cypriot refugees, was eager to share her story with me as part of her project to keep Cyprus and the refugee issue on the political agenda. However, she found certain aspects of the interview difficult, in particular when she referred to her brother, who has been missing since the war. About halfway through the interview she said, "I forgot to mention my brother. My, my, my brother's been missing. He was in the army in '74. He gave his life. This is a way I can do something. This is what is pushing me to get involved in those patriotic things, you know." It is unlikely that she had actually forgotten to mention her brother, but rather continues to find his disappearance understandably difficult to vocalize.

In addition to Maroulla's own exile and that of her family, her brother is the motivation for her activism. His loss is, of course, still painful for her, as she reveals when she talks of her first return visit to the village after the border opened. She was distressed to find her family house in ruins and being used as storage space for animal feed, and was struck by the fact that it was no longer the house she had dreamed of in exile. However, most important was the realization that if she could never return to the village she left, then neither could she bring her brother back. "I thought if I went back to the village, I would find my brother," she admitted. At the same time as she is committed to the political campaign of return, she also has to deal with the burden of her personal loss. The village she left behind now only exists in her memory, as she explains: "I dream of the church, my house, my grandma's house, my neighbour's house. I keep the memory."

Painful stories have impacts beyond those immediately involved, as they become wounds for the community as a whole to bear, symbolic of the hurt caused by war and exile. Dimitris, who is from the same village as Maroulla, also mentioned her brother during his interview: "I don't know if she had the heart to speak to you about him. Did she? She gets very emotional when she tells it. It's not easy for some people to, to talk about these things. I mean I was, emm, it's difficult. You know it, emm, it makes me shiver when I think about it." The loss clearly still affects Dimitris. Beyond his compassion for his fellow villager, and in spite of his confidence and ability to talk at length about both his personal experience of exile and the political situation in Cyprus, he too finds it difficult to talk about certain aspects of the war. Both the way in which Maroulla mentions her brother and the way in which Dimitris refers to her feelings about him suggest that she is indeed "caught between a morbid and necessary remembrance." Of course, she can never forget her brother, and his story is also part of the collective history of fellow villagers. For Maroulla, remembering her brother is part of a "patriotic" impulse to do something about the refugees and the missing. Yet it is not hard to sense the burden of retrieval for her and the fact that his loss remains in some ways inexpressible.

It is also the case that silences in refugee stories can be a result of the inequalities that preceded exile. As the minority community in Cyprus, Turkish Cypriots were marginalized during the 1960s and early 1970s, when many of them became refugees as a result of intercommunal violence. This led to a lack of confidence, which was transferred to Britain, and may explain a reluctance to talk about the past. Turkish Cypriots are less organized politically than Greek Cypriots in Britain and are generally more reluctant to be interviewed. Emine, a Turkish Cypriot woman, explained this to me: "We are always scared to talk, because we are used to being isolated. Because we keep quiet. Because we know what they did to us and we can't express it." The researcher needs to find a way, therefore, of listening to silences, being aware that absences form an important part of the truth of a community or individual's story. Indeed, it is often the things that are half said or spoken quietly that are the most illuminating.

Conclusion

Narrative methodologies can offer great insight into the lived experience of exile, but at the same time they challenge the forced migration researcher to meet head-on some of the debates about evidence-based research in the social sciences. As the discussion in this chapter has shown, the emotional truth about exile may be complex and not always easy to uncover. That is why narrative research has proved so powerful, allowing room for the expression of multiple, diverse and sometimes contradictory attitudes and feelings about exile. An obsession with factual accuracy, especially when listening to narratives about chaotic life events such as war, flight, and exile, can lead to an inability to hear the emotional truth about what it is really like to lose one's home and be forced to find another. While it remains necessary to engage with the ongoing debates about evidence, it is important to remember that the occurrence of historical or factual inaccuracies can be illuminating rather than obfuscatory.

In the context of hostile popular discourses about the refugee, the researcher has an additional responsibility to avoid contributing to a culture of doubt and suspicion. Starting from a position of trust and respect, it is necessary to find a way of being analytical without being inquisitory, especially when conducting research into the experiences of newly arrived or encamped refugees. The act of giving testimony about past injustices has allowed some refugees to take back control, so that they are recognized as actors in their own lives, rather than as passive victims. This testimonial impulse gives researchers access to life stories that form a collective story of exile and are, as a result, doubly valuable. Testimonies that have been repeated often or that bear the marks of collaborative construction do not represent compromised findings, but rather tell us about the prevailing opinions within a community as well as the narrator's personal sentiments about the past, present and future. At the same time, some refugees react to the difficulties of forced migration with silence and omissions. Although frustrating for the researcher, it is important to remember that these absences can themselves offer insight into the reality of exile and the marginalization that preceded it. It is apparent that there is no single, excavatable truth about exile waiting to be unearthed. What emerges instead is the realization that "truth" can be found in the interstices between personal memory and public history, between fact and story, between speech and silence.

Notes

1. See for example, Isabelle Allende, *My Invented Country* (London: Flamingo, 2003); Eva Hoffman, *Lost in Translation* (London: Vintage, 1989).
2. Interviews were not based on a strict interview schedule but allowed individuals to talk about their experiences with the introduction of key themes as prompts and follow-up questions. More men than women were interviewed (15 men to 7 women), and slightly more Greek Cypriots than Turkish Cypriots (12 to 10). Both of these factors illustrate the wider prominence of certain narratives, with Greek Cypriots more politically organized than Turkish Cypriots and therefore keener to talk, and first-generation Cypriot men more integrated in British society than women, making them more accessible.
3. Julia Powles, "Life History and Personal Narrative: Theoretical and Methodological Issues Relevant to Research and Evaluation in Refugee Contexts." *New issues in refugee research: Working paper no. 106,* http://www.unhcr.org/4147fe764.html (Geneva: UNHCR, 2004), 20.
4. Marita Eastmond, "Stories as Lived Experience: Narratives in Forced Migration Research," *Journal of Refugee Studies*, 20 (2007): 253.
5. Mark Freeman, "Science and Story," Unpublished paper delivered at the University of East London's Centre for Narrative Research's Methods in Dialogue Event, Hemingford Grey, Cambridgeshire (May 2005).
6. Mark Freeman, "Too Late: The Temporality of Memory and the Challenge of Moral Life," *Journal für Psychologie,* 11 (2003): 69–70.
7. Catherine Riessman, "Analysis of Personal Narratives," in *Handbook of Interview Research—Context and Method* eds. J.F. Gubrium and J.A. Holstein (Thousand Oaks, CA: Sage, 2001), 705.
8. Alessandro Portelli, *The Death of Luigi Trastulli and Other Stories—Form and Meaning in Oral History* (New York: State University of New York Press, 1991).
9. Ibid., 2.
10. Dori Laub, "Bearing Witness, or the Vicissitudes of Listening," in *Testimony: Crises of Witnessing in Literature, Psychoanalysis, and History*, eds.Shoshana Felman and Dori Laub (New York: Routledge, 1992), 59–62.
11. Ibid., 62.
12. Philip Marfleet, *Refugees in a Global Era* (Basingstoke, Hampshire: Palgrave Macmillan, 2006), 233.
13. John Chr. Knudsen, "When Trust Is on Trial: Negotiating Refugee Narratives," in *Mistrusting Refugees*, eds. E. Valentine Daniel and John Chr. Knudsen (Berkeley, California: University of California Press, 1995), 23; Marfleet, *Refugees*, 236.

14. Marfleet, *Refugees*, 235.
15. Knudsen, "When Trust...," 29.
16. Pseudonyms have been used throughout.
17. As in other conflict situations, the word "missing" in Cyprus generally refers to those who were killed in the conflicts of the 1950s, 1960s, and 1970s and remain unaccounted for. Recent work has been undertaken by international organizations to recover the bodies of the missing and return them to their families.
18. Rebecca Bryant, *Imagining the Modern: The Cultures of Nationalism in Cyprus* (London: I.B. Tauris, 2004), 198.
19. "Cyprus Icon Is Said To Weep," *New York Times*, February 10, 1997, http://www.nytimes.com/1997/02/10/world/cyprus-icon-is-said-to-weep.html?scp=1&sq=Cyprus+icon&st=nyt
20. Ibid.; Menelaos Hadjicostis, "Weeping Icon Moves a Nation," *Cyprus News Agency* (February 7, 1997) http://www.hri.org/news/cyprus/cna/1997/97-02-07.cna.html#03
21. Erica R. Apfelbaum, "'And Now What After Such Tribulations?': Memory and Dislocation in the Era of Uprooting," *American Psychologist*, 55 (2000): 1010.
22. Laub, "Bearing Witness," 61.
23. Ibid.; William Westerman, "Central American Refugee Testimonies and Performed Life Histories in the Sanctuary Movement," in *The Oral History Reader* eds. Robert Perks and Alistair Thomson (London: Routledge, 1998); Naomi Rosh White, "Marking Absences: Holocaust Testimony and History," in *The Oral History Reader*; Annette Wieviorka, "On Testimony" in *Holocaust Remembrance: The Shapes of Memory*, ed. Geoffrey H. Hartman (Oxford: Basil Blackwell, 1994).
24. Westerman, "Central American Refugee Testimonies," 225–7.
25. Ibid., 230.
26. Michael Jackson, *The Politics of Storytelling: Violence, Transgression and Intersubjectivity* (Copenhagen: Museum Tusculanum Press/University of Copenhagen, 2006), 15–16.
27. Ibid., 104.
28. Norman Denzin, "Foreword: Narrative's Moment,," in *Lines of Narrative: Psychosocial Perspectives*, eds. Molly Andrews, Shelley Day Sclater, Corinne Squire and Amal Treacher (London: Routledge, 2000), xii.
29. E.H. Carr, *What is History?* second edition, ed. R.W. Davies (London: Penguin, 1961/1987), 31, 55.
30. Andrews, et al., ed., *Lines of Narrative*, 1.
31. Samuel Schrager, "What Is Social in Oral History?" in *The Oral History Reader*.
32. Ibid., 293.
33. There are, of course, ethical implications in asking refugees to talk about difficult experiences. However, most of the participants in my study, unlike Adrienne, had told the story of their exile many times over the years and were eager to retell it. In Adrienne's case, the presence of her brother-in-law and cousin offered her additional support while she shared her story.
34. Geoffrey H. Hartman, ed. *Holocaust Remembrance: The Shapes of Memory* (Oxford: Basil Blackwell, 1994), 2.

4

Between Social and Individual Memory: Being a Polish Woman in a Stalinist Prison

Anna Muller

During one of my first meetings with a woman who had spent seven years in a prison in post-war Poland, I asked her how her experience as a prisoner compared to what is depicted in the well-known Ryszard Bugajski movie *Interrogation*.[1] For me, this masterful film, produced in 1982 at the height of martial law in Poland, fittingly captured the oppression and fear, the sense of being hunted, that female prisoners experienced. Krystyna Janda, in the role of the heroine, Tonia, commanded a powerful on-screen presence. Tonia is arrested after drinking heavily with a group of men in a nightclub. Still intoxicated, Tonia cries and screams during her first interrogations. Her hysteria is clearly visible in her facial expressions, gestures, and body language. Close-ups, which the director uses frequently, reveal Tonia's gray and swollen face, with heavy black circles around her eyes. She is tortured, sleep-deprived, and confused. During her captivity, Tonia's desperation is gradually transformed into silent stubbornness. After her husband comes to consider her an enemy of the party and divorces her, Tonia finds an empathetic partner in one of the guards, by whom she eventually becomes pregnant. Between this haunted woman and confused man a strange relationship emerges, marked by a mixture of distrust and desperation, of fear and hope. It seemed to me that there was no easier or more natural way of initiating a conversation with a woman who was a former political prisoner than by asking her opinion of *Interrogation*. Surprisingly, however, the woman with whom I spoke (who prefers to remain anonymous) did not agree.

Interrogation was banned soon after its making. Unofficial and illegal viewings of the film, attended by small groups of opponents of the Communist regime, became a political act. In many respects, the film was unique. Until the early 1990s, *Interrogation* was the only film and one of only a few sources about political prisoners. Moreover, it dealt with female prisoners, a theme that is rarely explored even today. And yet, many female prisoners assert that the movie is not about them.[2] They feel that the desperate Tonia does not accurately represent who they were and what they fought for in prison. Tonia's tears indicate weakness and confusion. While Tonia fought to survive and to understand why she was imprisoned, former female prisoners want to be seen as people who, even in prison, continued their fight for the dignity of Polish patriots and against their oppressor—the new Communist government established in 1945, which they perceived as illegitimate.

A prisoner's life after release from prison was difficult. Stigmatized by their incarceration, these women had great difficulty finding jobs or housing. The regime usually confiscated the land of prisoners who came from villages. The possibilities for receiving or completing an education were also severely limited. The alternative world of anti-Communist opposition that emerged in Poland in the 1970s did not seem to acknowledge them, either. The only book that appeared in underground circulation about political prisoners of the immediate post-war period dealt exclusively with men.[3] In this context, the women's disapproval of *Interrogation* is more than merely a rejection of what Tonia represented; it is also an attempt to join (or initiate) a debate on the place of women in the history and memory of the post-war anti-Communist struggle. This attempt to (re)gain a voice is also an effort to reconstitute part of the lost self.

This article examines a group of female political prisoners in post-war Communist Poland and their efforts to reestablish for themselves a space in the Polish historical narrative. I juxtapose certain aspects of the image of a political prisoner that women created in *Nike*, a periodical they established in 1992, with a more intimate understanding of their past that emerged in my interviews with them. To what extent did memories communicated through *Nike* silence certain, perhaps more difficult, aspects of their experiences in favor of a more univocal, heroic presentation of their past? In other words, what elements of autobiographical memories does *Nike* contain? There are some cultural constraints that dictate and inhibit the narration of certain stories. However, if that is true, to what extent is individual memory a reflection of a collective or a cultural template or script that we all learn during the socialization process? How much is individual memory socially or culturally determined? And finally, how much individual agency can we detect in the process of remembering?

Following James Fentress and Chris Wickham's study of social memory,[4] *Nike* can be viewed as representing the social memory of a particular group. *Nike* is the result of a specific dialogue between the women themselves, between their prison and post-prison past, and between their past and present. This dialogue is nevertheless imbued with the cultural meaning of Polish femininity. As Fentress and Wickham suggest, social memory "tells us who we are, embedding us in our past."[5] The women of *Nike* are their own historians, who created a forum that is an extension of the network of friendships they established in prison or shortly afterward. This network began as friendly conversations over coffee about post-prison life and about emotions, regrets, and even the kinetics they developed in a small prison cell. These informal gatherings and discussions eventually expanded into *Nike*, which was both a private exchange, a grapevine for information, and a space open to an outside audience.[6] The periodical provided the women with a chance to emphasize their contribution to the struggle for post-Communist Poland and reclaim a part of its history that the women felt had been lost to them.[7]

While reading *Nike* and talking to my interlocutors, I devoted special attention to the issue of gender. I realize that gender is usually overridden by other elements of self-creation, and an attempt to isolate gender may appear artificial. Nevertheless, since both *Nike* and many of my interlocutors were deeply involved in safeguarding the memory of women, it seems justified to focus on their understanding of femininity. Their criticisms of *Interrogation* suggest a certain cultural understanding of what it means to be a Polish woman. In *Exile and Identity*, a work about Polish women deported to Siberia during World War II, Katherine Jolluck argues that Polish women found it very difficult to talk about their gender identity and issues pertaining to their bodies. They based their identity on the fact that they were female prisoners but never quite consciously asked what imprisonment meant for them.[8] Narrating the story of a brave woman in the midst of violence and oppression worked toward both her heroization and her victimization. Similarly, the women of *Nike* used certain elements of their gender identity but concealed (silenced or simply chose to forget) others, especially their sexuality, as something shameful and stifling. The individual interviews I conducted do not reveal much beyond what *Nike* reveals in terms of gender. The women I interviewed had similar problems articulating what their distinct needs as women were. Their gender appears mostly as a source of weakness, but, interestingly, this does not prevent them from using certain cultural expectations in order to give their life stories coherence. Gender turns out to be "a shifting and contextual phenomenon . . . a complexity whose totality is permanently deferred, never fully what it is at any given juncture in time."[9]

As noted, my sources include articles from *Nike*.[10] The number of issues per year varies depending on the health of the main authors and editors. On average, *Nike* is issued four times a year. A second source are the interviews I conducted from 2007 to 2009. In this text, I use interviews with three former prisoners: Elżbieta Zawacka, Ewa Ludkiewicz, and Ruta Czaplińska. All three were autobiographical interviews, which were conducted in the form of an open conversation, during which I assumed the role of passive listener, ready to record their lists of regrets and wishes. The interviews were sometimes difficult. In more than one case, the interview turned into a political tirade about the fall of Communism and the interviewee's disappointment with the new, post-Communist Poland. I strove to maintain my role as an interviewer, although at times my strong disagreement with the political opinions my subjects expressed made this difficult.

The Women of This Study

After the Second World War, many former members of the anti-Nazi resistance joined various anti-Communist groups that sprang up as a reaction to Communism and the new political regime imposed on Poland after the war. For them, the war did not end. The first arrests had begun by 1944, and they continued through the early 1950s. There are no complete statistics regarding the number of prisoners in Stalinist Poland. According to rather modest estimates, from 1946 to 1953, 64,887 people were sentenced for anti-state crimes.[11] Women most likely constituted about ten percent of the entire population of prisoners.[12] Women were arrested for being couriers, liaisons, and members of espionage networks. Equally often, however, they were treated as a proxy for men: their sons, husbands, and fathers who, in light of the new political situation, decided not to take off their war uniforms. Regardless of whether they were actively involved or only accompanying various men, the women were treated by state authorities as "anti-state" prisoners, a term the women translated into "political prisoners." The ratio of political prisoners to criminal prisoners is impossible to determine. Moreover, these statistics include only Polish prisoners. Our knowledge about the social composition of female prisoners is rather skewed due to the nature of the sources and the class issues inherent in them. The majority of women who either wrote memoirs or remained in the network of former prisoners belonged to higher social strata, primarily Polish pre-war landowning groups or intelligentsia. As a result, most of the available documents do not represent a cross-section of society. Only a handful of recollections of women from lower social classes survived: for example, materials concerning imprisoned Communist women of working-class origins.[13] Nor is much known about women of peasant origins. Their stories have usually been preserved only in the recollections of others; at most, we know only their short biographies.[14] While an average imprisonment lasted from five to seven years, some women were sentenced to as many as fifteen years in prison. Most of these women were released by the mid-1950s.

Between an Interviewer and Interviewee: Creating Oral Histories

In contrast to the articles and vignettes from *Nike* that promote female prisoners' official reading of the past, interviews are more personal. Long conversations, in the safe surroundings of the women's private spaces, gave them a chance to reflect on their lives and sometimes, more or less willingly, to uncover tensions and worries that link their past with the present, which in turn provides us with insights into how they actively reconstruct their autobiographies. This was their moment—a chance to reinterpret their arrest, interrogation, and imprisonment, as well as an opportunity to explore their emotions: surprise, confusion, fear, and anger. The interview also constituted an opportunity for these women, on their own terms, to answer the questions they had been asked by interrogation officers decades earlier. After years of living with a sense that perhaps they could have answered some of the interrogation questions differently, they finally had a chance to articulate their point of view. In our conversations, there was none of the external coercion of the interrogations, just a feeling that some issues still need to be clarified.

Their autobiographical (individual) memory is organized by the prison experience—the defining moment of their lives. And long after their release, in the process of reinterpreting their past, the women view their time in prison as something that spans and explains their life narrations. Their knowledge about the past and their present experiences intertwine into complex nets, in which the present affects the way they interpret their past, and their past shapes the way they conceive of their present. Alessandro Portelli has shown how much can be learned from the mistakes, omissions, and exaggerations present in oral histories.[15] Oral histories take us beyond factual accuracy to the significance of certain experiences for an individual. Finally, these stories illustrate how these experiences are constantly (re)worked in order to accommodate one's understanding of the self.

Discussing the process of gathering oral histories, Ronald J. Grele suggests, "There are seemingly two relationships contained in one—that between the informant and the historian, and that between the informant and his own historical consciousness."[16] The more women I visited, the more I realized the role I played in their lives. As a person interested in their lives, I offered them a chance to be heard. And as a historian, my task was to give their life experience historical validity: the women I interviewed were essential to my project, but they benefited from the discursive space opened by the act of interviewing as well. In this sense, I was a witness who could (indeed, had to) testify that their lives were full of courage and bravery, without the hysteria and fear that Tonia showed in *Interrogation*. In both their own writings and the interviews, the women engaged in remembering with a similar aim—to reclaim their past and take a step toward empowerment. In this context, their private memories that I hoped to recover during a face-to-face conversation turned out to be not as private as I initially believed.

Together with my interviewees, I created research material in the reciprocal environment of a face-to-face conversation. My role in their eyes evolved from someone interested in hearing their stories to someone with a certain expertise as a historian, and finally to a witness who needed to present them to the outside world. Their role evolved as well, from that of women and former political prisoners to champions responsible for maintaining the reputation of all prisoners, especially women. While keeping in mind the dynamically changing roles between the women and me (as well as their transforming expectations of me), I read the stories that the women related to me through the mode of narrative that the particular women chose for themselves—irony, drama, or comedy. While it is relatively easy to heroize one's past on paper, in this case in *Nike*, it is more difficult to do so in an intimate conversation with a stranger, when silences, tears, hesitations, facial expressions, and gestures matter.

Nike: Life Stories "Written by Poland"

The beginning of the 1990s was a very exhilarating time in Poland. After the Round Table Talks in 1989, the Communist regime fell. Three years later, former female prisoners decided to share their experiences publicly.

The first edition of *Nike* was published in 1992. In June 2011, the women published the hundred and first issue. The first edition counted four pages, and 150 copies were distributed. Already in the first issue, it was evident that *Nike* had become the women's voice and their space to underline their roles as Polish patriots. The women, who on the pages of *Nike* became their own biographers, had a very clearly defined set of priorities. They wrote themselves back into the dominant historical narrative, which at the beginning of the 1990s focused on Solidarity, a free trade union established in 1980 that became a symbol for national revival and a peaceful movement that led Poland from Communism to independence. One of the *Nike* writers, Ruta Czaplińska, a woman who spent ten years in prison, writes, "I am sure we did everything that we were supposed to, while building this difficult road that connects the struggle for freedom from the time of war with its different form, which led through Poznań, Radom, Warsaw University and Gdańsk to Solidarity. In the second stage, months were important, in the first stage [meaning soon after the war] the struggle was counted in years."[17] Czaplińska maintains that the struggle that culminated in Solidarity began soon after 1945 and continued even in prison.

The mental and physical strength, uncompromised relations with prison guards, and resistance to any temptations to ease their sufferings in prison displayed by women and men testify to the principles that organized their life, the highest of which was a devotion to Poland. Independent Poland is an axiomatic and rather undefined ideal. It is an entity and an ideal for which people fight and suffer, about which they dream, and to which they commit their lives. The details and specifics regarding the future of Poland did not matter. Deeds committed for Poland created a sense of satisfaction from a fulfilled obligation. One former prisoner, Maria Walicka Chmielewska, writes, "From the perspective of long years, I look at my past with a bit of bitterness in my heart, with a conviction that these years were wrongly taken away from my youth, that my health and creative force were destroyed, forces which I could use for my homeland. But I don't regret what I did, because I did it for Poland."[18]

The women of *Nike* are strong and impossible to break. They are "unyielding" and "firm," as some titles suggest. Their life stories are "written by Poland" (*pisane Polską*). A crucial moment in their recollections is the interrogation—a rite of passage into prison life and a test of endurance. While writing about the former prisoner Halina Żurowska, the author emphasizes that Żurowska preferred to die rather than reveal anything to her interrogators.[19] Despite the use of violence and other techniques aimed at breaking an individual, the women of *Nike* won.

Their pure devotion to Poland, strength of spirit, and endurance had prevailed over those who persecuted them.[20] "Krysia," a nurse, suffered enormously during her interrogation, but she never revealed the identities of the people who had conspired with her. Later on, after her release, she had a chance to get revenge and kill the person who had beaten her. And yet, she did not do so. She did not kill because, she explained, she would not have been able to live with it.[21] In addition to being a great patriot, she remained sensitive and merciful. Such an understanding of their commitment to Poland allows the women to maintain agency and control over their lives. The injustice perpetrated by the Communist government deprived them of health and youth, but it provided their lives with a higher meaning. Poland created a sense of suffering, and the suffering created Poland. Poland is thus situated at the center of this logic, and as such it organizes the women's life narrations. The two are indispensable elements of the same story—that of the victory over violence and humiliation. It is a story in which the individual and her weaknesses disappear.

Nike's mode of narration is epic. Elevated and focused on deeds, it surpasses the usual and ordinary. There is no space for weaknesses and doubts, and the women are absorbed in events that they perceive as fundamental. To my knowledge, there is not one article in which the author openly admits that the fear or pain was so overwhelming that it compelled her to report on cellmates or collaborate with prison authorities—or even entertain that thought. Fear and regret are conspicuously absent. Czaplińska explicitly states that those who committed suicide were mentally weaker.[22] Being a political prisoner is not just a physical condition; it is a state of mind. From that point of view, Tonia, the semi-fictional hero from *Interrogation*, was an accidental (*przypadkowy*) prisoner: a woman imprisoned not for her behavior, stances, or even intentions, and a woman who cries and screams from fear and confusion. As Czaplińska stresses in *Nike*:

> The main hero enters a cell in the Ministry of Public Security, a cell that smells and is dirty, full of yelling, crying and hysterical women [*bab*]. I wiped my eyes. I spent over two weeks in the basement of this Ministry just after I was arrested. I saw only single rooms there . . . Women accidentally arrested were not there. There was no crying and no yelling. Silence and loneliness dominated. Despite everything, our cells were clean. We took care of them. There was no crying, hysteria, spasms, or yelling.[23]

In *Interrogation*, Tonia is tortured, stripped, humiliated, beaten, and starved, yet she does not portray a character with which the female prisoners wish to be associated. In the eyes of the female prisoners of post-war Poland, Tonia is everything they were not. Or, to put it differently, Tonia epitomizes the image or personality of an anti-hero. The nature of Tonia's imprisonment, however, becomes even more problematic due to the fact that she enters into a sexual relationship with her guard:[24]

> She is not someone committed to the Polish national struggle, and she does not respect her womanhood. She drinks, parties, sleeps with men she does not know, and finally gets pregnant with an interrogation officer. Tonia is an accidental prisoner and her child is accidental. As a result, she denigrates womanhood and motherhood. Apparently what we experienced in the prisons and then after our release was not enough. One had to slap us in the face publicly, creating false, hurtful personalities and false and dishonest situations. . . . Back then the prisons were full of women who knew their dignity, the dignity of a woman and of a political prisoner . . . There was no chance for any understanding between her and the interrogators, let alone sexual contact between victim and perpetrator.[25]

According to the cultural model that had been developed already by the nineteenth century, a woman is a guardian of the Polish family and Christian values, epitomized in the icon of the Polish Mother.[26] She is perseverant in her symbolic, mental, but also physical devotion to Poland or to those who represent Poland best. Strong during interrogation and during daily battles with severe living conditions in a cell, an individual body is a site of endurance. It is also a symbol for the national body. Sexual chastity, fortitude, and lack of intimate relations with the enemy symbolize a devotion to Poland (or to a struggle that the women continued in prison) and to those men who shared this devotion. But as the reaction to *Interrogation* reveals, the body can be also a site of weakness.

The women of *Nike* make a more or less conscious decision not to talk about imprisonment in terms of the potential vulnerability of women or problems that the female body might have experienced in a cell. This decision affects the way they think about gender violence.[27] They talk about beatings, kicking, interrogators jumping on their hands and crushing their fingernails, and yet they do not even hint that the male interrogation officers could somehow abuse their power over them in a way specific to their gender. For example, "little Danka's" interrogation officer beat her a lot, especially at night after he had been drinking alcohol. At times, he shocked her with electricity. The expectation that a drunk man could have abused her sexually in the middle of the night hangs in the air and yet is never expressed or implied.[28] Similarly, Jolluck argues that the Polish women sent to Siberia were able to talk about violence directed against them when it was generic, meaning common to both men and women.

Sexual or gendered violence remained taboo.[29] The body is both a symbol and a site of weakness; it is a space of empowerment (for example, through chastity) but also disempowerment (for example, through sexual assault). The model of the Polish Mother provides women with power as long as they perform within the limits of the model.

The agency that the women of *Nike* nevertheless display is located in a tactical understanding of the burden and responsibilities of the Polish woman. While referring to the suffering of women in prison, Maria Wiśniewska writes, "This fate has for ages been part of a Polish woman's life."[30] But the connection between being a Polish woman and making sacrifices, even if acknowledged, is rarely explored. This phenomenon is visible in *Nike's* relative lack of attention to the issue of motherhood. The prison mothers mentioned in *Nike* suffer from the longings for their children or the impossibility of taking care of those infants who were imprisoned with their mothers. But *Nike* does not reflect the torment that an arrested mother experienced during interrogations, in having to choose between concealing the identities of her (conspiracy or life) partner from the interrogation officers and protecting her children. That choice between competing obligations was at the heart of the drama that often took place in prison cells.

In the 1940s and 1950s, the authors of *Nike* were, for the most part, young. Most of them were in their early twenties at the time of their imprisonment. Their youth may account for the fact that the torment of mothers separated from their children is largely ignored on the pages of *Nike*. Conversely, perhaps while searching for coherence in their life narrations, the women of *Nike* rejected elements that could demonstrate weakness. Or, to put it differently, a search for empowerment is a search for agency and decisions of free will. Talking about the weaknesses (or love, pain, or attachments) that might have affected the way they had testified or behaved in prison does not advance the project of empowerment that *Nike* embraces.

A woman of *Nike* has clearly defined goals in life. She is a woman who strives to be almost equal to men in her agency. There is no gendered pain, fear, or worry. This reluctance to share gendered considerations reveals more than it hides. It reveals that the way to empowerment may lead through a denial of one's gender. Or perhaps it leads through a denial of the weaknesses that the women associate with their gender. Empowerment means searching for power as women—but as women who can be as strong and resistant as men, or as men are perceived to be and have been. The stories in *Nike* thus tell us more about how the *Nike* women want to be perceived than about how they experienced imprisonment. The three oral stories I present briefly below reveal another layer of the way former women prisoners reconstruct their life stories. Two of the women, Ewa Ludkiewicz and Ruta Czaplińska, are authors who often appear in *Nike*. The modes of narration and methods of achieving coherence that each of them uses, however, indicate even more ways of reinterpreting individual lives. In the end, the women I interviewed all show a variety of means through which an individual reestablishes oneself.

Elżbieta Zawacka: A Woman Soldier

Elżbieta Zawacka's narrative combines two closely entwined stories: a macrohistorical account of events of the last century of Polish history and her own personal narrative. The romantic mode through which she perceives her life helps her to individualize it. Even if Poland is in the background of all her activities, she remains a romantic hero on a mission to commemorate women soldiers. Although women occupy a central place in her narration, gender concerns are absent from her narrative. In this sense, her story is similar to those in *Nike*.

Elżbieta Zawacka, a Polish general, was an extraordinary woman.[31] During the war, Zawacka was a liaison for a cell of the underground anti-Nazi Home Army that was responsible for maintaining contact abroad. Speaking at least three languages fluently (German, French, and English), she travelled all over Europe, using different identities in various countries. In England, she was Elizabeth Kubica or Elizabeth Watson; in France, Elise Riviere; and in Sweden, Elżbieta Nowak.[32] One of her most important trips abroad was an illegal journey under a false identity to England. In London, she met with representatives of the Polish government-in-exile in order to convince them of the necessity of equalizing women soldiers with men soldiers (for example, in terms of bestowing ranks).

When I talked to her in 2007, she was already ninety-eight years old. While talking, she stared straight through me, as if I were not there and she was communing with history. She often stopped and tried to situate her story within a larger macrohistorical narrative. The commitment to become a soldier was a stable element in her long and rich life, and this ideal determined the way she recounted her life story. The first important moment came in 1919, when she was ten years old and watched Polish soldiers marching into Toruń, her home city. After over a hundred years of belonging to Prussia, Toruń again became a Polish city. Zawacka cried, when narrating that moment: "Their beautiful uniforms, these young shining faces . . . it was so beautiful." Her emotions clearly indicate that this was one of the cornerstone moments of her life. But she was also ashamed of her tears and asked me not to let anybody listen to her crying. She was very conscious of herself, of the role she played, and of the stories she told. She knew how she wanted to present herself in order to evoke strength and justify her consciousness as a historical actor, and she was also conscious of what she wanted to avoid. "Old crying women are ridiculous. People laugh at us," she said.

The second stage of her life came in the early 1930s, when she joined the Military Training for Women (PWK). Her participation in the Second World War was almost an extension of her work for the PWK. When the war broke out, Zawacka moved between various Polish cities, helping to organize a civil defense. From then on, she knew that to be a soldier was her destiny. In her second and final emotional outburst, she cried when mentioning the defeated Polish soldiers. The most important mission she had to fulfill during the war was to get the permission of Polish authorities in exile to grant equal status to women soldiers. She clearly downplayed her imprisonment after the war, as it was a time of forced passivity, which soldiers such as she despised. She emphasized that behind prison bars she behaved with the dignity of a soldier, but action is where she finds fulfillment. At this point, she ended her historical narration and moved on to describe her various activities. At age ninety-eight, she was still involved in several endeavors, such as a project to gather the names of all Polish women soldiers.

In a vein similar to *Nike*, Zawacka told her story in an epic and macrohistorical mode. As Daniel James argues, "an epic form implies the individuals' identification with the community and its values, and leaves little room for the expression of individual identity."[33] Zawacka was absorbed by the historical events that mark the foundational moments of her life. "I served Poland," she emphasized. "I had difficult moments, such as when my family was arrested. But my service was more important." But there is something that is not apparent in *Nike's* stories, but is at the core of Zawacka's narration. She romanticizes her life, which provides her with a chance to personalize it. It is the quest for the rights of women soldiers and later for the documentation of their lives that orders her life narration. These tasks have provided her with the agency of a soldier who has devoted her entire life to one mission.

Zawacka did not talk about family life, children, or stereotypical women's obligations. Only once she said, "I had a good life. This was my path. I had no husband or family . . . but that's what I have chosen."

Interestingly, I never asked her about her family situation, yet she felt a need to explain herself and to explain her commitment and her lifestyle. Perhaps she answered a question she expected to be asked. Perhaps it was something with which she herself struggled, examining choices she made that still subconsciously float to the surface. Regardless of what the answer may be, the very fact that she mentioned family indicates a certain tension in her life narrative. Struggling almost her entire life for the recognition of female soldiers—or perhaps for women to be treated like men—she professed (or only expressed) cultural sensitivities that make her think that family is the most natural way of life for women. The message conveyed is close to *Nike*'s. Gender considerations, worries, violence, fears, and expectations are absent from Zawacka's narrative. Women soldiers are like men, who can choose to avoid stereotypical expectations. The tension in Zawacka's story expresses the possibility of deciding between a commitment to your family (or stereotypical expectations) and a commitment to other ideals. Zawacka chose the latter and struggled for other women who shared her system of values, even if she was unwilling to elaborate on what her choice implies.

Ewa Ludkiewicz: Laughing through Misery

Ewa Ludkiewicz enjoys encounters with people: she entertains her interlocutors with stories about herself, about her family, her flowers and animals, her imprisonment, and recent developments in her life.[34] With the same enthusiasm, she talks about the significant and insignificant. There is everything in her stories: love, misery, joy, tears, enormous disappointment, and eventually pride in the things she has achieved, despite difficulties. Laughter and tears help her deal with a past filled with heavy losses and moments when expectations clashed with reality.

Ludkiewicz was born in 1923 into the family of a landowner. When World War II began, the entire family moved from Warsaw to Milewko, a small town outside Warsaw, where they owned a small villa. They lived there the entire war in a relative isolation from the tragedies of the war. Ludkiewicz developed a passion for poetry and fell in love for the first time. Even during our meetings, over seventy years later, she could not restrain her tears when mentioning the man. Her imprisonment in 1947 came unexpectedly. She helped her cousin, Władysław Śliwiński, deliver one illegal letter. She recollected, "I was such a bad conspirator. I was not even able to deliver a secret message. I walk up the stairs, knock, somebody opens the door, I say the password, but the guy does not seem to know what is going on . . . I felt lost." Ewa Ludkiewicz laughed, gesticulated, and modulated her voice so that I, even knowing that the consequences had been dire, could not help laughing. A few months later, she was arrested and sentenced to seven years in prison. Śliwiński, the man who asked her to deliver the message, was executed.

Ludkiewicz's narration is focused on microhistory. While narrating her life in prison, she remembered the smallest details: the different people she met in her cells, poems that accompanied different moments and moods, even the flowers she planted near a prison wall, and the tree she could see from her cell window. Her narrative has a theatrical quality. Laughing and crying, she often made fun of herself as a conspirator, her attempts to write poetry, her prison love affair, and eventually her efforts to be beautiful in prison. She laughed when mentioning her adolescent dream to become a scientist and her first naïve love, and she cried when admitting that this love turned out to be the strongest feeling she had ever experienced. She cried when she recited the poetry that reminds her of her childhood. She was serious in describing the fear she felt while walking down the stairs to the interrogation cell, and she became very sad when mentioning the deaths of those who were executed in Communist prisons. Talking about her interrogation, she jokingly said, "I was so scared that I told my interrogation officers how scared I am and that I don't know anything. I was so naïve in all of that, that they believed me." Many more times, she belittled herself, emphasizing how little she knew and how scared she was. Finally, she expressed the regret she felt at having lost her high social standing, the man she loved, and her beautiful home. Imprisonment hampered her chances for a university education and a better job. For decades after her release, she raised small farm animals. Laughing and joking, she described how she looked while performing such work.

Even though she is an author who often appears in *Nike*, in the conversation with me, she did not celebrate the Polish cause, nor did she depict herself as a serious political prisoner. She kept repeating the mantra: "I was imprisoned by mistake." She believes that being a political prisoner means maintaining a certain awareness and consciousness even in prison circumstances. Perhaps her arrest was a mistake on the part of authorities, but once in prison, she grew into her role as a Polish political prisoner, even if she now treats that role with a slight irony.

Throughout the interview with her, I wondered many times about the role of trust in oral history interviews. Is it possible that I trusted her more because she downplayed her role in conspiracy? Or is it that her use of self-irony made her testimonies more reliable? Irony, similar to an epic or romantic mode of narration, is a way to make sense of the past, to organize past events in a meaningful and coherent fashion. Interestingly, Ludkiewicz used irony to account for disappointments that are almost invisible in *Nike*: personal failures, unrealized expectations, and dreams that did not come true. What *Nike* silences, she faced and usually laughed at. This irony helps her gain some distance from herself. Even if her story is rather regressive (it moves from a happy childhood through the relatively stable war period to a miserable imprisonment and post-prison life, when she had to relinquish most of her dreams), the irony serves as a means of self-reflection and as such is an element of the healing process. Recently, eighty-seven-year-old Ludkiewicz told me that she does not want to talk about prison any more. She wrote one book and feels that this is enough.[35] A few months ago, she published her second book about and for her family. It is a book about those who died, and she wrote it for those who live.

Ruta Czaplińska: Celebration and Mourning

Ruta Czaplińska's mode of storytelling is romantic, full of melancholy brought about by senseless loss. The way she spoke about her participation in *Nike* and her former cellmates brings to mind a celebration of life despite difficulties. In this sense, her life story reflects the main message of *Nike*. But there is also a palpable, deep sadness and longing for a life that she and those who died were not able to experience: sadness in her prayers, in the tone of her voice, in her anger with the Communists, and in the loving words she chose in talking about those who died.

Ruta Czaplińska was a quiet and charming lady, eager to talk and be heard about her prison experience—the pivotal time of her life. She appeared rather withdrawn and concentrated on her inner world, a posture that stood in stark contrast to the feisty articles she wrote for *Nike*. After several meetings, our conversations became very intimate. We talked, had dinners, and drank coffee together in the little kitchen of her Wrocław apartment. She wanted to know everything about my family and wished that one day I would visit her with my small daughter. "We need to hurry up to listen to people, they go away so fast," she kept saying. Her small apartment was full of books about conspiracy and life in prison, as well as various memorabilia and photographs of close and distant family members. She did not have children of her own. Kind and resourceful, she lived for her sisters' children, her cellmates, and the memory of her "boys" (*moi chłopcy*), as she called her fellow conspirators who were executed in 1946. "I just have to say a little prayer for my dear ones, family and friends, and then I can go to sleep," she would say every time I called her in the evening.[36]

In 1946, following her brief involvement in the anti-Communist right-wing group *Narodowy Związek Wojskowy* (National Armed Union), Czaplińska was sentenced to ten years in prison. After her release in 1956, her fellow prisoners remained her closest friends. She participated in every initiative that was aimed at sustaining the memory of their time in prison, from organizing public meetings, through writing for *Nike*, to writing short articles for other periodicals. She talked about herself as a great patriot, as a person brought up and educated in the spirit of a commitment to Poland. But she perceived Poland through the prism of others: her late family members, those executed for their involvement in conspiracy, and, finally, those imprisoned. They became the main theme of her recollections, and a long list of people to commemorate accompanied every conversation I had with her. They were also on her mind when she wrote for *Nike*, criticizing the vision of the past, which, according to her, pushes them into oblivion.

In one *Nike* article, she wrote about the loneliness of a single woman and about the loneliness of a former prisoner, but she did not link the two. She used a rather pejorative term: "spinster" (*stara panna*), emphasizing the loneliness of a woman with a very low social status.[37] During one interview with me, however, while recalling the people close to her, she revealed that she regretted much of what had happened in her life, particularly that she had never managed to have a family of her own. She did not regret her engagement in subversive groups, but felt it was based on incorrect premises: on an impulse to act and not on any deeper considerations. "We did not know what we were doing. We claimed we had no fear. But we had no idea what that fear may be. And we did not know pain and what we were getting ourselves into. My boys . . ." She still suffered when mentioning those who had died. Each story from their conspiracy is burdened with the awareness that it resulted in the death of her "boys" and in the broken lives of many families.

Similarly to Zawacka, Czaplińska struggled to commemorate political prisoners. In a way, she was also a romantic hero on a mission, whose main quest was to reverse the wrongdoings committed by the Communist regime through remembrance. "If there is anything that remains to be done, it is to keep their memory alive. That's all we can do and that's so little in light of the suffering they experienced at the hands of Communists," she said.[38] A sense of deep sadness spoke through her. While Zawacka celebrates the bravery and commitment of the women who took the difficult road and decided to become soldiers, through various symbolic struggles Czaplińska mourned the lives lost.

Regardless of this sense of loss, Czaplińska did not regret her time in prison; it was not a lost time, she repeated often, in this way underpinning the main massage of *Nike*. "I met wonderful people and learned about myself and others," she maintained. She semiconsciously decided to remember only the positive moments, wise people, and good life lessons from her prison life. In a sense, Czaplińska carried two different visions of her life. On one hand, she appreciated what she experienced while positioning prison friendships at the core of her life. On the other hand, she was contemplative and full of longing for a life that she never had—a life without prison. There is a tension between life restored in prison versus death and misery brought about by prison. These two versions of her life story framed her active engagement in everything that concerns political prisoners, from mourning to celebration. These are supplemental but also competing versions of her life story, which are perhaps a result of the grief and issues she was still trying to cope with. In our last conversation, two days before her death, a seemingly weak Czaplińska still talked about "her boys" and their unnecessary deaths. During her funeral in February 2008, according to her will, a twenty-one-gun salute was fired: it was not for her but for her "boys."

Conclusion

Zawacka, Ludkiewicz, and Czaplińska's stories are very different. There is sadness in Czaplińska, power in Zawacka, and irony that helps Ludkiewicz maintain a sense of joy. Their ways of dealing with me parallel the ways they deal or dealt with their pasts. Czaplińska invited me to come more often, since she had so many more stories to tell, but once I arrived, she wanted me to guide her through her life story. She was full of sadness, melancholy, and hope that the people she cared for so much would not be forgotten. Zawacka emphasized action. She asked me to take the books she was writing and circulate them among my friends. No matter what I would like to ask, Zawacka was not distracted from what she wanted to say and the order in which she wanted to present it. Ludkiewicz did both: she narrated the stories she needed to tell but also searched her memory for answers to the questions I kept coming up with. She talked in a seemingly unorganized way but was always full of energy and optimism.

The three women I looked at used different key patterns to narrate their life stories. These specific narrative modes, through which the women explained their lives to others as well as to themselves, embody the fundamental sense of their lives. The stories are told in order to understand through sharing with others. All narratives strive for coherence and some sort of consensus with oneself, with others, and with the past. This struggle suggests that experience is a process, something that never ends and that needs to be constantly reworked. One question that still lingers for me is whether there is a difference between private (intimate) memory and a collective (or in this case, public) memory. The tensions that appear between *Nike* and individual memories are minor. The women interiorized *Nike's* epic mode, which focuses on celebrating their mental victory over those who persecuted them. They all did it, however, in a slightly different manner. The two sets of memoires, private as well as public, remain interconnected.

One final question remains, regarding the extent to which individual memories reflect a particular, broader set of cultural meanings and to what extent they manifest individual agency. A quick summary of the ways that the women conceptualized gender issues may shed some light on this question. To a large degree, gender issues and problems remain invisible, although most of the women are or were engaged in publicizing women's history. The most prominent model of a woman in Polish culture is that of the Polish Mother, devoted to the good of the country. Most of the women under examination here had a hard time situating themselves within these limits. The women of *Nike* mediated the dominant ideology, searching for their own agency outside these cultural boundaries. This was their individual contribution, an agency that gave them an impulse to tacitly silence certain aspects of the prevailing image of a Polish woman. Despite this, they had difficulty finding an alternative. Distancing themselves from Tonia in *Interrogation*, they nevertheless drew from elements of the traditional image of a woman. Searching for empowerment, they were not able to go beyond an understanding of the body as a source of weakness and vulnerability. Even if they tried to manipulate the dominant model of a Polish woman (or perhaps expressed tensions inherent in that model), it proved to be so strongly ingrained in them that this manipulation was very narrow in its scope and effect.

Notes

1. Ryszard Bugajski, *Jak powstało "Przesłuchanie"* (Warszawa: Świat Książki, 2010).
2. Barbara Otwinowska, "Wokół filmu Ryszarda Bugajskiego: *Śmierć Rotmistrza Pileckiego*," *Nike* 78: (2006): 20. Otwinowska adds, "When he (Bugajski, the director of the movie) was making *Interrogation*, he believed his own fantasy and trusted his contact with women who were not too representative of us . . . They were imprisoned,

but their recollections as well as their life stories are so different from ours. But in the movie you cannot see it . . . as a result of which the movie was warmly accepted by the audience as a touching film about political prisoners and their suffering. His choice of informers introduced elements of contempt for other prisoners: as a repulsive group of dirty and hysterical women. And even to this day, people are surprised that we have something against this movie . . ."

3. Czesław Leopold and Krzysztof Lechicki, "*Więźniowie polityczni w* Polsce 1945–1956" (Wydawnictwo Młoda Polska, Gdańsk, 1981).
4. James Fentress and Chris Wickham, *Social Memory: New Perspectives on the Past* (Malden, MA: Blackwell, 1992).
5. Ibid., 201.
6. "Zanim powstało środowisko Fordonianek," *Nike* 41 (1998): 3–6.
7. Janina Jelińska, "Na ogólniaku," *Nike* 31 (1996): 18.
8. Katherine Jolluck, *Polish Women in the Soviet Union during World War II* (Pittsburgh: University of Pittsburgh Press, 2002).
9. Judith Butler, *Gender Trouble: Feminism and the Subversion of Identity* (Routledge, 1990), 7.
10. "Jubileusz Nike," *Nike*, 40 (1997), 7–13.
11. Jan Paśnik, "Wybrane problem orzecznictwa sądów wojskowych w sprawach o przestępstwa przeciw państwu w latach 1946–1953," *Materiały Historyczne*, 1 (1991): 32, 34. Andrzej Paczkowski estimates that in 1948 there were 26,400 political prisoners, constituting 44% of all prisoners. In 1952, there were already 49,500 people deprived of freedom. Andrzej Paczkowski, *Pół wieku dziejów Polski 1939–1989* (Warsaw: Wydawnictwo Naukowe PWN, 1995), 260. See also, Andrzej Paczkowski, "Poland, the 'Enemy Nation'," in *The Black Book of Communism: Crimes, Terror, Repression* eds. Jean-Louis Margolin and Andrzej Paczkowski (Cambridge: Harvard University Press, 1999).
12. *Zawołać po imieniu. Księga kobiet-więźniów politycznych, 1944–1958*, eds. Barbara Otwinowska and Teresa Drzal, vol. 1 (Warsaw: Vipart, 1999), 11.
13. For example, Stanisława Sowińska and Halina Siedlik. Both were born in Łódź into working-class families.
14. For instance, Jadwiga Malkiewicz mentions peasant women who were imprisoned with her for helping AK partisans. Jadwiga i Krzysztof Malkiewicz, *W więzieniu i na wolności, 1947–1956* (Cracow: Platan, 1994), 82–84. Jacek Pawłowicz did meticulous work in collecting biographies of resistance fighters from northwest Poland, who were tried in Military Courts between 1946–1955 (662 biographical notes). He mentions dozens of women, many of whom were of peasant origins. Jacek Pawłowicz, *Chwała Bohaterom! Mieszkańcy Mazowsza Zachodnio-Północnego sądzeni przez Wojskowe Sądy Rejonowe, 1946–1955* (Warsaw: Oficyna Wydawnicza RYTM, 2003).
15. Alessandro Portelli, *Death of Luigi Trastulli and Other Stories: Form and Meaning in Oral History* (Albany: State University of New York Press, 1991).
16. Ronald J. Grele, "Movement without Aim: Methodological and Theoretical Problems in Oral History," *The Oral History Reader*, eds. Robert Perks and Alistair Thomson (Routledge: Taylor and Francis Group, 2005), 45.
17. Irena Bukowska, "Fordon w TV," *Nike* 3 (1993): 5.
18. Maria Walicka Chmielewska, "Wspomnienia," *Nike* 21 (1995): 29.
19. "Heniek - o Halinie Żurowskiej," *Nike* 14 (1999).
20. Lucyna Kuklińska, "Nieugięta. Wspomnienie o Stefani Broniewskiej," *Nike* 54 (2000): 8–15; Jadwiga Ejsak Chmielewska, "Bella. Wspomnienie Niepokornej," *Nike* 35 (1997): 9–12; Władysława Andruskiewicz, "Życiorys pisany Polską," *Nike* 33 (1996): 19–22.

21. "O Krysi pielęgniarce," *Nike* 47 (1999): 15.
22. Ruta Czaplińska, *Nike* 47 (1999): 8.
23. Ruta Czaplińska, "O *Przesłuchaniu* Bugajskiego," *Z Archiwum Pamięci . . . 3653 więzienne dni* (Warszawa: IPN, 2005), 317. In an article about Ryszarda Szelągowska (one of the prisoners), Barbara Otwinowska describes *Interrogation* as a film about "an actor-whore" (aktoreczce-kurewce). Otwinowska, "Z naszych rozmów z Rysią Szelągowską," *Nike*, 15 (1994): 23.
24. Interviews with Ruta Czaplińska, Wrocław 2007, and Barbara Otwinowska, Warszawa 2007–2009.
25. Ruta Czaplińska, "Trudna Wolność," *Nike* 3 (1993): 8.
26. Alicja Kusiak-Brownstein, "The Royal Tribe of the Piasts and the Missing Daughters of Wanda: Cultural Representations of Peasant Polishness at the Turn of the Twentieth Century," paper presented at AAASS, Los Angeles, 2010.
27. Another interesting issue is violence committed by women. Even if the women presented on the pages of *Nike* are soldiers or former soldiers, the violence that they could have participated in is never mentioned. Barbara Otwinowska, who wrote an article about the women soldiers from the first World War, made no reference to killings in battle or any activities of women that could involve taking life. Violence is experienced by women but never committed by them. In Otwinowska's story, the women are depicted as the best auxiliaries for men. With a slight irony, she recollects the story of Irena Tomalakowa, one of her cellmates, who had wished to become a soldier so much that she dressed as a man, only to be recognized by her supervisor, who subsequently married her. Barbara Otwinowska, "Kobiety dwóch wojen, 1914–18, 19–21," *Nike*, 46 (1998): 9–13.
28. Wspomnienie o Halinie Walickiej, *Nike*, 42 (1998): 12–13. "Wspomnienia "Malej Danki." W rękach kapitana Milczarka," *Nike*, 17 (1994): 21–24.
29. Katherine Jolluck, *Polish Women . . .*
30. Maria Wiśniewska, "Historia czy Pamięć," *Nike* 51 (1999): 24.
31. Interview with Elżbieta Zawacka, Toruń March 2008.
32. Natalia Iwaszkiewicz, "Zo Legenda AK," *Nike* 77 (2006): 7–12.
33. Daniel James, *Dona Maria's Story: Life, History, and Political Identity* (Durham, NC: Duke University Press, 2000), 162.
34. Interview with Ewa Ludkiewicz, Gdańsk 2007–2010.
35. Ewa Ludkiewicz, *Siedem lat w więzieniu, 1947–1955*, Gdańsk 2007.
36. Interview with Ruta Czaplińska, March–December 2007.
37. Ruta Czaplińska, "O samotności starej panny" *Nike*, 41 (1998).
38. Interview with Ruta Czaplińska, March–December 2007.

II

The Creation of a New History and the Integration of Collective Memory in the Story of One's Self

5

"They Didn't Rape Me": Traces of Gendered Violence and Sexual Injury in the Testimonies of Spanish Republican Women Survivors of the Franco Dictatorship

Gina Herrmann

> ... the question of gendered violence during the Spanish Civil War—analyzed as such—very rarely constitutes in itself an object of history.
> —Maud Joly[1]

Sexualized Violence from the Holocaust to Franco

Women are raped in wartime and during periods of political repression by dictatorial regimes. We take this statement to be true, its truth founded on physical and testimonial evidence across nations and time. And yet extended, interdisciplinary scholarly discussion of sexualized violence during two of the most studied military conflicts of the twentieth century—the Spanish Civil War and World War II—have arisen only in the wake of the very recent genocidal rapes in Rwanda and the former Yugoslavia.[2] Even though the feminist movements of the 1970s lifted, to a degree, the social prohibition and stigma of first-person reports of rape, the filth of the crime perpetually besmirched victims. They were more stigmatized than the perpetrators. For women survivors of sexualized violence before the 1970s, the prohibition against communicating cases of rape could be attributed to generational, religious, familial, or political reasons, which explains why so many survivors of war rape and gender humiliations dealt with their trauma in the realms of the unspeakable, since neither language nor images for the expression of these memories, nor a validating audience for this story, were available.

Our understanding of how Spanish Republican women negotiated experiences of sexualized violence is greatly enhanced by excavating the Spanish case with the research tools and questions posed in the pioneering 2010 collection, *Sexual Violence against Jewish Women during the Holocaust*, edited by Sonja Hedgepeth and Rochelle Saidel. This interdisciplinary volume is the first English-language book devoted to the multiple forms of sexualized violence wielded against Jewish women during the *Shoah*. The cruelties analyzed in this volume, including the shearing of body hair, rape, obligatory prostitution, forced sterilization, and other tactics of gendered humiliation correspond to the types of abuses experienced by Republican women during the Spanish Civil War (1936–1939) and the ensuing Franco dictatorship (1939–1975). We can never know how many Republican women witnessed or experienced sexualized violence during the Civil War, in detention centers, concentration and labor camps, or prison. As historian Paul Preston writes, in his 2011 *The Spanish Holocaust*,

> a central, yet under-estimated, part of the repression carried out by the rebels—the systematic persecution of women—is not susceptible to statistical analysis. Murder, torture and rape were generalised punishments for the gender liberation embraced by many, but not all, liberal and left-wing women during the Republican period.[3]

Like the Nazis, the Francoist authorities did not maintain official documentation about sexual violation, and so we have to rely primarily on survivor testimony rather than on efforts at empirical assessment.

In both the literature on the Holocaust and Spanish fascism a paradox arises wherein testimonial evidence of gender violence, on one hand, abounds, and yet we simultaneously have the impression that stories of sexualized violence have been smothered by discomfort and shame on the part of scholars, perpetrators, and survivors alike. A further parallel in the testimonial records of women survivors of the Shoah and Spanish women is the researcher's perception of the scarcity of first-person accounts and the concurrent presence of references to and memories about the rape of *other* women. I have observed that in the Spanish testimonial record, penetrative rape is more likely to be narrated as the experience of someone else, as first-person speakers appear more willing to own non-penetrative encounters: namely, acts that caused pain to sexual organs (shocks to nipples and genitals, whipping of naked buttocks) or acts of humiliation with sexual undertones (shaving of hair, forced ingestion of cod liver oil so that women would defecate uncontrollably), and attacks on maternity, including beatings during interrogations that focused on the lower abdomen with the intention to cause permanent damage to the womb and thus prevent the enemy from reproducing, thus wiping out the "red" opposition to the regime.[4]

Testimonies of Spanish Republican women have been studied by scholars from many vantage points, and yet the subject of rape and gendered humiliation and torture has been taken up only very recently by historians Maud Joly (2008), Irene Abad (2009), and Paul Preston (2011). This investigation is the first effort to perform close readings of sexualized violence as described or alluded to as traumatic personal experiences in the life stories of individual women. The attention to Spanish political women's experience during incarceration in all its grisly practices and spectacles of horror allows us to understand the Francoist dictatorial apparatus with greater precision and complexity. My focus in this essay is on the consequences of two separate but related testimonial processes in the oral histories of Esperanza Martínez (1927–) and Remedios Montero (1926–2010), Communist women who joined the armed resistance against Franco in the 1950s; both narrate scenes of sexualized torture. First I analyze how each woman has transformed, over approximately three decades, her life story, particularly descriptions of torture and sexual or gender-inflected injury during captivity. The second traces the interpretations by historians, filmmakers, and novelists in the course of employing their oral histories in the production of testimonial-based popular artifacts, in particular, a feature-length docudrama, Pau Vergara's 2007 *Memorias de una guerrillera*.

The *Maquis*: Esperanza Martínez and Remedios Montero

After the fall of the Spanish Republic (1931–39) to the forces of General Franco, the internal resistance to the new Catholic-Nationalistic military regime took shape as guerrillas who maintained increasingly defensive positions mainly in the mountainous regions of Spain. In Cuenca, Spain, in 1949, two women—best friends—escaped with their sisters, brothers, and fathers to join up with the *Agrupación Guerrillera de Levante y Aragón* (AGLA), one of the most active and well-organized of the Communist resistance groups. Remedios Montero and Esperanza Martínez had served as *puntos de apoyo*, or support contacts, for the men hidden out in the countryside around their villages. When the rural civil guard discovered their clandestine cooperation, the women abandoned their homes and were incorporated into the guerrilla movement. By the early 1950s, the Communist Party ordered the retreat of all armed resistance groups and set in motion plans for the remaining fighters to cross into exile in France. Montero and Martínez, employed by the party to serve as guides for their comrades, were exposed as Communist agents, savagely tortured, and sentenced to long terms in the infernal prisons of the dictator. Montero served eight and a half years in prison, while Martínez did not see freedom for fifteen years.

In their respective testimonies Esperanza Martínez and Remedios Montero describe daily life with the guerrilla movement as physically uncomfortable and largely dull. With respect to gender relations under such harsh conditions, Montero and Martínez paint a picture of "absolute equality" with their male comrades: they were not expected, they insist, to do dishes, do laundry, or cook. Along with some men, the women attended a makeshift school where they were taught to read and write. The women, who were not asked to do guard duty or descend into the outlying villages to secure supplies, carried small pistols for defensive reasons, while the men carried rifles. In print and on film, Montero and Martínez vociferously refute the Francoist "myths" that the few women who joined the *maquis* did so in the capacity of lovers or prostitutes. Romance and sex were, they aver, strictly forbidden. Despite the atmosphere of camaraderie and high morale the women report, their participation with the *maquis* was fraught with intense pain: each lost their fathers in shootouts with the Civil Guard, and Remedios's younger brother was hatcheted to death by *contra-partida*, spies within the Civil Guard.[5]

In 1951, Montero and Martínez, guided out of Spain and across the Pyrenees on foot, placed themselves at the service of the leadership of the Spanish Communist Party in exile. Their assignment, to cross back into Spain and to themselves guide comrades into safety in France, went terribly wrong when a traitor revealed their mission. The Francoist authorities detained both women, who survived weeks of torture in detention centers before being sentenced to long prison terms. Eventually Remedios chose self-exile in Communist Prague, where she married one of the leaders of the *Agrupación*—Florián, "*el Grande*"—a charismatic militant whom Remedios thought had been killed in his attempt to escape Spain in the early 1950s. Upon the death of the dictator Franco, the couple returned to Spain, where they remained active in the Communist Party. Remedios lived until 2010 in Valencia, courted by historians, journalists, directors, and writers. Her narrative reached even wider audiences when it featured prominently in a best-selling novel and an acclaimed 2002 documentary film by Javier Corcuera, *La guerrilla de la memoria*. After her liberation, Esperanza Martínez married a comrade and had a child, and the family remained active in the movement for democracy. She too participated in the interviews for the very same books and films. Thus by the close of the nineties, Montero and Esperanza Martínez became the "go-to" women for a series of popular artifacts produced about the resistance.

The various iterations of the oral testimonies of Montero and Martínez have proved integral to this memory/testimonial "boom." In order to follow the paths these oral histories have taken, I outline for the reader which texts this essay will discuss. The first recording of the Martínez and Montero testimonies took place sometime in the first part of the 1980s when Tomasa Cuevas, a Communist militant with her own remarkable story of survival of the Francoist penitentiary system, embarked on her third collection of oral histories of female political prisoners. These quite telescoped life stories, first published in Cuevas's *Mujeres de la Resistencia* (1986), constitute the original narratives of each woman's life as members of the armed resistance and later period of incarceration. Here we find, in the case of Martínez, the single instance of a richly described episode of sexual torture, which I will analyze in detail in the pages ahead. This scene does not reappear in any of her later testimonial accounts—including her own 2010 memoir—nor does it have a place in the video-taped interviews she gave for three non-fiction film productions.[6]

The case of Remedios Montero is even more complex and convoluted. In the various versions of her life story, Montero details three tortures she suffered during interrogation sessions with the Francoist police: the crushing of her fingers, being made to kneel on a board laid with hard chickpeas and coarse salt (causing extensive damage to her knees), and beatings on her lower abdomen (an abuse she determined prevented her from having children). Both Montero and Martínez enumerate the verbal assaults and insults on their womanhood during torture sessions, including accusations that they were the whores of the male fighters; thus their captors framed the women's political crime of armed resistance in plainly sexual terms. Montero, however, is known for relating one particular story about the time she refused to kiss a figurine of the baby Jesus during a mass in prison. As I argue later on, I have come to understand this episode as an allegory about forced sexual contact between women political prisoners and members of the Francoist prison personnel (priests, guards, etc.). Montero has recounted this episode repeatedly: in the testimony she gave to Tomasa Cuevas (1980s); in oral histories[7]; and in interviews with the novelist Dulce Chacón, whose best-selling 2002 novel *La voz dormida* is based in part on Montero's life.[8] The baby Jesus story is the most humorous and spirited anecdote of her entire life story. For this reason it is, at first glance, puzzling that while the story holds an important place in the enormously popular Chacón novel, it disappears entirely from Montero's own memoirs, as well as from Vergara's film about her.

By their own accounts, Montero and Martínez experienced on their bodies various forms of sexualized violence during interrogation sessions. But let me make clear that the object of this essay is not to figure out whether Montero and Martínez were personally raped or forced to engage in sex acts, but rather to locate narrative techniques—silences, troping, smokescreens, and evasive language among them—suggestive of a Francoist culture of abuse and incarceration in which sexualized violence was one order of the day. I explore how Montero and Martínez, over time and in multiple versions of their life-stories, reveal or occlude, detail or evade descriptions of an atmosphere of sexual danger and impositions of nonconsensual sexual contact characteristic of women's penitentiary experience during the dictatorship.[9]

Before turning to Martínez and Montero, we need to pause and survey the geography of gender violence against Republican women in the early years of the dictatorship. Paul Preston, in his 2011 *The Spanish Holocaust*, draws a chilling portrait as he describes how "thousands . . . were subjected to rape and other sexual abuses, the humiliation of head shaving and public soiling after the forced ingestion of castor oil."[10] He further reports that "Rape was a frequent occurrence during interrogation in police stations. Transfer to prisons and concentration camps was no guarantee of safety. At night, Falangists took young women away and raped them. Sometimes their breasts were branded with the Falangist symbol of the yoke and arrows."[11]

By studying testimonial evidence, some of it overt, some difficult to detect, we accord social legitimacy to the survivors and bring necessary added dimension—in this case, that of sexualized violence—to the landscape of repressive and murderous practices carried out by the henchmen of the Franco dictatorship. My examination focuses on one distinct aspect of the Montero and Martínez oral histories, admittedly to the detriment of a more multifaceted exploration of many other important episodes. Readers should not see a uniform narrative or homogeneity of experience indicated in my readings, for as we will see, the memories and attitudes of Republican women demonstrate great dimensionality and polyphonic complexity.

Esperanza Martínez: "Me Quiere Dominar"

In the collection of women's prison testimonies recorded by Tomasa Cuevas in the early 1980s, Esperanza Martínez recounts how she was tortured in the infamous dungeons of *Dirección General de Seguridad*, a Francoist detention facility in Madrid:

> They shoved dirty rags into my mouth, my whole mouth filled so that I couldn't scream, because you could imagine that what I had coming was going to be serious. Then they told me to lie down on the floor. I refused to lie down and so they forced me down under a rain of blows. They put me face down and after having covering myself they lifted up my skirt and pulled off my underpants. With one of those rubber truncheons [*una verga de esas de goma*], and with one of the men on either side of me, they serenaded me with that song "*María Cristina me quiere gobernar y yo le sigo la corriente* . . ." [María Cristina wants to boss me around and I follow her commands]. And one of them gave it to me and the other gave it to me, and when they saw that the whipping didn't hurt me anymore because it was numb [*lo tenía adormecido*], they let me rest . . . but it was always the same way. That I should get down on the floor, that I should get naked. I denied everything and then with a bare-knuckled punch they would give it to you from one side and then from the other.[12]

What we have before us is an encounter that Esperanza would not consider rape or sexualized violence since "rape" for a woman of her generation and cultural position would be considered an exclusively penetrative act. But it is hard not to hear the obvious suggestions of rape scattered about. First, we should admit that upon hearing this story, we find ourselves in territory we, sadly, recognize: a group of men alone with a female prisoner, charged with the task of torturing and interrogating her. We imagine, indeed, we anticipate that the woman will also become a target of their sexual assault. Let us scrutinize three aspects of this harrowing passage, in which hints of rape abound in Esperanza's diction. First, she employs the word *verga* to describe the hard rubber billy club that the police used to beat her. While the word *vergajazo* in Spanish means "whipping," the definition of *verga* is "penis." Second, Esperanza speaks evasively of some part of her body turning numb under the continual blows; the reader cannot know what the masculine object pronoun *lo* in Spanish refers to, but the removal of the panties limits the possibilities. Her buttocks (*el culo*)? Her vagina? (Slang would be the masculine *el coño*.) The emphasis on getting it from both sides suggests sodomy with the truncheon in both orifices.

Not surprisingly, this depiction of torture counts among only a handful of first-person reports of explicitly sexualized violence at the hands of the Francoist police. To the best of my knowledge, Martínez never again recounted this episode for public consumption. She has, however, emphasized in at least two subsequent interviews that while she endured horrific and demeaning abuse, she was never "raped": *tengo que decir que no me violaron*—"I have to say they never raped me" (Vergara). If Esperanza has maintained as recently as 2010 that *no me violaron*,[13] she has shifted the graphic descriptions of her sexualized torture from her 1980s interview with Cuevas to more ambiguous language that nonetheless suggests the degradation of her body. Here follows the episode as related to historian José Antonio Vidal Castaño in 2001:

> They beat me again and they leave my face swollen like a loaf of bread and of course the other women prisoners protested . . . So then they no longer beat . . . in the face. They beat me in other places. I remember that I lost a lot of weight and they beat me all over . . . the *organismo* changed to such a degree that well . . . Once in jail [as opposed to the interrogation chamber] I felt good! Uf! I am relieved, now they don't lift me up or take me down [*ya no me suben ni me bajan*], they don't give it to me [*ni me dan*] . . . nor do they do *eso* [that].[14]

The language of evasion here is especially interesting from a gender perspective if we read it in conjunction with "*María Cristina me quiere dominar*," the popular song the police sang as they delivered their blows or thrusts. As we will see, the choice of this particular song brought added gender and political dimension to the encounter between Esperanza and the police. Wildly popular in the early 1950s, this Cuban song was written by one of Cuba's most famous guitarists, Nico Saquito, renowned for his four-line stanzas and humorous lyrics. A Spanish singer, José de Aguilar, aligned with the Spanish Francoist regime, recorded it in 1951 or 1952.[15] The subject of this cheerful *mambo guaracho* is a young man who bemoans that his girlfriend, María Cristina, is domineering and bossy. He wants to refuse her commands but cannot resist her, and feels embarrassed that people will know that he follows her around like a puppy dog. The male singer offers a litany of physical tasks he is forced to perform by his girl, many of them involving exaggerated movements with his body. Witness one verse from the song that Esperanza's captors may have sung:

> Let's go home, and so I go
> Go upstairs, and I go up
> Get in the bath, and I get in
> Take off your clothes, and I take them off . . .
> Throw yourself down on the sand, and I throw myself down[16]

The command forms of the verbs in the lyrics are echoed by Esperanza in her interviews with Cuevas and Vidal: *desnudara*, "to get undressed";

subir and *bajar*, "to go up and down" (*ni me suben ni me bajan*). Her appropriation of commands to tell her own story resemanticizes the Francoist intention to beat and violate her until she is no longer "like" María Cristina. By making some of the lyrics her own, Esperanza rejects the conservative gender alignments that the male singer laments have gone awry. For her Francoist torturers, Esperanza Martínez appeared before them as a "red whore," a woman whose progressive politics spilled into the sexual arena. Like the girlfriend in the song, Esperanza would be seen to have presumed to have power over men by the mere fact of her participation in the armed resistance. Esperanza's account of the musically-scored abuse of her naked body, as told to oral historian Tomasa Cuevas (one of Esperanza's best friends and prison-mates), must be understood in the larger context of a narrative about resisting the trials of interrogation. Esperanza proudly asserts that she gave up no names or information that could have jeopardized her Communist comrades still in the field. Thus the grisly explicitness of the episode correlates to the valor Esperanza mustered in order to save her fellow anti-Francoist agents. And yet the nauseating sexual sadism of the scene runs the risk of overwhelming its political message. Little wonder, therefore, that Esperanza radically changed her testimonial account of torture in future interviews, continually diminishing the references to her body and nudity, to the point that torture vanishes altogether from her 2010 memoir *Guerrilleras, memoria de una esperanza*.[17]

Remedios Montero and the Baby Jesus

> ... The story is one that no one wants to hear: "it's not," as the grandmother remarks, "one of those stories that audiences love."
> —*Sexual Violence Against Jewish Women in the Holocaust*

In 1953, in Valencia's prison for women, female political prisoners gathered in the chapel for Christmas Day mass. Remedios Montero recalled mass this way:

> One Christmas day all the top brass attended—the Director, the priests from outside—to observe the women prisoners' mass. And after the service, they forced us to file out down an aisle and the priest held out a figurine of the Baby Jesus. The prisoners paused to kiss the baby. So then when it was my turn to pass by, an evil woman prison official, named Purification, came up behind me. I looked at her and I walked right by the Baby Jesus without kissing his feet. Suddenly she grabbed me like this, by the back of the head, and she hit me in the head, forcing me to bend over, and she said to me: "Kiss him!" In that moment I felt so much rage that instead of kissing the baby, I bit him, on that little foot that the Baby Jesus has, and like this, the little toe went flying up and

up. I bit him. And in front of the whole staff, for them it was . . . well . . . that woman took hold of me and I spent another two or three months in solitary confinement.[18]

This vivid and sinister anecdote functions as a mise en abyme for the total memorial enterprise surrounding the unruly Montero, whose life story chronicles the making of her communist self and, from a Marxist, working-class worldview, describes the tension between a unique, unorthodox female subject and the pervasive female compliance with conservative, nationalistic, Catholic scripts of womanhood.

The public trajectory taken by Montero's testimony illustrates the problematic consequences brought on by the instrumentalization of the oral histories of the *guerrilleros* by what I would call their compassionate "cultural interpreters." In his excellent book on the memories of surviving members of the ALGA Guerrilla unit, Vidal Castaño calls Remedios Montero "an emblematic figure of the antifascist resistance."[19] An enigma inheres in Montero's attitude toward her public persona, and it remains troublingly unclear whether she concedes uncritically to the desire for her story or whether she, in fact, endeavors to manage the circulation and proliferation of her image. By repeatedly presenting herself to an audience that promises to disseminate or absorb her story faithfully and with ideological and historical precision, we imagine that Remedios would perform as a willing subject of her own testimony. And yet she enacts, in her reiterations, a powerful will to resist her interlocutors' efforts at proximity. On closer inspection, each of the many versions of her life story turns on a silent affective distance from her interviewer as well as from narrative produced through the act of collecting the oral history. Over the years, as I have come into contact with and analyzed various versions of Montero's testimonies (including my own 2002 interview), what comes to light is that her guarded bodily and vocal expression safeguards her sense of agency through the volitional deployment of secrets, silences, ambivalence, hesitation, withholding.

In order to delve into the scripted and imagistic reconstructions of Montero's testimony, I began to think about the cinematic retellings by way of the concept of "reenactment," or historical restaging. Traditionally understood, "reenactments," according to Bill Nichols, are the "more or less authentic re-creation of prior events."[20] Nichols's rethinking of reenactment through the figure of the specter and the fantasmatic allows us to correlate reenacted events in cinema with the production of desire in *testimonio* (Doris Sommer) and oral history (Luisa Passerini).[21] All three performances—the cinematic, the testimonial, and the oral historical—depend on meaning-bearing silences or refusals that reveal a gap that stimulates "our craving to know."[22] Put another way, reenactments in film and the retellings of oral history "introduce a fantasmatic element that an initial representation of the same event lacks."[23]

Unable to bridge the gap between original events and their narrative restagings, the historian, interviewer, or spectator might feel deceived upon realizing that the reenactment is an interpretation that has lost its indexical bond to that for which it stands and instead functions as evidence for the "voice of the filmmaker" or writer, or journalist.[24] By way of these critical approaches to the representation of difficult memory, we can explore further Montero's oral history as a fraught project that reveals her discomfort with the prospect of entering sexual elements of her experience into history. In drawing out how these concepts converge, I attempt to think through how Montero's oral testimony pushes back against the friendly appropriation of her story in two specific cases, significantly the texts produced closest to her death and the versions of her life story that do not include the episode of the baby Jesus: Montero's own 2004 memoir, *Historia de Celia: Recuerdos de una guerrillera antifascista* and Pau Vergara's 2007 historical docudrama, *Memorias de una guerrillera*.

In Vergara's film, predictability reigns. It borrows from the least inspired tradition of tired television docudrama or the made-for-television "true story," but it also demonstrates pretensions to historical fiction. These attributes become evident not only in the poor production values, but also in the use of the oft-employed pattern of intercutting interview sequences with dramatized reenactments. In *Memorias de una guerrillera*, the director alternates interview footage of Montero with recreations of scenes from her life between 1949 and the 1960s. In the film, the spectator may detect something subtle in the way Montero holds her body in the film that seems deliberately apotropaic: there is a language to her wordlessness and in her body that "deflect[s] an audience's rapport even as [it] summons us."[25] Like many subaltern testimonial speakers, Montero meets us "performing a defensive move in the midst of her seduction."[26]

At this point, let us return to the scene of the Christmas Day mass and the Baby Jesus. In the versions of the story by Montero told to Tomasa Cuevas and Vidal Castaño, the episode is linked temporally and narratively to an anecdote in which Montero explains to a hostile priest that she refuses to pray and take Communion because she does not consider herself a Catholic. Montero's aggression toward the Baby Jesus stands out as the most cinematic and perversely humorous of the core chapters she has narrated on dozens of occasions. Why is the event erased from public view in the memoir and the film—the most recent iterations of her story?

Because the reenactment forfeits its representative bond to original events in its execution, the recreation has the potential to retrieve something—an object or a state of mind—redolent of the original historical representation. Although Vergara does not reproduce the story of the prison mass, I posit that in *Memorias de una guerrillera*, the complex valences of the disfigurement of the Baby Jesus seep through in sequences suggestive of the same sexually and institutionally inflected dialectic between repression and rebellion that the original incident puts on display.

Vergara produces two scenes in his film in which he has directed the real-life Montero to enter into a reenacted scene of her past. The first is the ambush in which her father and other comrades of the *maquis* were shot and killed by the Spanish Civil Guard. Here Remedios walks among the actors playing the cadavers and leans forward, kissing her hand and placing the kiss on her father's head. In the second reenactment, today's Remedios walks into an interrogation room where the actress playing her much younger self lies unconscious against a wall, bloodied and bruised from the torture the audience has just witnessed. Here too, Remedios has been directed by Vergara to incline over the victim and place a kiss on her cheek.

In order to unpack how these two reenactments echo the Baby Jesus story in their suggestion of sexual threat, we need to take note of the complex and layered representational network operative within the Catholic ritual of the kissing devotion. Although the ubiquitous figurine or doll of the Baby Jesus in mid-twentieth-century Spain renders him a light-skinned, blondish infant in *pañales* and perhaps a simple gown, the iconic image of the Baby Jesus in his full regalia is that of the internationally venerated Infant of Prague, originally a Spanish Carmelite object of devotion brought to Bohemia in 1628. The Infant of Prague, increasingly venerated in Spain around the 1930s, is significantly an infant king, and symbolizes authority and royalty. Because the infant is connected to Christmas, there would have been, as Montero and other women prisoners describe, a kissing devotion that day. The doll of the Baby Jesus would have had little feet under his gown, and we can imagine a devotion where people would have come up to it, an attendant would have lifted the hem of the gown, and the women inmates would have kissed the feet.

Montero's refusal to place her mouth on the feet of the figure of the infant Jesus is cast in strictly anti-clerical tones. Her hatred of the church, mere disinterest in her youth, came on full force, she explains, when the Francoist police who tortured her would take breaks between beatings—delivered at "sexual range"—so they could attend mass.[27] If the torture she endured before prison reinforced her anti-clericalism and thus explains her repulsion for the mass and its symbols, the sexual overtones of the pantomime Montero refused to act out remain nevertheless striking: pushing her head down to kiss the toe evokes both oral sex and the penitent Magdalene kissing the feet of Christ. By doing violence to the figurine, Montero in essence reverses the image of coerced fellatio, and therefore the story of the baby Jesus becomes an important signifier of a double resistance: to the Church and to the gendered abuses and humiliations wielded against Republican women inmates. It is a gripping tale—both mythology and fact—that beautifully captures Montero's defiance, but its subtext is sexual coercion. What is more, the surprising violence of the tale makes the story not only one that Montero loved to tell, but part of the prison lore passed on by women who had witnessed the scene or heard of it from others.

It should not strain credibility to imagine that women prisoners were forced to fellate their torturers or the priests assigned to their jails. Furthermore, during torture sessions, Montero and Martínez were pressed not only to reveal the names of their comrades, but also to "confess" that they had joined the resistance as the lovers or whores of their men. According to the discursive logic of their torturers, sexualized torture could be justified because the women were "whores" to begin with. Let us revisit the two reenactments in *Memorias de una guerrillera* to see how they supplement the absence of the spectacle described above. Let us recall that the first reenactment entails Montero, playing herself in the present, utterly alone among the carnage, gazing detachedly down upon the still-bleeding body of her father. She kisses her own hand, and bends over to place her kiss on her father. In the second sequence, blocked by Vergara in a fashion troublingly like the first, the director shoots the actress playing the young Montero framed in a high-angle medium shot. The assaulted character lies unconscious on the concrete floor. Again the present-day Montero appears in the mise-en-scène, a medium close-up focuses on her feet stepping into place behind the unresponsive body on the hard floor. Cut to a low-angle camera that peers up at today's Montero, who bends over to stroke the forehead of the actress playing her former self, and again, places a kiss tenderly on the cheek. Yet, as in the previous reenactment, Montero does obeisance badly, perfunctorily. Her facial expression, even in close-up, gives away no overt meaning.

Refusing the Will to Intimacy

If Vergara's actors overplay their roles throughout the film, Montero, playing herself, stalwartly rejects the kind of therapeutic dramaturgy that Vergara imputes to her in the hope that "seeing" her father's corpse, and witnessing her own torture will illicit in her (and in us) the cathartic release that has eluded her compassionate cultural interpreters up until this moment. These crucial scenes oblige the audience to bear witness to a clumsily manufactured effort at something like "making peace with one's past," or "putting to rest inner demons," or more likely still, a coming to terms with the traumas of loss and torture. In a moving article about Holocaust testimony, Patricia Yaeger describes how the speaking survivor's body wards off our efforts for intimacy. Like Yaeger, I read Montero's desubjectivized participation in the reenactments looking for "the effect of a gesture or glance, an undecidable moment when the act of witnessing confounds identification. As secondary witnesses, we may feel a redoubled empathy in such a moment, and yet it is exactly in this moment that as witnesses her "body language marks our nonentry into the place of intimacy."[28] Vergara shoots Remedios alone and exposed, amid bodies (dead or beaten) who cannot come to her aid. But Montero does not succumb to the bathos of the scene; her face disconnects, refusing to meld with the story as Vergara has interpreted it. The narrative and the body go in separate directions.

And still, the threat of the male perpetrators remains in the filmic frame. Remedios in her eighties stands on stages of male destruction on which the men, Civil and prison guards, were certain to return to torture, murder, and violate again. We do not see rape in the Vergara film or in any of Montero's testimonies. What we do see in both the Montero and Martínez stories are "abandoned female bodies, susceptible to rape."[29] In both of the reenactments, the past threat of torture, murder, and sexual assault still looms over the scenes in a present made that much more threatening for the camera's focus on Montero's elderly 2007 body—a body that interacts only with the dead or the unconscious. The spectator does not need the recourse to a confession of rape to understand the signs of sexual danger lurking among the thick trees of the *monte* or beyond the walls of the interrogation chamber momentarily abandoned by the police.

In restaging her rebellion to sexualized violence and clerical ritual, Montero's corporeal and psychic recoiling from the mise-en-scène of Vergara's design ruptures the indexical relation between the historical event and the memory he attempts to reproduce in the present. The rigidity of her bodily stance cannot be attributed only to her advanced age. Rather, the reluctance we observe in her movements—heavy, it seems, with memories—as Passerini explains, transmitted without words, "such as those incorporated in gestures, images and objects."[30] She held on to her secrets and her silences even to her grave, for they endowed her precarious self, so brutalized psychically and physically, with agency.

Although compelling for its efforts to employ reenactments and interview in order to bolster its truth effects, *Memorias de una guerrillera* is more failure than success. This is so for a variety of reasons, among them the showy effect of shifts into black and white in order to create a simulacrum of historical footage; luridly stylized dramatizations of executions and torture; and the surprisingly poor acting by seeming nonprofessional actors whose theatricality undermines the attempt at authenticity. When Vergara casts the real Remedios Montero as a future specter of her own past, the director strives for a cathartic "Shoah effect," produced by "an unsettling combination of Freudian technique and method acting to unearth traumatic histories through harrowing on-location interviews."[31]

Still, despite the film's many flaws, Vergara cannot be accused of naive filmmaking. He manipulates familiar canonical techniques of documentary, including the talking-head interview and the return to the scene of the crime. In the scenes of forced kissing, cast in the mold of Nichols's "realist dramatizations," Vergara too understands that reenactments "fulfill an affective function . . . contribut[ing] to a vivification of that for which they stand . . . an inflection that resurrects the past to reanimate it with the *force of a desire*."[32] The force of desire remains ours, the spectators', and Montero walks off the scene unmoved by the performance she has ultimately refused to deliver. And through her stiff, refractory gestures and the lack of emotional reactivity in both the restagings and the interviews, Montero unveils reenactment as a "discipline, with both punitive and critical valences."[33] Her act, not unlike reenactments of tortures in more recent times, "provokes us to consider not only where we reenact elements of the structure of power that makes torture possible, but also where these reenactments constitute central and paradoxical components of our oppositional discourse."[34] The reenactment of torture Beckman refers to here is the re-performance (most famously by Christopher Hitchens) of waterboarding performed at Abu Ghraib. Montero's witnessing of an actress reenacting her own tortures and suffering might not appear, at first glance, to warrant comparison with the employment of a repeat performance of torture in another culture and time. But Beckman's point sheds light on Montero's physical involvement in the Vergara film, a participation that presses her into an unwilling collaboration of sorts with the structure of power that tried to destroy her and that simultaneously opens a space for her to exercise her capacities for opposition and survival.

The erasure of the Baby Jesus narrative from Montero's 2004 memoir could be explained a number of ways. Perhaps she did not want to be remembered for her hatred of the Church. But I suspect that the episode's subtext of resistance to sexual victimhood is what troubled her as she contemplated whether or not to include it in her own book. Montero's affective noncompliance with Vergara's reenactments suggest that she determined to project herself as an always-resisting political militant who has comprehended better than her sympathetic interpreters that techniques of historical restaging foil the desire to present the past and confound the spectators' will to intimacy.

Conclusion

Tracing different versions of Martínez's and Montero's life stories over time allows us to observe how the entire oral testimonial project of these women is fraught with a tension between competing discourses of heroic activism, resistance, and political bravery on the one hand, and memories of sexualized violence on the other. Our task in interpreting the testimonies of Republican women survivors of the Franco penitentiary system involves exposing the dynamic of resistance that inheres in both memories of political action and solidarity, and in narratives alluding to sexualized violence. But we must also exercise caution in our efforts to know more, as we coax the images in the testimonies to speak of acts that Montero and Martínez illustrate through figurative language—metaphor and simile, detours, vacillations, and euphemism. As compassionate cultural interpreters, we should not expect traumatic testimony to be literal or directly representational, and certainly not in the sense that it is immediately comprehensible to us. The Montero and Martínez life stories are not expository artifacts, and perhaps they simply cannot be, for they register some of the ways (both sublimation and storytelling) in which their speakers survived and still survive at the moment of testimony. By the time they composed their respective memoirs, in the heat of the Spanish memory boom, more than sixty years after they were first arrested, their self-closure regarding sexualized violence is complete. The memoirs ask the audience to be attuned to the power of the Republican ideal, not the power of the regime that employed violence to make its victims believe in the torturer's version of the world.[35] In excluding the Baby Jesus story and the "María Cristina" torture from their autobiographical publications, Montero and Martínez assert control over the dissemination of their memories by imposing protective boundaries around their lives as *maquis* and by rescuing their publicly celebrated militancy from the stain of rape and sexual torture.

Notes

1. Maud Joly, "Las violencias sexuadas de la guerra civil española: Paradigma para una lectura cultural del conflicto," *Historia social* 61 (2008): 89–107. See also Irene Abad, "Las dimensiones de la 'Represión sexuada' durante la dictadura Franquista," *Dossier—Guerra civil: Las representaciones de la violencia*, eds. Javier Rodrigo and Miguel Angel Ruiz Carnicer. Jerónimo Zurita 84 (2009): 65–86.
2. The language that best encompasses the phenomena of unwanted sexual contact I trace in the testimonies of Montero and Martínez is "sexualized violence." Brigitte Halbmayer defends the term "sexualized violence" because it "covers direct physical expressions of violence that are bodily attacks, an unauthorized crossing of body boundaries. They range from flagrant sexual advances to rape . . . This definition also allows for the inclusion of indirect, often emotional expressions of violence, such as imposed public nakedness and accompanying feelings of shame, infringement on intimate space, deplorable hygienic conditions, leering stares, suggestive insults, and humiliating methods of physical examinations. . . ." See Brigitte Halbmayer, "Sexualized Violence During Nazi 'Racial' Persecution," in *Sexual Violence against Jewish Women during the Holocaust* eds. Sonia Hedgepeth and Rochelle G. Saidel (Lebanon, NH: Brandeis University Press, 2010), 30.
3. Paul Preston, *El holocausto español: Odio y exterminio en la Guerra civil y después* (Barcelona: Random House, 2011). The English edition, *The Spanish Holocaust*, is forthcoming 2011.
4. For accounts of sexualized torture, gang rape, and gendered humiliations, see Maud Joly, http://www.historiacritica.org/anteriors/anterior3/tesis/tesis02.htm; Juana Doña, *Desde la noche y la niebla: Mujeres en las cárceles franquistas* (Madrid: Gráficas Monedero, 1993); García Consuelo, *Las cárceles de Soledad Real: Una vida* (Madrid: Alfaguara, 1982); Francisco Moreno Gómez, *La resistencia armada contra Franco: Tragedia del maquis y la guerrilla* (Barcelona: Crítica, 2001); Tomasa Cuevas, *Testimonios de mujeres en las cárceles franquistas* (Huesca: Instituto de Estudios Altoragoneses, 2004). The Cuevas collection from 2004 is a compilation of three previously self-published volumes: *Cárcel de Mujeres: 1939–1945, Tomo 1* (Barcelona: Sirocco Books 1985); *Cárcel de Mujeres: Tomo 2* (Barcelona: Sirocco Books, 1985); and *Mujeres de la Resistencia* (Barcelona: Sirocco Books, 1986). In Cuevas's collections of testimonies, none of the interviews carry dates.
5. The primary first-person accounts of Esperanza Martínez's life story appear in José Antonio Vidal Castaño, *La memoria reprimida: Historias orales del maquis* (Valencia, Spain: Publicacions Universitat de València, 2004); Cuevas's book *Testimonios* (1986); Corcuera's film *La guerrilla de la memoria* (2002); Pau Vergara's film, *Memorias de una guerrillera* (Maltes Productions: Valencia, Spain: 2007); the film *Historia de una guerrillera*; and Esperanza's own memoir, *Guerrilleras: La ilusión de una Esperanza* (Madrid: Latorre Literaria, 2010). Those of Remedios Montero also appear in Vidal Castaño, Cuevas, Corcuera, and Vergara, and in addition, Montero's memoir, *Historia de Celia: Recuerdos de una guerrillera antifascita* (Valencia: Rialla-Octadero, 2004). All translations are mine.
6. In the films by Corcuera and Vergara, but also for a filmed interview produced by investigators at a women's studies institute at the University of Zaragoza, *Esperanza Martínez: Una luchadora por la libertad* (SIEM, 2007).

7. Remedios Montero, interview, October 2002, Valencia, Spain; Esperanza Martínez, interview, October 2002, Zaragoza, Spain. Montero died in 2010, and I never had the chance to talk to her about my interpretations. There is, however, a short interview with Montero, posted on YouTube, in which she expressed her ambivalence about the Vergara film based on her life: http://www.youtube.com/watch?v=SyFiiPIHUT8.
8. Dulce Chacón, *La voz dormida* (Madrid: Alfaguara, 2002).
9. José Antonio Vidal Castaño, *La memoria reprimida: Historias orales del maquis* (Valencia, Spain: Publicacions Universitat de València, 2004); Remedios Montero, interview with *La Gavilla verde*, Santa Cruz de la Moya, Spain, 2003, http://www.lagavillaverde.org/centro_de_documentacion/materialesIV/entrevflorianreme.htm; Remedios Montero, interview, October 2002, Valencia, Spain.
10. Preston, *The Spanish Holocaust*, xix.
11. Preston, *The Spanish Holocaust*, 511.
12. Cuevas, *Testimonio de mujeres*, 601–2.
13. Esther López Barceló, *Testimonio de la memoria* (Agepv.com. 2011), 55.
14. Vidal Castaño, *La memoria reprimida*, 164–5.
15. José de Aguilar y su Orquesta. Odeon Catalogue number: 184768 Matrix: SO 10689 / SO 10687 Title: Mambo Guaracha - María Cristina me quiere gobernar (A. Fernández "Ñico Saquito") / Huapango - Torito bravo (F. de Val). Most likely it was Aguilar's performance that would have been familiar to Esperanza and her captors. Aguilar rose to fame with his recording of "Hala, Madrid," the hymn of the Spanish soccer team, the *Real Madrid*—known as the soccer club of the regime.
16. Complete lyrics in original Spanish can be found at http://www.lyrics85.com/%C3%91ICO-SAQUITO-MAR%C3%ADA-CRISTINA-LYRICS/389700/
17. Esperanza Martínez, *Guerrilleras: La ilusión de una Esperanza* (Madrid: Latorre Literaria, 2010).
18. Vidal Castaño, *Memoria reprimida,* 116; Cuevas, *Testimonio,* 613.
19. Vidal Castaño, 95.
20. Bill Nichols, "Documentary Reenactment and the Fantasmatic Subject," *Critical Inquiry* 35 (2008): 72–89.
21. Doris Sommer, "Rigoberta's Secrets," *Latin American Perspectives* 70 18(2) 1991: 32–50. Luisa Passerini, "Memories between Silence and Oblivion," in her book *Memory and Utopia: The Primacy of Intersubjectivity.* (London: Equinox, 2007): 15–32.
22. Sommer, "Rigoberta's," 34.
23. Nichols, "Documentary," 72.
24. Ibid, 88.
25. Yaeger, Patricia, "Testimony without Intimacy," *Poetics Today* 27 (Summer 2006): 399–423, 405.
26. Sommer, "Rigoberta's," 36.
27. The term comes from David Grossman's *On Killing: The Psychological Cost of Learning to Kill in War and Society* (Boston: Back Bay Books,1996) and suggests that in the invasion of bodily and psychic privacy in acts of torture, even if the assault is not intended, conceived, or experienced as "sexual," per se, the intimacy of the violation approximates sexual contact.
28. Yaeger, "Testimony," 417.
29. Ariella Azoulay, "Has Anyone Ever Seen a Photograph of Rape?" *The Civil Contract of Photography* (Cambridge: The MIT Press, 2008): 217–288, 264.
30. Passerini, "Memories," 27.
31. Jonathan Kahana, "Introduction: What Now? Presenting Reenactment," *Framework: The Journal of Cinema and Media* 50 (2009): 46–60, 49.

32. Nichols, "Documentary," 88. Italics in text are mine.
33. Kahana, "Introduction," 57.
34. Karen Beckman, "Gender, Power, and Pedagogy in Coco Fusco's Bare Life Study (2005), A Room of One's Own (2005), and Operation Atropos (2006)." *Framework: The Journal of Cinema and Media*, 50 (2009): 125–138, 135.
35. This idea about the linguistic dimensions of torture come from Elaine Scarry's well-known account in *The Body in Pain*, by which interrogation itself is part of torture, and that pain under torture is produced by being faced with the torturer's vision of reality. Elaine Scarry, *The Body in Pain: The Making and Unmaking of the World* (New York: Oxford University Press, 1985).

6

On Testimony: The Pain of Speaking and the Speaking of Pain

Srila Roy

In *On the Genealogy of Morals*, Nietzsche says that pain is the most powerful aid to mnemonics.[1] For Nietzsche, the inscription of pain on the body is the medium through which the body is integrated into the moral community. Here, pain is not an inherently alienating experience[2] but the very condition for the individual's entry into the social. In contemporary trauma studies, a "remaking" or reconstitution of selfhood in the face of trauma is often premised on the ability to transform traumatic memories into a linear, coherent narrative that can be told and heard.[3] Telling a story of trauma transforms traumatic memory into narrative memory, thereby remaking the survivor's sense of self and her relation to the world[4]: "testimony attempts to bridge the gap between suffering individuals and ultimately communities of listeners, whose empathic response can be palliative, if not curative."[5] The survivor does not bear witness to a private life or strictly for herself but always for the sake of an other and to an other, to whom the testimony is addressed.

The task of telling the untellable is, however, ridden with contradictions, not least of which is the sheer inexpressibility and inaccessibility of pain in language.[6] Women's testimonies to political violence, in particular,

---

* This essay has been a long time in the making, starting its life as a presentation to the Thirteenth International Oral History Conference at Rome in 2004. I would like to thank, for their engagement and encouragement along the way, Parita Mukta, Molly Andrews, Steve Fuller, Anirban Das, Rafael Winkler, and especially, Terry Lovell.

are said to speak through the language of silence, and on more than one historical occasion, they have been observed to testify to the sufferings of others while rarely speaking of their own.[7] While some have viewed this mode of silencing the private voice as undermining the universal (and patriarchal) basis of contemporary human rights discourse,[8] others have linked the compulsion to "narrate the other" to normative gendered roles, of which the testimonial one becomes an extension.[9] Even when women's stories have been speakable, they have been received with disbelief. Patriarchal categories of speech also compromise women's testimonies and the communicability of injury.[10] Besides the gendered complexities of testimonial practice, the study of testimony must address the implications of traumatic memory when it assumes a testimonial form, or examine how such forms of representation can rob survivors of their voice and agency.[11]

This chapter engages with the testimony of political violence in the context of the extreme left Naxalbari movement of eastern India, to offer some reflections on the politics of bearing witness and testifying to violence and pain. It raises some questions regarding the privileged position of testimony (especially in feminist politics) as a conduit for understanding and even ameliorating women's suffering. In doing so, it points to certain limitations of telling stories of trauma for individual women.

Custodial Violence and Naxalbari

The Naxalbari movement began in 1967 as a peasant uprising in the northern village of Naxalbari in West Bengal, a singular iconic episode that introduced a major shift in the Indian left, besides spawning a range of militant Maoist struggles in the subcontinent that continue to this day. What began as a peasant rebellion over issues of land soon gave way to a large-scale urban guerilla battle, staged primarily in the city of Kolkata (formerly Calcutta). Youths and students emerged as an important locus of support for the movement, imparting to it the character of the student radicalism that marked the 1960s globally. The political line of annihilating "class enemies," first instigated against landowners in rural areas, escalated into what has often been referred to as an orgy of violence. Small guerrilla units, composed primarily of men, killed anyone from traffic policemen to local schoolteachers as representatives of the state. Even more legendary is the state's violent onslaught that followed. Notorious "encounter" killings, arbitrary jail firings and deaths, and custodial abuse and torture have rendered the early 1970s one of the darkest periods in the history of independent India. Popular representations of the movement are replete with images of the victimization of young Naxalites at the hands of the state.

A majority of these activists (both men and women, whom I interviewed as part of a larger project[12]) were incarcerated for anything between three to seven years, and suffered varying degrees of police torture and prison violence. The trauma that their stories speak of suggests a relationship with violence that persists through the passage of time, infuses portraits of the self, and permeates their relationship to normality. There are, however, remarkable differences in the ways in which traumatic experiences are remembered, constructed, and told, and in the subject-positions that survivors choose to inhabit in order to do so. I have looked at these stories extensively elsewhere.[13] Here I want to explore the politics of testimony in the case of one woman, Latika.

The Burden of the Witness

In 1974 Latika, her sister in-law Archana, and a close family friend, Gauri, were arrested in their home.[14] Archana was tortured in a way that has made her name synonymous with the reality of custodial violence in West Bengal. Physical torture, particularly the use of *falanga*, the systematic beating of the soles of the feet, left Archana's lower limbs completely paralyzed. Latika's husband, Saumen, a middle-ranking activist, was arrested soon after and tortured as well. Although Latika suffered much less physical torture than the others, she bore the solitary burden of witnessing the ordeal, and took upon herself the responsibility of nurturing the wounded (which continued post-incarceration). Since their release from prison, the entire Guha family has been involved in a case against the policemen for the torture inflicted upon Archana. The legal battle against custodial violence is nothing short of historic in West Bengal, given that it has no precedent, and it inaugurated a new chapter in the civil rights movement in the state.[15] In the last year of trial, Saumen appeared as the defense council on behalf of his sister, the plaintiff, Archana. Amnesty International subsequently sent Archana to Denmark for rehabilitation. In a landmark victory in 1996, after nineteen years of struggle, the primary accused, Runu Guha Neogi was sentenced to a year's imprisonment. (At the time of my interviews, the case against one other policeman was pending.)

I interviewed Latika and Saumen at their home in Kolkata over several meetings that spanned a few months in 2003. As the interviews progressed, I realized how it was practically impossible to elicit a conventional life story from Latika, given that her memory remained tightly tethered to certain key moments that unite in a single, dominant story. The story begins with her marriage to Saumen in 1973; her subsequent arrest, torture, and incarceration in 1974; and an afterlife of loss and insecurity that has seemingly left her with few material or psychological resources to "work through" trauma, let alone to begin the work of mourning. Needless to say, the legal battle is the pivot upon which her entire story hinges. The "Archana Guha case," which Saumen describes as "the most beloved baby in the bosom of the then childless couple, my wife Latika Guha and me,"[16] has imbued the memory of the event with new significance, besides transforming Latika's status from a victim of torture to a crusader against human rights violations. The event and its afterlife comprise a master narrative that pervades Latika's speech, memory, and sense of self. As she puts it, "This, in my life, has been a major event, you know, I mean, you can say, the last event in my life, the impact of which I will have to carry till my death."[17]

Much like her legal testimony, her interview with me was structured around the precise temporal coordinates of her arrest, her movements within the Lalbazar police station, a detailed description of the people encountered, names, faces, and designations, and finally the moment of torture itself:

> We had to walk half a mile to the main Dum Dum Road where the van was parked. It was drizzling. We walked all the way, getting wet. They took us straight to Cossipore *thana* where they kept us waiting.... There was one officer and two constables. Then after a while they came back, past 3–3:30 ... Then they took us to Lalbazar at 4:30. (*You remember the exact time?*) Yes, morning was approaching ... [At Lalbazar] The officer, Manas called us and asked mother's, father's name, husband's name, where does he live, do you do politics or not, all that ... They kept us waiting. Runu Guha had created a special cell only for Naxalites, just for their torture. We sat outside this room. There was a huge, long corridor ... [detailed description of the building] ... it [the "special cell"] was part of the detective department but only for the repression of the Naxalites. Then it became morning, between 10–10:30. First Archana was called in ...

What follows is the turn-by-turn torture of the three women in Inspector Runu Guha's notorious "special cell." Latika's published memoir conveys a similar depth of detail while bearing witness to the collective strength shared by the women in the face of humiliating torture: "My body trembled with anger. I would not weep in the face of such tremendous uncertainty. I would not shrivel up. I would listen quietly, watch, I would bear everything. I didn't tremble the slightest. I didn't get perturbed. None of us did."[18]

Evoking the burden of the witness that Felman describes,[19] Latika emphasizes how she feels that it is her "responsibility" to speak out against custodial violence, even though the process itself makes her feel "very bad":

"But then I feel that writing is my responsibility, so I continue to write. What I've seen, there's a need to write that . . . this is a responsibility. The whole of history has to be recorded and the event definitely has a place there."[20]

Such a sense of responsibility is common to survivors of state terror.[21] When Latika says, "it is my responsibility to write what I have seen," she speaks as a subject in history who uses her own speech as material evidence for truth.[22] To the extent that testimony infuses pain with historical/political agency, it can be recognized as a performative speech act. For Brison, testimony is performative by virtue of its curative quality for the trauma survivor: "saying something about a traumatic memory does something to it."[23] For such performative utterances to be felicitous, they must accord with the cultural norms, rules, and conventions of the "language game" in which they are performed.

Testimony and Individual Healing

Latika's testimony has been instrumental to her entry into the public domain. It has enabled individual pain to win public recognition and acknowledgment, a move that is perceived as central to the process of healing past wounds. Her status as witness has enabled a transformation of the subject from one that passively submits to oppression to one that actively resists it. The act of testimony can be considered as both empowering and redemptive for the trauma survivor. The question of agency, however, is tricky, and we need to be cautious before replacing the discourse of victimology with that of agency, especially when it comes to women.

While the testimony to violence might fulfill the ethical demand for justice, I am uncertain to what extent it responds to the need for individual healing. Latika's testimony is an instance of the way in which individual pain can be silenced in its testimonial transformation for the sake of bearing witness on behalf of an other or a victimized collective. The transformation of individual suffering into a collective narrative does not always entail an acknowledgment of pain in ways that would initiate the process of healing for the individual trauma survivor. On the contrary, the very structure of testimony, as a genre, conditions the articulation and reception of suffering in the public domain in ways that seriously compromise a representation of the individual subject in pain. This makes the question of healing a lot less straightforward than present trauma studies are wont to assume.

In what follows, I argue that while the act of testimony gives voice to the silence of pain, it forecloses the possibility of listening to and acknowledging individual suffering. This can be attributed to at least three structural limitations: first, the duality between individual and collective that is inherent to the act of testimony; second, the politics of listening that make testimony *a priori* possible; and finally, the possibility of sharing in the experience of pain.

The Erasure of the Self

In the act of testimony, the subject is witness to something other than *itself*; to bear witness is "to speak *for* others and *to* others."[24] Trauma testimonies demand an effacement of the individual voice in their commitment to speak on behalf of those who are not able to bear witness, those who have been silenced. They necessitate a privileging of the collective and symbolic "we" over the individual "I," to the extent that the latter might accede to the former.[25] While some have thought of this as imparting a degree of political agency to the survivor,[26] others have thought of it as significantly complicating the process of individual recovery and healing. Molly Andrews, for instance, draws on the case of the South African Truth and Reconciliation Commission to suggest that "testifying in public about private pain might ultimately lead to a silencing of the individual sufferer" even as it might fulfill other goals of reconciliation and nation-building in the aftermath of trauma.[27]

Latika can be recognized as a witness in the legal sense, who can produce evidence in a trial, but also as a survivor who can bear witness to something she has lived through.[28] Yet there is a tendency in her testimonial act to subsume her representational status as a survivor beneath that of being a legal witness. In Latika's oral and written discourse, there is a slow erasure of the speaking subject or, as Caruth (drawing on Dori Laub's work with Holocaust survivors) observes, "[an] ability to witness the *event* fully only at the cost of witnessing oneself."[29] Her subjectivity is overridden by her agency as witness to *someone else's* pain (namely Archana's) and not her own. The "other" in this instance expands from a singular Archana to a plural "us," a community of torture victims, and the testimonial act becomes intimately bound up with a politics of suffering. She almost always has recourse to the collective, impersonal "we" (referring to herself, Archana and Gauri) when narrating her experience of police custody and jail. Common to such "judicial models of witnessing,"[30] emotions and subjective interpretations of events are also kept to a minimum. Even where the individual voice is employed (as in her memoir), the experience of physical torture is narrated as a record of happenings, a series of events that the victim passively undergoes:

"Runu's cohorts pushed me up against the wall and began to madly slap my left cheek. I realized the cheek had swollen up."[31]

Such a mode of writing does not reveal a personal side of pain, or any personal truths, in its emphasis on historical truth. It seems to uphold, instead, the legal imperative to keep "a trauma narrative straight, for the purpose of a trial."[32] The legal compulsion to "get it right" results in a "forgetting" of one's own wounded subjectivity. We have no way of "reading" the private impact of state-inflicted torture on Latika from her testimony, or how she, as an individual, has come to terms with a traumatic past. Indeed, we have no way of recognizing Latika herself as a victim or even as a survivor. I often forgot, in my interactions with Latika, that she too was beaten, slapped, and verbally abused while in police custody. While the erasure of the self might fulfill the political impetus to testify on behalf of a collective of victims, it also radically reproduces, rather than disables, the "already Other" positioning of women.[33]

Latika's self-identity as a witness to someone else's pain has also meant a more circumscribed role for her even in the public domain since the only story that she deems worthy of sharing is her testimony; all other life experiences and opinions are subsumed under the voice of Saumen. Latika's identity is, in fact, deeply entwined with that of her husband, to the extent that she appears, frighteningly, as his alter ego, agreeing to everything he says or simply letting him speak on her behalf.[34] This made it extremely hard to elicit any independent response from her, and the usual remarks that I encountered were "He has said all that I had to say" and "I don't have very much to say."[35]

This conceding of agency is characteristic of the dualism on which the testimonial act is built: that of the individual and the collective. Testimony involves, as Miller and Tougaw note, a double function of "producing social discourse and initiating individual recovery," and yet, "these two effects do not necessarily coincide."[36] They are not the first to show how the creation of collective memory on behalf of a victimized community, or even the nation, can take precedence over personal healing—either because listeners can exert a powerful force on the kind of testimony they wish to hear or because of the symbolic force of testimony that exceeds personal suffering.

The Politics of Listening

It is not uncommon for a trauma survivor to feel alienated from her own words in the ways that I have noted of Latika. There is an important gendered dimension to this biographical effacement that bespeaks more than a sense of alienation. It introduces an important element of power into the analysis of trauma stories, suggesting that the elision of the personal voice could be a mode of patriarchal silencing. In the written version of Latika's story, self-identity is constructed through the self-effacing and self-sacrificial qualities of motherhood that are traditionally valorized and culturally specific. The rhetoric of martyrdom and self-sacrifice is the *leitmotif* of the Naxalbari movement, explicit in its written literature and still dominant in the sensibility of many of its supporters.[37] Latika's written text emphasizes the heroism and sacrifice of all three women, noting their resolve not to "break" under torture. Like her, the women are constructed as resisting subjects who show no weakness, remain resolute, and bear suffering for the sake of others—namely Saumen, about whom they were questioned. The only time they break down is when they think of their ailing mother (or mother-in-law) alone at home. The figure of the mother is, in fact, a dominant one in Latika's memoir; "a beacon of will, patience and love," she inspires them to bear suffering and "not to break."[38] What is also notable is the manner in which pain is here construed as weakness, to the extent that the very expression of physical pain is derided as a sign of possible betrayal.

In other texts, such as newspaper reportage, Latika's representation is governed by similar terms: "Particularly Latika, less severely tortured stood like a rock by the side of the other two ignoring her own injuries."[39] It is also interesting that the "Archana Guha case" itself is feminized in the language employed by both husband and wife, and located in a discourse of motherhood. The case is spoken of as a "beloved baby" as well as a vulnerable "daughter" that requires nurture and care, protection and safekeeping, especially against the threat of rape and violation. In a culture where motherhood is traditionally valorized, the use of the maternal trope to speak of past suffering has enormous emotional affectivity whether employed by men or women. Across cultures, gender plays an important part in what Berlant calls the "practice of making pain count politically."[40]

In testimony, the language game does not begin with the speaking subject; it begins with a community of listeners that command certain representations of self for this particular speech act to be performed. This makes the retreat into culturally sanctioned (and often nonthreatening and non-subversive) roles an *a priori* necessity in order for testimony to "speak." It also explains why certain kinds of trauma stories (such as human rights abuses) find more ready circulation in the public field of memory than do others (rape, incest). It is thus not surprising that women invariably have recourse to traditionally acceptable female stereotypes to gain public acknowledgment for violation and pain.[41] Latika cannot refuse the position of sacrificial woman/mother; these are the only subject-positions that a politics of listening will allow her. The retreat into traditionally acceptable roles also prevents patriarchy from invalidating or discrediting women's speech in advance.

Testimony has always enjoyed a position of privilege in feminist politics. As Sunder Rajan notes, the conversion of women's silence into speech through the act of testimony is "a specific attribute of feminist politics."[42] But perhaps greater reflection is required on what forms of subjectivity are conferred upon the gendered speaking subject. Female agency in testimony is seriously compromised, to the extent that women can only be legitimate users of a language that is not of their own making. Perhaps, as feminists, we can only engage with personal testimony on the assumption that "speech is a 'contaminated' area for research into women's subjectivities."[43]

The Sharing of Pain

Testimony might impede the process of individual recovery to such an extent that individual pain remains unrepresented and, by implication, unacknowledged. The need to resort to particular subject-positions ("victim," "martyr," "mother") to represent pain also constrains the agential capacity of the survivor. In both cases, the trauma story remains tethered to the demands of a universal narrative of suffering, on behalf of a community of listeners. In the aftermath of Naxalbari, this is a community that the legal battle around "Archana Guha" has helped to construct. One of my interviewees recalled how when the case began, it was construed as being on behalf of the entire victimized community, who were *all* victims of police torture. Yet as the case progressed, Saumen and Latika isolated themselves from this very moral community that their own acts of witnessing had willed into existence. The plaintiff herself, Archana, on whose behalf the case was fought, was severed from all family ties. Today all that remains are bitter memories on both sides, with strong boundary lines being drawn between "us" and "them."

One of the assumptions behind the reparative force of testimony accrues from its ability to bind the speaker and the listener through a collective sharing of pain. By contrast, Latika's act of testimony posits a radical separation between the self and the other. The "other"—namely, her ex-comrades—are presented as traitors to the cause, not victims of custodial violence like herself and her husband: "The intellectuals, progressives are very untrustworthy, undependable and short of traitors, they are the enemies of society . . . after the police-military, I think of them." Selfhood, in Latika (and Saumen's) testimony, is constructed in strongly oppositional terms, positing a heroic and sacrificial "us" against a weak and effeminate "them." The repeated evocation of "us" and "them" within a discourse of blame and resentment makes it difficult to perceive the self as formed in relation to and sustained through others in a social context. It also makes one question the degree to which the act of testimony has enabled a reintegration into the community. Bonds of friendship formed between Latika and the other Naxalite women in jail, which were often key to survival, are forgotten—as is their initial help with the Archana Guha case. Such acts of almost willful forgetting make it difficult to envision the possibility of communicating pain in a meaningful manner, which is often perceived as being central to the social recovery of the trauma survivor.

How are we, then, to understand the act of testimony as "an invitation to share"[44] and collectively experience individual pain? In her discussion on an "anthropology of pain," Veena Das grapples with the following problematic of "whether pain may be seen as providing the possibility of a new relationship, the beginning of a language game rather than its end (as Wittgenstein saw it), or whether it destroys the sense of community with the Other by destroying the capacity to communicate?"[45] It is this possibility of sharing pain that creates a moral community out of the injured and generates healing. Latika's pain is not intrinsically incommunicable, as has been posited of pain as such. Taking from Das, I would argue that the gaps, silences, and "forgettings" in women's narratives like hers are less about individual failings than about a collective failure, on the part of society, to share in the pain of an other.

Concluding Reflections

Latika's testimony has clearly offered her benefits, especially with regard to the forms of social recognition that it has enabled. But while it has offered her recognition as witness, I am uncertain as to how redemptive or empowering it has been for her, as a survivor or as a subject in pain. My uncertainty stems from the way in which her testimony fails to give voice to individual pain, while giving voice to the silence of torture in the public domain. In its political and historical force to represent a collective struggle against the crimes of the state, Latika's testimony circumvents a representation of individual pain, which has now become incidental to this larger, historical struggle. Her agency is also constrained to the extent that she needs to resort to traditionally acceptable gendered roles in order to gain social recognition. I have also raised the question of the communicability and sharing of pain through testimony. The act of testimony seems to disable the possibility of sharing pain given the manner in which the self is constructed within an identity politics of victimization.

Much of my discomfort concerns the duality of individual–collective, which is intrinsic to this particular speech act. Testimony is, in the final instance, a speech act that draws its meaning from a collective, plural "us" rather than the "I" who is in pain. It is equally governed by a politics of listening that grants a powerful role to the listener. The speaking subject can be perceived as an effect of the act of listening; the subject in pain comes to be only within the requirements of a community of listeners. In Judith Butler's reading of the *On the Genealogy of Morals*, the subject is retroactively produced as a moral, responsible agent (who is worthy of blame or guilt) on the occasion of pain: "A being is hurt, and the vocabulary that emerges to moralize that pain is one which isolates a subject as the intentional originator of an injurious deed."[46]

The act of listening in testimony, similarly, requires a subject; it instantiates a particular kind of subject as an effect or as a "consequence of that requirement."[47] The testimonial subject is neither the originator nor the owner of pain to the extent that the experience of pain is, in testimony, always and *only* a socially mediated one. On the contrary, the subject is "fictively secured" through discourses of legality and gender (and that of the political movement), as we have seen. At its extreme, the act of testimony can be perceived as a process of subjection to hegemonic and regulatory social norms whereby one becomes a testimonial or a speaking subject. Perhaps, then, it is only as a "failed performative"[48] that the testimony can rupture its fixity in convention, and signal new and potentially subversive ways in which the subject-in-pain can be (re)constituted.

Notes

1. Friedrich Nietzche, *On the Genealogy of Morals; Ecce homo*, trans. with commentary by Walter Kaufmann (New York: Vintage Books, 1969), 61.
2. Lawrence Langer, *Holocaust Testimonies: The Ruins of Memory* (New Haven: Yale University Press, 1991), and Elaine Scarry, *The Body in Pain: The Making and Unmaking of the World* (New York; Oxford: Oxford University Press, 1985).
3. See Susan Brison, *Aftermath: Violence and the Remaking of a Self* (Princeton, NJ: Princeton University Press, 2002). For recent overviews of trauma and memory studies, see Nancy Miller and Jason Tougaw, "Introduction: Extremities" in *Extremities: Trauma, Testimony, and Community* eds. Nancy Miller and Jason Tougaw (Urbana: University of Illinois Press, 2002), 1–21; Mieke Bal, Jonathan Crewe and Leo Spitzer Hanover, eds., *Acts of Memory: Cultural Recall in the Present* (Hanover, NH: University Press

of New England, 1999). On testimonial studies, see Sara Ahmed and Jackie Stacey, "Testimonial Cultures: An Introduction," *Cultural Values*, 5, 1 (2001): 1–6; and Anne Cubilié and Carl Good, "Introduction: The Future of Testimony," *Discourse*, 25, 1&2 (2003). The two most representative sources within this field are Cathy Caruth, ed., *Trauma: Explorations in Memory* (Baltimore, MD: Johns Hopkins University Press, 1995), and, Shoshana Felman and Dori Laub, *Testimony: Crises of Witnessing in Literature, Psychoanalysis, and History*, (New York: Routledge, 1992).

4. The distinction between "narrative memory" and "traumatic memory" is ascribable to the work of Pierre Janet, one of the first psychologists to draw out the effects of psychological trauma. On the curative function of narrative memory or testimony as a means of healing, see Felman and Laub, *Testimony;* and Brison, *Aftermath*. For critiques of the "narrative cure," see Jenny Edkins *Trauma and the Memory of Politics* (New York: Cambridge University Press, 2003); Kathryn Robson "Curative Fictions: The 'Narrative Cure'" in Judith Herman's *Trauma and Recovery* and Chantal Chawaf's *Le Manteau noir*," *Cultural Values*, 5 (2001): 115–130; and Caruth, *Trauma*.
5. Miller and Tougaw, *Extremities*, 11.
6. Scarry, *The Body in Pain*.
7. Fiona Ross, "Speech and Silence: Women's Testimony in the First Five Weeks of Public Hearing of the South African Truth and Reconciliation Commission," in *Remaking a World: Violence, Social Suffering, and Recovery* eds. Arthur Kleinman et al. (Berkeley: University of California Press, 2001), 250–279; Elizabeth Jelin, *State Repression and the Struggles for Memory*, trans. Judy Rein and Marcial Godoy-Anativia, (London: Latin America Bureau, 2003); and Nthabiseng Motsemme, "The Mute Always Speak: On Women's Silences at the Truth and Reconciliation Commission," *Current Sociology* 52 (2004): 909–932.
8. Anne Cubilie, *Women Witnessing Terror: Testimony and the Cultural Politics of Human Rights* (Fordham University Press, 2005).
9. Jelin, *State Repression and the Struggles for Memory*, 83.
10. Rajeswari Sunder Rajan, *Real and Imagined Women: Gender, Culture and Postcolonialism* (London; New York: Routledge, 1993).
11. See Veena Das and Arthur Kleinman, "Introduction," in Veena Das et al., ed., *Violence and Subjectivity*, (California: University of California Press 2000), 1–18.
12. Srila Roy, *Remembering Revolution: Gender, Violence, and Subjectivity in India's Naxalbari Movement*, (New Delhi: Oxford University Press, 2012).
13. Srila Roy, "Testimonies of State Terror: Trauma and Healing in Naxalbari" in *States of Trauma: Gender and Violence in South Asia* eds. Parama Roy, Piya Chatterjee, and Manali Desai (Delhi: Zubaan Books, 2009), 141–71.
14. None of the names or personal details of any of the interviewees have been changed. Latika and Saumen Guha always insist on being named in any form of publication or media, given their association with a fairly significant legal case to which they wish to draw national and international attention. Anonymity, for them, would violate their will to testify against custodial violence. I have also chosen to keep all the details regarding the case the same, including the names of the other two women involved in the case—Archana, the plaintiff, and Gauri, who was arrested with Latika and Archana. Since I refer to works published by the couple in which all the women have been named, anonymity would be futile.
15. For details regarding the historic nature of the case, see Subhas Ganguly, "The Forgotten Decade: Archana Guha Case," in Saumen Guha, "*The Battle of 'Archana Guha Case'*," (Kolkata: Human Justice in India, 1997), 297–326. Latika's legal testimony appears in full here as well.
16. Ibid., xiii.

17. Interviews were conducted in Bengali, spanning four meetings, each interview lasting 3–4 hours.
18. Latika Guha, "Narak Prokash Hok" [Let Hell be Exposed], in *Porichoy* (February–July, Kolkata, 2001): 28. All translations from the original Bengali text are my own.
19. Shoshana Felman, "Education and Crisis, or the Vicissitudes of Teaching," in Felman and Laub, *Testimony*, 3.
20. Interview July 2003.
21. See Cubilie, *Women Witnessing Terror*.
22. Felman, *Testimony*, 5.
23. Brison, *Aftermath*, 56.
24. Felman, *Testimony*, 3.
25. See Orly Lubin, "Holocaust Testimony, National Memory," in *Extremities: Trauma, Testimony, and Community* ed. Nancy Miller and Jason Tougaw (Urbana: University of Illinois Press, 2002), 131–142.
26. Cubilie, *Women Witnessing Terror*.
27. Molly Andrews, "Beyond Narrative: The Shape of Traumatic Testimony," in *Beyond Narrative Coherence* eds. Matti Hyvarinen et al. (Amsterdam: John Benjamin, 2010), 147–166.
28. Giorgio Agamben, "The Witness," in *Violence in War and Peace: An Anthology* eds. Nancy Scheper-Hughes and Philippe Bourgois (Malden, MA: Blackwell Publishers, 2004), 437–442.
29. Caruth, *Trauma*, 7.
30. Das and Kleinman, "Introduction," 26.
31. Latika Guha, "Narak Prokash Hok," 27.
32. Brison, *Aftermath*, 102.
33. Cubilie, *Women Witnessing Terror*, 212.
34. Recognition of her subjectivity as witness might explain this dynamic, which is not reducible to male dominance on his part or "false consciousness" with regard to her. I believe that it has more to do with their differential roles with regard to the legal case that has, in turn, enabled them to inhabit different subject-positions in the public world. While Latika has been the key witness in the case, Saumen has been its public voice throughout. This division of labor structured their interviews with me, as well, where Saumen dominated speech, and Latika spoke only to give her testimony. Saumen's life story is also remarkably different from that of his wife, in that it is not overdetermined by the experience of torture and pain.
35. Here it must be made clear that it was practically impossible to interview Latika on her own and not in the presence of her husband. Even though I always chose the schedule for an appointment with Latika, Saumen would be invariably present at the time of the interview.
36. Miller and Tougaw, *Extremities*, 12.
37. See Roy, *Remembering Revolution*
38. Latika Guha, "Narak Prokash Hok," 27.
39. Ganguly, *The Battle of 'Archana Guha Case'*, 302.
40. Lauren Berlant, "The Subject of True Feeling: Pain, Privacy, and Politics," in *Transformations: Thinking Through Feminism* eds, Sara Ahmed et al. (Routledge, 2000), 40.
41. See, for instance, Mamphela Ramphele, "Political Widowhood in South Africa: The Embodiment of Ambiguity," in *Social Suffering* eds, Arthur Kleinman, Veena Das, and Margaret Lock (Berkeley: University of California Press, 1997), 99–117; and Maya Todeschini, "The Bomb's Womb? Women and the Atom Bomb," in *Remaking a World: Violence, Social Suffering, and Recovery* eds. Veena Das et al. (Berkeley: University of California Press, 2001).

42. Sunder Rajan, *Real and Imagined Women*, 84.
43. Ibid.
44. Veena Das, *Critical Events: An Anthropological Perspective on Contemporary India*, (New Delhi: Oxford University Press, 1995), 194.
45. Ibid., 176. Das here draws on two seemingly incompatible notions of pain: one as being an inherently private experience that cannot be communicated to anyone outside of the self (not dissimilar to ideas of pain's unrepresentability in speech and in language alike) and another that speaks of the possibility of communicating pain, and indeed, of "relating to the pain of others." Das invokes Wittgenstein to speak of the possibility of the latter. She manages to move our attention from the individual experience of pain to its broader context, especially to society's responses to pain. The onus is ultimately on society to experience and understand the pain of the other.
46. Judith Butler and Sara Salih, eds., *The Judith Butler Reader* (Malden, MA: Blackwell, 2004), 215.
47. Ibid.
48. Ibid., 213.

7

Memories of Argentina's Past over Time: The Memories of Tacuara

María Valeria Galván

Tacuara, a right-wing nationalist group, was one of the first radical organizations to emerge in Argentina after the fall of President Juan Domingo Perón in 1955. Notorious for its violent anti-Semitic and anti-Communist actions during the sixties, public representations of Tacuara depicted the group as a bunch of nonconformist upper-class adolescents and, at the same time, as dangerous criminals. More than thirty years after the dissolution of Tacuara, some of these mixed and contradictory representations have revived.

In the nineties, Tacuara was depicted by the print media as merely a part of a shameful and obscure past of politicians connected to the Carlos Saúl Menem presidency. Nonetheless, at the beginning of the new millennium—following a deeper reconsideration of the guerrillas of the seventies, to whose formation Tacuara contributed, and driven by the new memory policies of President Néstor Kirchner—the discourses on Tacuara changed once again. Tacuara, well-known to be a breeding ground for militants and warfare know-how for the leftist groups of the seventies, profited from the new appreciation of the leftist militancy, and a new public image of Tacuara was born.

In this context, the main objective of this article is to analyze the consequences of changes in the recent past's memory of this political organization from the years 1996 to 2008. These repercussions have been traced in the print media, in the editorial industry, and in the field of audiovisual productions. Likewise, the changes in the public's current representations of Tacuara influenced the present discourse on the former activists. In order to briefly describe the relationship between both, an analysis of two representative oral testimonies has been included at the end of this article.[1]

On Tacuara

Origins

After the self-proclaimed *Revolución Libertadora* ("Liberating Revolution") overthrew the Peronist government in 1955, a long period of political turmoil followed. Within this framework of political uncertainties, social upheaval, consolidation of the Peronist identity, and local repercussions of the Cuban Revolution, a group of young Catholic school students and radical nationalists got together and founded a political group, the *Movimiento Nacionalista Tacuara* (MNT, Tacuara Nationalist Movement), commonly known as Tacuara. This organization was famous in its time for being involved in several episodes of political violence and for expressing anti-Semitic, anti-liberal, and anti-Communist ideas.

However, the heterogeneity of the original movement's ideology, in a context of limited democracy and political radicalization, soon influenced a split of the MNT into different groups. The first division of the MNT originated the far right *Guardia Restauradora Nacionalista* (GRN, The Restorative Nationalist Guard) in 1960. A year later the Peronist-sympathizing *Movimiento Nueva Argentina* (MNA, New Argentine Movement) separated from the original group, and the leftist *Movimiento Nacionalista Revolucionario Tacuara* (MNRT, Tacuara Nationalist Revolutionary Movement) did the same in 1963. While the GRN separated due to the radicalization of its right-wing and anti-Semitic tendencies, the second group separated because of the growing influence of the Peronists. Lastly, the MNRT had ideological discrepancies with the original group, and was formed under the influence of the Cuban Revolution.

Despite the extreme differences described above, originally the ideology of Tacuara had roots in Catholic nationalism, historic revisionism, and European fascism. This heterogeneous set of ideas not only laid the foundation for a violent political praxis against the Communists, liberals, and Jews, but also became evident in its aesthetics, its rituals, and its iconography. Moreover, they perceived liberalism, capitalism, democracy, socialism, and Communism as enemies, and promoted a strong corporatist state. This was influenced by the Argentine nationalists of the thirties, whom the young members of Tacuara started reading at a very early age.[2] Their works also emphasized the importance of a strong male political leader, and waxed nostalgic about lost models of social harmony and the supremacy of tradition.[3] Tacuara incorporated these elements as well.

Tacuara as Seen by its Contemporaries

Tacuara was famous for its exotic use of symbols. These symbols had Nazi overtones, and it was hard to separate them from the numerous anti-Semitic attacks that Tacuara perpetrated. Nonetheless, contemporary public opinion was sufficiently benevolent toward the young Tacuara activists; they were considered troubled teenagers who used political ideals in vogue at that time to rebel against the tediousness of the upper classes, to which they all belonged.

These considerations were heightened by the end of February 1964, when a riot involving MNT militants and Communists broke out at a *Confederación General del Trabajo* (CGT, General Confederation of Labour) meeting in the city of Rosario, in which three people were killed.[4] Among the deceased were members of the MNT.[5] These facts impacted every cell of the MNT throughout the country. A few days later three MNT activists retaliated and broke into a Jewish Communist militant's apartment in Buenos Aires and assassinated him. The victim, Raúl Alterman, was not a public political figure, and he was chosen only as an example. Immediately afterward, the national print media began to publish lengthy editorials full of colorful speculations on the true nature of these political organizations. People were trying to understand why these upper-class, well-bred kids were playing cowboys and Indians.[6] Nonetheless, even before the Alterman case, there already had been famous anti-Semitic attacks perpetrated by these Tacuara activists against individuals and institutions.

The wave of anti-Semitic aggression had broken out after the Mossad's capture of the Nazi war criminal Adolf Eichmann in Buenos Aires at the beginning of 1960. These violent anti-Semitic attacks continued for several years.[7] One of the most controversial attacks was the kidnapping and torture of the Jewish student Graciela Narcisa Sirota by a group of Tacuaras in June of 1962.[8] Sirota was released a few days after her abduction, with a tattoo of a swastika on one of her breasts.

While the MNT was becoming famous for its anti-Semitic attacks, the MNRT, led by Joe Baxter and José L. Nell, kept its distance from the anti-Semitism and right-wing symbols; this group was strongly influenced by the Cuban Revolution and the events of the Algerian War.[9] Under these influences, the MNRT started to promote and practice the *lucha armada* (armed struggle). The urban guerrilla methods required material means in order to be fulfilled. Accordingly, the MNRT took part in a series of armed robberies of military storehouses and factories[10] and, as part of this strategy, perpetrated the famous robbery of the *Policlínico bancario* of Buenos Aires (Bank Labor Union's Hospital) on a payday. Two guards were killed during this incident. Part of the loot of fourteen million pesos was found a year later by Interpol, discovered when two young nationalists were spending it at a cabaret in Paris.

When the public found out that the criminals of the Bank Labor Union's Hospital robbery were members of the MNRT, the representation of Tacuara changed. The fact that these activists were spending stolen money—destined to pay salaries—on a dissipated and immoral life (with prostitutes instead of the supposed "military training" that they proclaimed they were interested in) was unforgivable. The breaking news about the true story of a band of common criminals who used political idealism (they declared that they wanted a "National Revolution") to shield their lowly private lives was soon on the front pages of the most influential national newspapers.[11]

This case drew the public's attention to the importance of "Tacuara," considered as a homogeneous gang of young people who called themselves nationalists, guerrilla-militants, revolutionaries, and even Peronists. This shows that, by then, all the very different Tacuara groups (MNT, MNA, GRN and MNRT) were viewed as one, resulting in a conglomeration of their characteristics. However, media attention for Tacuara began to dissipate several months later until finally, the news about these groups disappeared completely. The groups themselves disappeared soon afterward as well,[12] and in the following decade many of its members would take part in guerrilla groups such as Montoneros, etc. After the dissolution of Tacuara, the group endured a long period of silence and oblivion in the Argentine public opinion, which was preoccupied with a traumatic period of political violence and State terrorism. However, with the consolidation of democracy, the social discourses on Tacuara returned, though they were radically changed.

Current Public Representations of Tacuara

Early Characterizations in the Print Media

Triggered by a denunciatory report published by the *Noticias* weekly magazine in the nineties, Tacuara once again became a central focus of journalistic discourse. In 1996, *Noticias* denounced the Minister of Justice at that time, Rodolfo Carlos Barra, for having belonged to the "Nazi-sympathizer group" Tacuara in his youth.[13] In the context of the recent, shocking attacks on the Embassy of Israel (1992) and on the offices of the *Asociación Mutual Israelita Argentina* (AMIA, Argentine Israelite Mutual Association) in the city of Buenos Aires (1994), such reporting unleashed a scandal in the media that ended in the officer's resignation. When light was shed on his dark past, Barra declared that he was ashamed of that "sin of youth."[14] Regardless of this late exculpatory declaration, the political price to pay for the revelation was already too high, and Barra had to resign. In 1999 this case stirred controversy once again, when Barra was appointed National Auditor-General.[15] This is interesting not only because the infamy this officer earned would bring Tacuara back to the Argentine public memory, but also because this political affiliation in his youth was the only point in Barra's political career that could not be forgiven by public opinion under any circumstances. (The public had apparently been able to get past the earlier numerous reports on long, corruption-ridden terms when he was public officer and Minister of Justice.[16])

However, looking at the historical context of this case, it is possible to see that his participation in Tacuara—briefly defined in the nineties as a Nazi organization (a description confirmed by the minister himself[17])—could not be forgiven because it seems to be closely related to the open wounds in the social imagery, exacerbated by the dramatic events of the attacks on the Embassy of Israel and the AMIA on Argentine territory. These also appear to be linked to the memory of the great number of disappeared Jews during the last military dictatorship (1976–1983) and to the intention to remove anything that could relate Peronism (the political party to which President Menem belonged) to Fascism or National Socialism. This was part of the realignment of Menem's government with the United States. In this scenario, it did not seem prudent to leave the investigations into the attacks committed on the Jewish community in the nineties in the hands of a Minister of Justice who had confessed to being a Nazi in his youth.

Apart from the exclusively negative connotation that Tacuara took on after that journalistic denunciation, it is important to highlight that a connection was established between "having been a Tacuara activist" and harboring a "shameful past." This dark past correlated, in Barra's case, with a corrupt present as well. In this sense, the chain of interrelations pertaining to this particular case was soon to be applied in general to all those who had taken part in any of Tacuara's groups.

Due to this resounding return of Tacuara to the print media, the despicable activities of the extreme right-wing nationalist group in the seventies would be mentioned often and in varied circumstances, including the breaking up of a criminal band that robbed vaults in 2001. One of the members of this band was Horacio Rossi, former activist of the MNT and the MNRT, who had taken part in the robbery of the Bank Labor Union's Hospital in 1963. The headline of the article published in *La Nación* leaves little room for doubt: "Rossi: almost 40 years of criminal history. His first big blow was in 1963."[18] This also helped bring back from the shadows the criminal side of Tacuara that had prevailed after the attack on the Bank Labor Union's Hospital. In this sense, the present state of affairs seemed to confirm what the print media had asserted at the time. These representations of the criminal activities performed by the ex-Tacuara activist can be seen as part of a long and painful prelude to the current corruption cases, unveiling the real nature of the movement's character. Thus, the news article reminds readers that:

> Far from being an ordinary criminal, or better said, a thief of these times, Horacio Francisco Rossi is a link to the most violent days of the unrest typical of the sixties and seventies . . . Rossi participated in the first criminal blow aimed at raising funds for the operations of an extremist group in our country: he was a member of the extreme Nationalist Tacuara group that on August, 29, 1963 broke into the Bank Labor Union's Hospital in Caballito, and before running away with a loot worth almost 14 million pesos at that time—money allotted for salaries—killed two people and left three wounded . . . [Tacuara] was in the 60s what the *Triple A* (Argentine Anticommunist Alliance) would be at the beginning of the next decade. . . .[19]

A year later, the death of Rodolfo Galimberti gave a new excuse to highlight these representations of Tacuara. Galimberti[20] was considered proof of what the country had inherited from the militancy of that time. However, the fact that he was introduced into the political and public spheres by Tacuara was also not overlooked:

> Galimberti, better known as Galimba or El Loco [the Deranged], embodied many of the evils that beset Argentina over the last three decades: the end of utopias, the celebration of violence, the apology for torture, the inconsistencies, the arriviste features, the deceitful agreements, the shallow culture, the hunger for power, the egotism, the total lack of self-criticism . . . He started his political life in the early sixties when he was sixteen, in Tacuara, the Nationalist group, where he learned to drop his first Molotov cocktails.[21]

Regarding his beginning with Tacuara, *Clarín* states that Galimberti

> . . . was a Catholic and Right-wing fellow, as was the whole embryo of the Montoneros' guerrilla movement. Barely a teenager, when the sixties had not yet turned into turmoil,

he participated in the Nationalist group named Tacuara, the youngest members of which used to wear slicked-down hair, a poor imitation of Hitler's iron cross as key ring and they had a pathetic lack of ideas.[22]

So the biography of such a paradigmatic character in Argentine history demonstrated how despicable the ethical standards of Tacuara were. Described as an extreme right-wing and nationalist group that was Nazi-oriented and lacked ideas and ideals, the group was also used to discredit the left-wing groups of the seventies, many of which were made up of former Tacuara members. However, the negative representations of Tacuara were about to change with the switch of human rights and memory policies by the national government, from which the popular representations of this group would ultimately benefit.

Changes in the Memory Regimes

Over the last few years a change in memory policies brought about a significant transformation in how public opinion viewed Tacuara. Immediately after the return of democracy put an end to the darkest period in Argentine history, in which the state terrorism of the military dictatorship left 30,000 disappeared (1976–1983), the belief that there was a civil war between the military and the leftist guerrillas became the hegemonic narrative. More than a decade later, this way of remembering the military dictatorship and the circumstances of the state terrorism began to be questioned. In fact, the thread of the memory regimes[23] relating to the dictatorship was disrupted for the first time in 1995, with the public confession made by the former Lieutenant Commander Adolfo Scilingo, in which that he admitted participating in the "death flights."[24] After this, the Lieutenant General at that time, Martín Balza, performed his "self-criticism," putting an end to the marginal place assigned to the denunciations for human rights violations and the nostalgic memory of the seventies left-wing groups that prevailed during the first half of the nineties.[25] This meant that the public debate on state terrorism in the seventies was opened once again and that it would gradually start to change the discourse trends about this topic.

When Néstor Kirchner began his presidential term in 2003, he immediately removed the military leaders from their positions and declared that he was in favor of invalidating the laws of *Obediencia Debida and Punto Final* (Laws of Due Obedience and Full Stop),[26] encouraging that this case be treated by the Supreme Court. During his term, the decree that prevented repressors from being extradited was declared void; the long-time human rights activist Eduardo Luis Duhalde was appointed Human Rights Secretary, and his policies gained the support of human rights groups, including the Mothers of Plaza de Mayo.[27]

On March 24, 2004, the portraits of the ex-dictators Jorge Rafael Videla and Leopoldo F. Galtieri were removed from the *Escuela de Mecánica de la Armada* (ESMA, Navy Mechanics School), and a ceremony took place in which Kirchner made a public apology on behalf of the state. During that event he announced the objective of building a memory museum on that site, formerly a clandestine center of detention and torture, in honor of those who had been imprisoned there. This recovery of the revolutionary leftist militancy helped cast a veil of mysticism over the tradition of the seventies that included the revolutionary groups (JP, Montoneros, *Ejército Revolucionario del Pueblo* [ERP, People's Revolutionary Army], etc.).[28] Furthermore, in 2006 the National Human Rights Secretariat re-edited the notorious report of the National Commission on the Disappearance of Persons, *Nunca Más*, with a new foreword.[29]

In this context of profound changes in memory and human rights policies, Tacuara appeared again in the print media in 2008, but this time the discourse on the group had no negative connotations whatsoever. The news report is about one of the last grandchildren kidnapped by the military and illegally adopted under a false identity to be recovered by the *Asociación de Abuelas de Plaza de Mayo* (Association of Grandmothers of Plaza de Mayo) and by other human rights entities. The media that addressed this topic mentioned that the father of the grandchild, Jorge Guillermo Goya, had been the disappeared named Franciso Goya, who had been a militant of the *Juventud Peronista* (JP, Peronist Youth), Montoneros, and Tacuara (specifically, MNT).[30]

In this sense, the changes in memory regimes fostered by the state paved the way for a vindication of the history and struggle of the seventies armed organizations, which ultimately favored Tacuara, as it started to be considered as a "preparatory" or "training" ground for those who would later participate in the left-wing guerrilla groups and become victims of the state terrorism during the last military dictatorship. In this context, various books and audiovisual Argentine productions that offered an alternative discourse on Tacuara were launched.

The Editorial Industry Takes an Interest in Tacuara

Two new historical narratives about the young nationalists generated great public interest. These works, published almost simultaneously, were the research of the journalist Daniel Gutman in 2003 and Roberto Bardini's memoir as a former Tacuara militant, in 2002.[31]

The publicity of these books should be understood under the new conditions that characterized the editorial industry of Argentina after the economic, social, and political crisis of 2001. Non-fiction readers' taste was drawn at that time to non-academic history books and biographies of prominent people in national history. This switch in readers' taste after the crisis came as a result of the generalized dissatisfaction inherited from the events of 2001. In this context, readers began a quest for narratives of Argentine history with an explanation of the "national defeat" they felt they were going through at that time.[32] This search for meanings in the past to explain present problems—together with the change in the memory regimes of the recent Argentine past—contributed to the editorial success of the books of Gutman and Bardini.

Gutman's book, based on the journalist's research on the history of Tacuara, emphasizes the fact that the group constituted the "first urban guerrilla" movement in the country. According to his hypothesis, Tacuara is a good example of the political commotion that led to the violent seventies. Notwithstanding this link Gutman establishes between the young nationalists and the origins of the political violence of the seventies, and aside from the far-right affiliations of the group in its origins, the author introduces a more human side of Tacuara.

In the same sense, the memoir of former Tacuara militant Roberto Bardini presents the subjective point of view of the militancy. This self-exculpatory narrative, despite being the first published book on Tacuara, did not have the same impact as Gutman's on the editorial market. Nonetheless, the main contribution of Bardini's work was that it was the first written testimony ever made public by a former Tacuara member. The subjective perspective of the book intends a transformation in the collective memory that associates Tacuara with Catholicism, anti-Semitism, political extremism (right- or left-wing), and nationalism. Mainly, the author sets forth a revision on a Tacuara that, according to him, has been stereotyped and stigmatized by public opinion. As a result, the book succeeds in presenting a de-Nazified version of the group. That is to say, starting from the several splits of the original MNT, Bardini takes some distance (as former member of MNT and MNRT) from the Fascist, Catholic, Hispanic, and Nazi-sympathizing right-wing Tacuara. Within this same framework, Bardini discredits the criticism of Tacuara.

In a similar manner, several subtle turns in his account allow his public to read between the lines to find hints regarding the existence of a "right-wing" Tacuara (very politically incorrect), opposed to a second Tacuara, that is eventually exonerated by its affiliation to leftist Peronism and its opposition toward and victim-like quality in the last military dictatorship. In this way, it is possible to find titles that read: "A Tacuara member—like many others—that did not read Hitler or paint swastikas," "March 24th, 1976: the first victim, a Nationalist," or "The Nationalist sin," supported by quotations like the following from Edgar Morin:

> Recently, I was asked: 'Did you know that Emile Cioran sympathized with the Nazis when he was young?', to which I replied: 'Yes, and it's terrible, but it's not possible to reduce people to what they were in the past, their youth. He certainly evolved afterwards.'[33]

Thus, Bardini emphasizes, or rather justifies, Tacuara's ideological diversity. In all, the key pattern[34] of this discourse is a narrator who takes distance from the prototypical Tacuara activist. Bearing in mind that this pattern accounts for the relationship between the narrator and the dominating social models, it is possible to determine that Bardini's testimony is strongly influenced by the aforementioned human rights policy recently brought into force. This policy would make it possible to assign a present quality to the public denouncement of the crimes committed in the last military dictatorship and allow a vindication of the activist past. Within this framework, Bardini presents himself as regretting the shameful past of the first MNT, but this falls into the background when faced with its "avenger" and "redressing" role. In other words, he was denouncing the acts committed against Tacuara activists who "didn't read Hitler" and would later become the victims of state repression.

The articles that promoted these books[35] showed the repercussions that the change in the memory regimes as well as the new tendencies of the editorial industry had in the social discourse on Tacuara. The print media only described the different paths covered by the books and the authors' hypotheses, but this simple fact motivated readers to go beyond the obvious and poorly grounded articles that simplified Tacuara, portraying it as a Nazi and extreme right-wing group.[36]

The renewed interest in the vicissitudes of this dark political group, about which society knew but little, continued in the bookstores. In this context, in 2006 a biography on MNT former militant and MNRT leader Joe Baxter,[37] and the edited memoirs of MNT and MNRT militant Jorge Caffatti[38] (who would die in the seventies as a victim of the state terrorism), were published.

In Baxter's biography, written by journalists Alejandra Dandan and Silvina Heguy, the militancy in Tacuara is depicted as the inopportune right-wing beginning in the political life of a figure who would later become emblematic in the leftist guerrilla and the seventies' political violence. Similarly, in Jorge Caffatti's memoirs,[39] edited by journalist Juan Gasparini, former member of the left-wing party FAP[40] (and member of the MNT and MNRT in his youth), Caffatti remembers his activism in Tacuara with a strongly self-critical tone. However, even when this text is not free of justifications—such as the proper ignorance of the age or repentance for the ignorance or trusting quality of early youth—the key theme in the structure of this account is the belief that all past experiences would cultivate martyrdom in him, and this was one of the highest positions that the ideal activist could reach.

In this way, Caffatti's biography, retrieved by Gasparini in 2006, as well as the book on the life story of Baxter, present Tacuara's militancy as a juvenile mistake that—when the militant becomes a leftist activist—is somehow turned into an asset and serves as preparation for the harsh road the seventies hero had to walk toward his or her tragic end. Finally, in 2008 Juan Esteban Orlandini published his BA thesis on the MNT.[41] Despite the academic claim of Orlandini's book, he was a former member of the group and, therefore, could not avoid a subjective perspective when revisiting and discussing the hegemonic memory of the MNT. In this sense, the author intends to offer the "true" version of Tacuara that results, once again, in a "heroic and de-Nazified" history of the group. All these biographies clearly have a close relationship to the social discourses available at the time they were published, and as testimonies to the changes in the representations on Tacuara, they do not stand alone. Apart from the recently enriched bibliography on these nationalist militants, three audiovisual productions on the group were launched during recent years. Similar to the books, these films reflect the way in which changes in the memory regimes on the Argentine recent past affected social discourses on Tacuara.

Tacuara on the Screen

The first of a number of film productions about Tacuara is the documentary movie *Los malditos caminos*.[42] The structure of this expository documentary[43] is divided into three life stories. An omniscient narrator tells the story of three brave, idealistic progressivists, who were closely related to the left-wing Peronism of the seventies and were tragically killed. One of them was José Luis Nell, who as an MNRT leader had participated in the attack on the Bank Labor Union's Hospital and had been in contact with the leftist Tupamaros in Uruguay. He eventually joined the equally leftist *Fuerzas Armadas Peronistas* (FAP, Peronist Armed forces) and Montoneros. In the voice-over of this documentary the oral testimonies of relatives, friends, and acquaintances are intertwined. Thus used, documentary interviews are aimed at stirring emotions in the viewer by centering their attention on the remembrance of the main character's subjectivity. To do this, a rhetoric mainly based on emotional trials is used: testimonies appealing to arouse empathy in the viewer, images from news programs' archives of that time or movies to portray the historical context in which these facts occurred and to emphasize certain topics that would reinforce the argumentation of the film. The purposively constructed biographical narratives and the abundance of archive material make the story of these tragic heroes of the seventies militancy seem objective and credible.

In this documentary, Tacuara always appears in relation to Nell and, more specifically, to his beginnings as a militant. No efforts or resources are spared to justify Tacuara's actions, which had been and still were reprehensible. Thus, by interviewing former militants of other leftist guerrilla movements (all of whom had been friends of Nell), the movie describes the militancy in Tacuara so vaguely that on several occasions in the interviews the characteristics of the MNT and MNRT may be confused. On the other hand, the attack on the Bank Labor Union's Hospital perpetrated by the MNRT in 1963 is described in great detail. Nell was the only one to shoot and kill workers. The movie also resorts to personal and subjective testimonies of former MNT and MNRT militants, who downplay Nell's participation in the event. Finally, his escape closes this first epic cycle and starts a new and difficult stage in Nell's life: the path of clandestine living and commitment to the Peronist movement, which would make him a hero in the public's eye. Thus, imitating the narrative structure typical of the modern novel,[44] this film discourse adheres to the thesis that was faintly emerging at that time about Tacuara: the group was a sort of "preparatory limbo" on a road full of trials to be trodden by the hero on his way to redemption.

The movie reveals the beliefs, intentions, and imagery of the society in which it was made.[45] Therefore this film's objective of presenting a heroic version of a Tacuara militant is well situated within the general framework that was starting to emerge, which vindicated the popular fights from the seventies and eventually paved the way for the implementation of new policies on human rights.

Closer in time (with this general and now legitimized frame of reference), on April 26, 2007, a short television film appeared as part of a fictional series about the 1964 murder of Raúl Alterman by MNT. The series, called *9 mm*, devoted each chapter to a political assassination in Argentine history. Alterman's case is the first episode.[46] The point of view in the film is that of the killers, as it tells of the motivations, insecurities, and childish behavior of a reduced group of Tacuara activists from the city of Buenos Aires who want to take revenge for the death of their last martyrs, fallen in the confrontations at the Salón de Cerveceros (Beer Workers Union Hall) in Rosario in 1964. As the scriptwriter describes, this episode depicts an essentially subjective approach, developed from the perspective of the murderers.[47] He recognizes that

> Shedding light on the murderer's viewpoint is not easy, but it enables us to see other things, what is at stake in everyone's conscience. To many of them, killing was a source of anguish. But it was something they had committed themselves to. A painful commitment that was taken as a mission. These murderers were not bloodthirsty *gurkas*. They were real human beings who had a problem to solve.[48]

This representation of Tacuara would have been impossible ten years earlier, because the perspective of the murderer, portraying all their insecurities, fears, and idealism, implies a subjective approach by the viewer. On the other hand, just as with *Los malditos caminos*, this episode raises the issue of what kind of historical reality has been rebuilt. This one is completely different from that which prevailed in the nineties. While at that time the representatives of the Menemist corruption had a dark, Nazi past, the reality put forth by these new films is that of some idealistic guys who were a bit confused, fearful and insecure (just like "any of us"), and who made some "mistakes."

However, these representations of the young members of Tacuara as idealist youths coexist with parallel representations that continue to demonize them. A clear example of this is a television special on the attack on the Bank Labor Union's Hospital, broadcast only a few months after the television airing of *9 mm*. On June 26, 2007, TN cable channel broadcast a forty-minute special named *Operación Rosaura: el comienzo de la guerrilla urbana*. This expository television documentary shows the attack as the "social introduction of Tacuara," a "right-wing group that represented the beginning of the urban guerrilla" movement. In this way, the voice-over leads the viewer along the development of the "history of Tacuara." With the intention of validating the narration of the case, journalists specialized in the subject are invited to the studio to give their expert opinion. Documentary pictures are shown in the background while these testimonies are being given. These include newspaper clippings from that time on the case of the attack on the Bank Labor Union's Hospital and other cases lead by Tacuara. After the first four minutes of consolidation of an objective discourse evidencing the serious quality of the narration, testimonies of former members of MNT are inserted. These emphasize youth and the idealism that moved them, making the point that they did not belong to "the right or the left"; they were simply nationalists. Following this apparent objectivity, the program juxtaposes these claims of innocence by former Tacuara activists with one of the expert opinions that recalls anti-Semitic attacks (the images in the background portray swastika graffiti signed by Tacuara). It points out that the worst of all crimes committed by Tacuara was the attack on the Bank Labor Union's Hospital.

The narration of the case itself is presented in a "police crime fiction novel" format and includes witness testimony. Documentary images of the hospital building accompany the audio presentation; present-day images are included, all of them in black and white. On the one hand, this intends to strengthen the credibility of the account, and on the other hand, it tries to establish the close relationship to the case that needs to be created due to the time gap between the viewer's everyday life and the moment when the events took place. Similar to how the facts were presented by the print media at the time, the case is closed with Nell's spectacular escape from the *Palacio de Justicia* (Hall of Justice); the narrator takes advantage of this opportunity to tell the legend of José Luis Nell. The documentary report ends with the affirmation of one of the specialists who claims that Tacuara was Nazi, and with a close-up of the front page of *Ofensiva* (*Offensive*), the MNT publication, which included Nazi iconography.

This narrative makes the viewer wonder about two things: in the first place, the perpetration of a crime of such magnitude (in which employees were deprived of their salaries and innocent people were killed); in the second place, what happened to the criminals. Both questions get the same answer: armed struggle. That is to say, the robbery took place, as the host of the show concludes, with the only purpose of raising funds for the "preparation of the armed propaganda," which ended up being utilized in the political upheaval and military coup of the following decade.

It is interesting to see that the different Tacuara organizations are never presented independently, and their separate existence is not mentioned.

This program not only does not recognize the separation that took place in the original MNT, but it also attributes MNT characteristics (Nazi tendencies, anti-Semitism) to the MNRT, a group that had turned away from anti-Semitism and extreme right-wing politics, leaning toward a Peronist left, which was the true perpetrator of the robbery. Finally, in accordance with the present dominant memory, the show recognizes Tacuara as the immediate predecessor of the seventies' guerrillas, but this does not contribute to creating an epic discourse on Tacuara. On the contrary, within the framework of the narrative structure of a crime novel, it is used as another argument to condemn it.

Former Activists' Memories

The transformations in the general public opinion discourse on the history of Tacuara and its activists have affected the present reports of former members of Tacuara. In order to understand this dialogic interaction, it is important to bear in mind that reports on the recent past can only be interpreted through the lens of the memory. As a consequence, access to the past through personal subjectivity is necessarily influenced by present representations of that past.[49] In this way, former Tacuara activists' testimonies need to be considered within their cultural and sociopolitical context, without disregarding their possible current individual interests and expectations. Any use of oral testimonies requires being able to distinguish in the interviewee's discourse both explicit information and implicit information related to certain mental, cultural, and ideological structures.[50]

Furthermore, it is important to emphasize that oral testimonies provide information on the meaning that the sources attribute to the fact being reported, not only on the fact itself.[51] In order to identify present subjective representations of Tacuara among former activists, two in-depth semi-structured interviews were conducted with former members of MNT (one of whom had also been a member of MNRT). The first interviewee[52] began his account by justifying his approach to Tacuara with the admiration he felt for the organization, its symbols, and its patriotism. At the same time, as an excuse for many actions his activism would lead him to take, he pointed to his barely fourteen years of age at the time he started his militancy. It is interesting to focus on the fact that, without any specific prodding on the part of the interviewer, the interviewee tried to justify his affiliation to Tacuara all throughout his account of the facts. Thus he mentions, for example, that he had been a Leftist activist in the seventies and that he had been forced to go into exile abroad to survive during the dictatorship. He also points out that former brothers-in-arms hold public offices in the government today (as did he), possibly trying, in this way, to delete or throw a cloak of legitimacy over the stigma to which former Tacuara activists were condemned.

In a similar vein, he claims that anti-Semitism was understandable if one bears in mind the context of the post-war times in which Tacuara developed. In general, he claims, Tacuara admired Hitler and his nationalism, the economic recovery the Axis countries achieved; there were even "people who felt captivated by European Fascism." As he explains, "there are some things that wouldn't be understood today." In relation to this, the interviewee made constant reference to Daniel Gutman's recently published book on Tacuara. The condemnatory tone of Gutman's investigation of Tacuara—which, according to the interviewee, was triggered by the false preconception that the group was anti-Semitic—was insinuated into the interview as a kind of interlocutor hidden behind open and general questions. In consequence, the main factors guiding his account were not only the image the interviewee had of the interviewer, but also the image he believed was dominant in public opinion, especially after the success of Gutman's book. It was an image he wanted to reach through the interview.

In the framework of this discourse, and setting forth the exonerating trend of former militants' biographies, the interviewee separates himself from a group of "others" whose activism he claims was different from his for including everything that is seen today as blameworthy. These "others"—the sectors that were most criticized for their anti-Semitism and Fascist influences—were the ones who had watched over Eichmann's home in 1960, after it was made public that he had been captured by the *Mossad* and extradited to Israel as a war criminal.

The second person interviewed,[53] a former activist of the MNT and a friend of the first interviewee, was much more relaxed and at ease with being interviewed. In general terms, he thought his interaction in Tacuara was almost a childish mischief, telling funny, nostalgic anecdotes. Instead of trying to justify questionable actions performed by the group, he discredited their truth and diminished their importance. For example, when asked about the initiation rituals performed at the tombstone of the martyr hero of Tacuara, Darwin Passaponti, he claims that it was only a myth. "Yes," he says, "there might have been some night owls doing it . . . someone came up with this delusional idea of giving an oath at the grave . . . a necrophiliac delirium came out of that . . . Nazi rituals . . . but that's total BS." In the same way he downplays Tacuara's violent actions through a particular selection of vocabulary—for example: "we did make some noise."

Regarding political violence, he claims Tacuara was actually a conciliatory movement that was obliged to change its nature when society was not conciliatory to its members. This means, according to this testimony, that the MNT has always been persecuted for their revisionism, which can be explained in the context of the proscribed Peronism from which the movement emerged. He adds to this affirmation, "at that age you're totally and absolutely unaware." However, when asked why they were referred to as Nazis, he admits there were sectors in the organization that sympathized with Nazi ideology, but only on a romantic level. In this regard, he claims, "there is a very romantic quality to this, the admiration for the lost fight. Some admired Berlin's resistance. (They were fighting in debris . . . with nothing!) Same thing with the Italian Republic . . . they were fighting for their honor, after everything had been lost . . . This is fascinating for young people." In this sense, the "fascination over fighting to defend your honor" slowly surfaces in his account as the key pattern. At first the interviewee does not seem preoccupied with justifying his activism in Tacuara. However, gradually this implicit justification presents itself, and he tries to reconcile with his personal past through his present. From his point of view, heroism and struggle gain new meaning in his discourse. Thus he tries to keep a safe distance from the political history of the movements he himself mentions.

The literature of adventure gives the interviewee the interpretative framework for these "heroic struggles." According to his own account, this is due to the influence of Emilio Salgari's novels, which young Tacuara members read obsessively in childhood. A particular sense of existence was imbued in the group's everyday life through the Malta Cross; it was based on this romantic heroism represented both by Partisans, Italian Fascists in the last period, Spanish Republicans, and Medieval knights. "This has to do with the admiration of those who fight for their ideals without caring for winning or losing. Struggle for us is an end in itself, better if crowned by victory but you have to fight regardless," he added. In that way, he strove to recover an image of Tacuara as a group that made an effort to fight for their ideals, even if those ideals turned out to be a little childish from the perspective of the present, he admitted.

These representations and valorizations of former Tacuara activists are in permanent dialogue with discourses analyzed in the previous section. Thus, by recognizing and adopting contemporary memory and human rights discourse, the lens through which former Tacuara members look at their past makes them set foot in the present, where they cannot ignore the hegemonic narratives about their own activism. In this way, they make a point in their account of either separating themselves from a Nazi Tacuara or from an extreme right-wing one, or justifying their belonging to the group with the excuse of their youth. Romanticism and idealism are added to the equation. As a result, resorting to purity and innocence sanitizes their "mistakes of youth." A large number of these accounts cannot avoid subscribing to the narrative structure of the fictional novel. Despite the fact that not all of them participated in the armed struggle that took place in the seventies, most of them believe that their innocence, triggered by idealism in youth, was lost when they became adults.

Conclusion

In recent years, the social discourses on Tacuara have undergone profound changes. Decades after its dissolution, Tacuara was believed to have been a Nazi organization, formed by young nationalists who would turn into corrupt and morally questionable politicians in their adult life. But the emergence in the last ten years of testimonial books and audiovisual productions about Argentina's recent past shows a turn in the public's image of Tacuara as well. This turn was induced by the newly appreciated leftist militancy of the seventies, whose memory was revived by the official discourse. In this regard, some of the biographies analyzed here made explicit reference to the fact that Tacuara was a mere first step toward the immolation that these individuals would offer for their ideals ten years later. Thus, Tacuara is revived in the hegemonic memory as a necessary preparation period for the ultimate sacrifice of the leftist militants of the seventies. Even though not all the Tacuara activists became leftist militants later, the representative "heroic cases" helped to construct an analytical model, from which all the former Tacuara members can profit today. However, these representations coexist with other ones that expose Tacuara as the source of violent guerrilla actions that are still demonized by some sectors of the public in Argentina. In their present narratives, some former Tacuara activists still portray themselves as heroic tragic figures, while others simply struggle to keep their distance from the memories of a "Nazi" Tacuara. The documents analyzed in this article reveal how past and current fluctuations in the memory of Argentina's recent past determined and configured important changes in the social discourses on Tacuara.

Notes

1. The selected corpus is only a representative sample of a broader selection of documents. The study of the complete documents can be consulted at María Valeria Galván. *El Movimiento Nacionalista Tacuara y sus agrupaciones derivadas: una aproximación desde la historia cultural* (M.A. Thesis, IDAES, Universidad Nacional de San Martin. Buenos Aires, 2008).
2. Cristián Buchrucker, *Nacionalismo y Peronismo: La Argentina en la crisis ideológica mundial, 1927–1955*, (Buenos Aires: Sudamericana, 1999); Marysa Navarro Gerassi, *Los Nacionalistas* (Buenos Aires: Editorial Jorge Álvarez, 1968); Fernando Devoto, *Nacionalismo, fascismo y tradicionalismo en la Argentina moderna* (Buenos Aires: Siglo XXI, 2002).
3. Federico Finchelstein, *Fascismo, liturgia e imaginario: El mito del General Uriburu y la Argentina nacionalista* (Buenos Aires: FCE, 2002).
4. The meeting took place at the local Salón de Cerveceros (Beer Workers Union Hall) and was meant to discuss the strategy to be followed by the CGT, the National Trade Union Centre of Argentina.
5. Mario Glück, "Tradición xenófoba y violencia política: Tacuara en Santa Fe a principios de la década del 60" en *Jornadas Historia, etnicidad y literatura latinoamericana: La experiencia del judaísmo contemporáneo* (Fundación Auge and Universidad Hebrea de Jerusalén, Mendoza, 2000); *La Nación*, 26 February 1964; *La Nación*, February 27, 1964; *La Nación*, February 28, 1964; *Clarín*, February 28, 1964; *Primera Plana*, March 3, 1964.
6. *Primera Plana*, March 10 and 17, 1964, *El Popular*, March 18, 1964.
7. *La Luz*, November 2, 1962; *Mundo Israelita*, September 15, 1962; *Nueva Sión*, December 14, 1962; *La Prensa*, January 22, 1963; *Correo de la Tarde,* January 23, 1963; *Clarín*, January 23, 1963; *Clarín*, January 26, 1963; *Nueva Sión*, February 8, 1963; *Así*, March 31, 1964; Comisión Provincial por la Memoria, File 1609, Daños, Mesa "DS"; File 1715, Daños, Mesa "DS"; File 1829, Daños, Mesa "DS."
8. Leonardo Senkman, "El antisemitismo bajo dos experiencias democráticas: Argentina 1959/1966 y 1973/1976" in Leonardo Senkman, *El antisemitismo en la Argentina* (Buenos Aires: CEAL, 1989).
9. Daniel Gutman, *Tacuara: Historia de la primera guerrilla urbana argentina* (Buenos Aires: Ediciones B, 2003).
10. Ibid.; Luis Fernando Beraza, *Nacionalistas: La trayectoria de un grupo polémico (1927–1983)* (Buenos Aires: Editorial Puerto de Palos, 2005).
11. *Pregón*, March 24, 1964; *Crónica*, March 25, 1964; *La Nación*, March 24, 1964; *Clarín*, March 25, 1964; *El Siglo*, March 25, 1964, *Clarín*, March 26, 1964, *La Voz del Interior*, March 26, 1964, *La Nación*, March 28, 1964, *Careo*, April 1, 1964 and *Ocurrió*, April 10, 1964.
12. According to Gutman and Beraza, Baxter's MNRT was dissolved right after the assault of the Bank Labor's Union Hospital. On the other hand, the MNT survived for a few more years. The GRN disappeared with Ongania's coup in 1966, because many of its members took part in his government. Finally, the MNA joined the forces of right-wing Peronism. Last Tacuara press releases are from 1971.
13. *Noticias*, June 22, 1996.
14. *La Nación*, August 6, 1996. Even two years later, Barra was still trying to exculpate himself: "it was a childish situation . . . I was no Nazi, I mean I did not know what being a Nazi implied. But I did have an anti-democratic tendency. I really despised the political party system. I am ashamed of that today . . . but they were the tendencies of that time" (*Clarín*, January 5, 1998).
15. *La Nación*, December 20, 1999, and *Clarín*, December 14, 1999.

16. See, for example, *La Nación*, December 20, 1999.
17. According to *Noticias*, Barra declared "if I was a Nazi in my youth, I regret it" (*Noticias*, June 22, 1996).
18. *La Nación*, April 25, 2001.
19. *La Nación*, April 25, 2001.
20. Rodolfo Galimberti was a Tacuara activist in the seventies and became a Montonero militant in the seventies. During the presidency of Héctor Cámpora in 1973, Galimberti was a delegate of the JP. As such, he called for the formation of armed militias. When Perón found out, Galimberti was removed. As a Montonero, he organized numerous kidnappings, including the famous kidnapping of the businessman Born. After the coup in 1976, he exiled himself to Brazil, Mexico, and France. In 1989, after a presidential pardon granted by Menem, he started doing business with Jorge Born, one of his former hostages, thus becoming an important businessman of the nineties. During this time, Galimberti participated actively in the frivolous and corrupt culture and politics of the Menem administration. He abhorred his militant past and became friends publicly with his torturers of the seventies. Finally, as part of Menem's government, he became a double agent and exchanged Argentinean state secrets with France and the American Central Intelligence Agency (CIA) (*La Nación*, February 13, 2002; *Clarín*, February 13, 2002; Marcelo Larraquy and Roberto Caballero, *Galimberti*, Buenos Aires: Grupo Editorial Norma, 2000).
21. *La Nación*, February 13, 2002.
22. *Clarín*, February 13, 2002.
23. Emilio Crenzel, who defined it as "the emblematic memories that become hegemonic," coined this term. According to Crenzel, memory regimes "define the parts of our past that are worthy of being remembered, how to interpret these memories and which narrative styles are to be used to evoke, think and pass on the memorable past" (Emilio Crenzel, *La historia política del* Nunca Más. *La memoria de las desapariciones en la Argentina*, Avellaneda: Siglo XXI, 2008, 24).
24. "Death flights" were the practice of dumping the bodies of the illegally detained political prisoners of the dictatorship into the River Plate and Atlantic Ocean from a military plane.
25. According to Lvovich and Bisquert, "the general pardon granted by President Carlos Menem was meant to close the past, in order to start a new period of 'national pacification' . . . at a time when the issue of the state terrorism was not so relevant for the public opinion" (Daniel Lvovich y Jacquelina Bisquert, *La cambiante memoria de la dictadura militar desde 1984: Discursos públicos, movimientos sociales y legitimidad democrática*, Buenos Aires: UNGS—Biblioteca Nacional, 2008, 7–8).
26. Amnesty laws passed by President Raul Alfonsin in 1986 and 1987 to protect the military accused of state terrorism.
27. Ibid.
28. Ibid.
29. Crenzel, *La historia política* . . .
30. La Nación, July 31, 2008.
31. Gutman. *Tacuara* . . .; Roberto Bardini, *Tacuara: La pólvora y la sangre* (México DF: Editorial Océano, 2002).
32. Pablo Semán, *Bajo continuo: Exploraciones descentradas sobre cultura popular y masiva* (Buenos Aires: Editorial Gorla, 2006).
33. Ibid., 153.
34. Daniel James, *Doña María's Story: Life, History, Memory, and Political Identity* (Durham, NC: Duke University Press, 2000).
35. *Clarín*, May 11, 2003, 10 June 2003, 29 August 2003; *La Nación*, November 16, 2003.

36. *Clarín*, July 12, 2003.
37. Alejandra Dandan and Silvina Heguy, *Joe Baxter: Del nazismo a la extrema izquierda—La historia secreta de un guerrillero* (Buenos Aires: Grupo Editorial Norma, 2006).
38. Juan Gasparini *Manuscrito de un desaparecido en la ESMA: El libro de Jorge Caffatti* (Buenos Aires: Grupo Editorial Norma, 2006).
39. This was the first written testimony from a former Tacuara activist. However, his account was written in captivity, during the last dictatorship, and this is why it was not published until 2006, when the already-mentioned historical conditions allowed for the reception of a text with these characteristics.
40. *Fuerzas Armadas Peronistas* (Peronist Armed Forces).
41. Juan Esteban Orlandini. *Tacuara . . . hasta que la muerte nos separe de la lucha. Historia del Movimiento Nacionalista Tacuara 1957–1972* (Buenos Aires: Centro Editor Argentino, 2008).
42. DVD premier: November 14, 2002; 200 minutes.
43. Bill Nichols, *Representing Reality* (Bloomington: Indiana University Press, 1991).
44. The novel describes the actions of a protagonist who engages in trials of either physical or moral strength in order to prove his or her worth as hero. The hero of the modern novel struggles to configure a vital totality, to which he no longer has access. He lives in a chaotic world now, where the communion between the subjectivity and the totality is lost (György Lukács, *Theory of the Novel*, Baltimore: John Hopkins University Press, 2000).
45. Marc Ferro, *Cinéma et histoire* (Paris: Éditions Gallimard, 1993), and Siegfried Kracauer, *Theory of Film: The Redemption of Physical Reality* (New York: Oxford University Press, 1960).
46. The script and idea came from the historian Marcelo Larraquy; it was directed by Ulises Rossel.
47. *Noticias*, July 14, 2007.
48. *Clarín*, April 25, 2007.
49. Elizabeth Jelin, "La conflictiva y nunca acabada mirada sobre el pasado," en *Historia reciente: Perspectiva y desafíos para un campo en construcción,* Florencia Levin y Franco Marina (Buenos Aires: Paidós, 2007).
50. Ronald J. Grele, "Movimiento sin meta: Problemas metodológicos y teóricos en la historia oral," in *La Historia Oral*, ed. Dora Schwarzstein (Buenos Aires: Centro Editor de América Latina, 1991): 129.
51. Alessandro Portelli, "Lo que hace diferente a la historia oral," in Dora Schwarzstein, *La Historia Oral* (Buenos Aires: Centro Editor de América Latina, 1991).
52. E.R., interview, Buenos Aires, February 28, 2007.
53. Y.G., interview, Buenos Aires, April 18, 2007.

8

History, Memory, Narrative: Expressions of Collective Memory in the Northern Cheyenne Testimony

Sachiko Kawaura

For Native American people, tribal history and mainstream national history are often in conflict. Therefore, accounts of historical events from the point of view of the tribes inevitably have testimonial overtones, and such tribal testimonies are supported by the collective memory of their communities.[1] In the case of the Northern Cheyenne, "the Exodus from Indian Territory" (1878)[2] resides at the heart of their collective memory. Against the forced removal from their Northern Plains homeland, Chief Dull Knife and Chief Little Wolf fled the Darlington Agency in Indian Territory (in present-day Oklahoma), and led their people back to the north. The tribe attributes this historical event, in which many lives were lost, to an "ancestral sacrifice" that resulted in the creation of the Tongue River Indian Reservation (in present-day Montana) in 1884. The consequential interpretation is expressed through tribal governance and local museum exhibits created by tribal production teams. The tribal members' self-narratives, gathered through interview research,[3] indicate that collective memory of the ancestral sacrifice functions as an important part of the foundation of the tribal identity.[4]

This paper discusses a cross section between history and memory by studying the expressions of collective memory in Northern Cheyenne testimonial narratives. Halbwachs defines collective memory as memory of small communities, such as family, local, and regional community, which deals with the relatively recent past. According to him, collective memory expresses how a community reconstructs its own past. Halbwachs considers that collective memory is deeply entrenched in daily consciousness and that it functions as a living tie between people and their ancestors.[5] The concept of collective memory embraces the acts of "recalling" and "narrating." In the case of the Northern Cheyenne, collective memory of the "ancestral sacrifice" has been used to assert their rights to live on their homeland, and the relevance of the collective memory has been tested by the people's ongoing act of recalling and narrating the Exodus.

In order to illuminate how the tribe's testimonial narratives have been supported by the work of collective memory, first I present a brief history of the Cheyenne people, consisting of contrasting elements with mainstream national history of the United States. Then, I discuss how testimonial narratives of the tribe are expressed in public domains as well as at the individual level.

History of the Cheyenne People

Legends and Migration

Today, the Northern Cheyenne are known as a Great Plains Indian tribe. While the tribe's reservation resides in the southeast corner of Montana, according to legends, their original homeland was the vast area between Hudson Bay and the Great Lakes. The tribe expresses itself as "people of Tsetséhestáhase and the So'taeo'o,"[6] and their heritage is rich and complex. Crossing the great marshlands of southern Ontario and northern Minnesota, Tsetséhestáhase people first migrated into the Mississippi River region and later to the west of the Minnesota River. There they had lived in permanent earth-lodges, growing crops and hunting game. By the mid-eighteenth century, they owned horses. They had encountered a band of the So'taeo'o who spoke a similar language and had similar cultural practices. Eventually, Tsetséhestáhase adopted the lifestyle of the So'taeo'o and became buffalo hunters on the Plains. By early nineteenth century, Tsetséhestáhase and the So'taeo'o merged to be one tribe, today known as the Cheyenne.[7]

During the early 1800s, the Cheyenne were involved in trading guns and horses to other tribes on the Plains. After Bent's Fort in Colorado was built in 1834, many Cheyennes and Arapahoes moved into the Arkansas River region, mainly for trading. This movement led to the initial separation between the Northern and Southern Cheyenne bands.[8] In the mid-nineteenth century, European emigrants' westward movement was accelerated by the discovery of gold. As conflicts between frontiers and

Native tribes deepened, a series of military campaigns against Plains tribes was launched. In 1865, the Powder River Expedition was organized, but it achieved little. However, the Cheyenne's north–south travel route was virtually cut off by the expedition. Consequently, those who stayed in the south became the Southern Cheyenne, and those who remained on the Northern Plains became the Northern Cheyenne.[9]

Today, among the Northern Cheyenne, Tsetséhestáhase and the So'taeo'o still hold their unique heritage. Tsetséhestáhase honor teachings and prophecies of Sweet Medicine, who received the Sacred Arrows from the Creator, Ma'heo'o, at Bear Butte (in present-day South Dakota) and brought governing systems such as the Council of Forty-Four and military societies to his people. Today, among the Northern Cheyenne, the military society system is still in practice.[10] For the So'taeo'o people, Erect Horns, who brought the Sacred Hat, has been central to their cultural practices and belief.[11] While the Sacred Arrows stay with the Southern Cheyenne, the Sacred Hat has been with the Northern Cheyenne, and as a service to the whole community, the Sacred Hat Keeper attends to the spirit of the sacred buffalo woman as his daily duty.

Establishment of the Northern Cheyenne Indian Reservation

The Northern Cheyenne Indian Reservation consists approximately 444,000 acres of land, and about 4,800 enrolled members reside on the land.[12] For the Cheyenne people, the sense of connection to the land is the very basis of their identities. While it is important to mention that their historical connection to the land encompasses territories beyond boundaries of the reservation, for the tribe, having their own reservation and possessing control over their ancestral lands is essential to the succession of their cultural practices and sovereignty. The Tongue River Indian Reservation was established by the Executive Order of 1884, but it was not specifically granted to the Northern Cheyenne tribe. The Executive Order of 1900 officially granted the reservation to the tribe, and through the Order, the reservation was renamed the Northern Cheyenne Indian Reservation and expanded to its current borders.

The Northern Cheyenne is a federally recognized tribe and has its own constitution as an IRA (Indian Reorganization Act) tribe.[13] Getting federal recognition and/or being an IRA tribe does not necessarily guarantee reserved land. As of 2005, 562 federally recognized indigenous entities existed in the US, and there were only 314 reservations.[14] For the Northern Cheyenne, making their ancestral land their own reservation has been a long and treacherous process. In the treaty-making era, the Northern Cheyenne were not recognized as an independent tribe, and in fact, the Fort Laramie Treaty of 1851 did not treat the tribe as a separate entity from the Southern Cheyenne and Arapaho. The Treaty with the Northern Cheyenne and the Northern Arapaho of 1868 was the only treaty that the Northern Cheyenne actually signed, and yet, this treaty did not grant a reservation to the tribe. Instead, the treaty forced the tribe to choose among the Crow, Sioux, or Southern Cheyenne and Arapaho Reservation and attach itself to the chosen tribe.[15]

As the treaty-making era ended in 1871, the tribe fought a series of battles against the United States along with ally tribes such as the Sioux and Arapaho. In subsequent battles such as the Battle of the Rosebud Creek (1876) and the Battle of the Little Bighorn (1876), the Northern Cheyenne won victories, which ironically led them to be removed from the Northern Plains and sent to Indian Territory. In August of 1877, 937 of the Northern Cheyenne were enrolled at the Darlington Agency, and soon many of them suffered from illness due to congested living condition and unaccustomed weather. In response to the people's wishes to return to the Northern Plains, on September 9, 1878, Chief Dull Knife and Chief Little Wolf led 353 of them and fled the agency. With the skilled maneuver of the chiefs and the legendary medicine of North Woman, they managed to dodge the chase. However, in the end, Chief Little Wolf's band was captured and sent to Fort Keogh (in present-day Miles City, Montana) and Dull Knife's band to Fort Robinson (in Nebraska).[16]

The Northern Cheyenne, as a tribe, honor the heroic journey of Chief Dull Knife and Chief Little Wolf back from Indian Territory.[17] Especially, the determination of the Dull Knife band is recognized by tribal members as a direct cause that brought a reservation to the tribe. Held captive at Fort Robinson, the Dull Knife band refused the order to go back to Indian Territory. They attempted to escape from the barrack where they were being held, and in their attempt, many were gunned down. The tribe commemorates their efforts to return home every January, the month when the incident took place, by organizing the "Fort Robinson Breakout Spiritual Run."

Testimony against US History

Contradicting "Manifest Destiny"

Most often, US national history employs the doctrine of "manifest destiny" that justified the westward expansion of emigrants and their acquisition of land. The covert plot of the mainstream national history assumes "assimilation" as a natural progression of tribal communities. In order to testify against this trend, Native tribes need to make claims contradicting national history and communicate their perspectives on historical events. In the case of the Cheyenne, the Sand Creek Massacre (1864) and the Battle of the Little Bighorn (1876) are good examples of how the tribe laid claim against the US national history.

The Sand Creek Massacre was long treated as a "battle." Chief Black Kettle's camp was attacked by Colonel John M. Chivington, despite the fact that they put out the American flag along with the white flag. Most of the victims were elders, women, and children, and bodies of the victims were butchered to pieces and taken as trophies.[18] The site in Colorado was long left without much recognition. Through the efforts of the Northern Cheyenne Sand Creek Massacre Historic Site Project team,[19] in 2007, the site was dedicated as a historical site and rightly named the Sand Creek Massacre National Historic Site.

The Little Bighorn Battlefield National Monument used to be called the Custer Battlefield National Monument where the acts of General George A. Custer and the US Army's 7th Calvary were commemorated. There was no place for the recognition of the efforts of Native warriors who died defending their way of life. In 1925, a daughter of a Cheyenne chief killed at the battle sought ways to put up a marker for her father. Long after her request was dismissed, in 1991, the site was renamed. In 2000, red granite markers for Cheyenne warriors were erected, and the Indian Memorial was dedicated in 2003.[20] Today, on the anniversary of the Battle of the Little Bighorn, the tribe facilitates traditional ceremonies and various events at the site to commemorate the ancestors' efforts to defend their homeland. In both cases, perspectives of the tribe on historical events had been denied, and the tribe fought to make marks on national history.

The Collective Memory and Re-interpretation of the Past

For the Cheyenne, the Sand Creek Massacre and the Battle of the Little Bighorn are seminal historical events to be remembered. However, the Exodus from the Indian Territory, especially the Fort Robinson Breakout, has a special function in the succession of tribal sovereignty.

In the American Indian Tribal History Project (2003–2009), facilitated by the Yellowstone Western Heritage Center in Billings, Montana,[21] the tribal production team decisively made a significant tribute to the Fort Robinson Breakout. The tribal production team states, "It is only through their selfless sacrifice, their skill, their intellect and their undying love for future generations of Northern Cheyenne that we are alive today and residing in our beautiful ancestral homeland."[22] The exhibit, which covered the period from 1876 to 1884, was titled "Coming Home: The Northern Cheyenne Odyssey," drawing public attention to the tribe's emotional tie to their hard-won reservation. Employing Homer's *Odyssey*, which speaks of the universal human desire to reach home, the exhibit redefined "reservation" as "homeland." Considering a long history of anti-Indian sentiment in Yellowstone County, the exhibit could be seen as a testimonial narrative of the tribe expressed toward general public of the regional community.

Today, many of the tribal members consider the Exodus from Indian Territory in 1878 as a major milestone to the establishment of their reservation. In reality, it required a much more complex process for the Tongue River region to be officially and stably recognized as the homeland of the Northern Cheyenne. In fact, the Executive Order of 1884, which set up the Tongue River Indian Reservation, did not specify the reservation boundaries, and that caused serious problems to the tribe. Since the survey result of the region had not been approved by the Commissioner of the General Land Office, the District Land Office in Miles City kept allowing intruders into the reservation. There were cases of violent clashes between the tribe and neighboring ranchers, and a series of anti-Cheyenne movements were launched.[23] Consequently, the Tongue River Indian Reservation came close to revocation more than once.[24] On each occasion, the investigators and inspectors proposed plans to transfer the Northern Cheyenne to the Crow Indian Reservation, and each time, the consulted chiefs unanimously refused the proposed relocation. The chiefs argued that the region had been their home, and General Nelson A. Miles had promised the land to them as a reward for the scouting efforts done by Two Moons, White Bull, and others at Fort Keogh. Miles supported their argument even after leaving Fort Keogh.[25]

The "Miles' promise" was often used in the tribe's argument against the proposed relocation plans. Once the Northern Cheyenne Indian Reservation was established in 1900, the memory of the Exodus, which had been translated to an "ancestral sacrifice," became the tribe's central defense against national Indian policies that put many Native tribes into a state of disintegration and dissolution. In defense against such Indian policies, the "Miles' promise" could not fully convey the tribe's determination to keep their land and sovereignty, but the "ancestral sacrifice" could. In accordance with the changing political climate, the discourse of the tribal testimony may shift, and the collective memory works as resources that make re-interpration of the communal past possible.

The Work of the Collective Memory in the Tribal Governance

Throughout the last century, the Northern Cheyenne tribe had protected their land against inconsistent Indian policies, and in their decision making, the work of the collective memory of the "ancestral sacrifice" has been visible.

The General Allotment Act came to the Northern Cheyenne tribe in 1926. The Act promised 160 acres of land to heads of households, with the rest of the reservation land declared "surplus." Due to the Act, nearly ninety million acres of tribal lands were lost to the United States.[26] Fortunately, the General Allotment Act did not affect the Northern Cheyenne Indian Reservation. However, as House Concurrent Resolution 108, adopted by Congress in 1953, set the termination policy in motion,[27] sixty sections of reservation land were sold through the Billings Area Office of the Bureau.[28] In 1959, the tribal councils under the initiative of President Woodenlegs launched the Unallotment Program, getting government loans in order to buy back the lost land. In his speech at the Association on American Indian Affairs Annual Membership Meeting in 1960, Woodenlegs stated, "To us, to be Cheyenne means being one tribe—living on our own land—in America, where we are citizens. Our land is everything to us . . . It is the only place where Cheyennes remember same things together."[29] He spoke of his grandmother's journey back from Oklahoma, conveying the importance of preserving the tribal lands for which his ancestors devoted their lives. Today, 99 percent of the land in the Northern Cheyenne Indian Reservation is owned by either the tribe or individual tribal members.[30] The efforts of Woodenlegs carried out over years have resulted in today's high percentage of tribal ownership of reservation land.

In the 1970s when the energy crisis hit the United States, major energy companies flocked to the reservation in the attempt to mine coal. Pressured by the Bureau of Indian Affairs, the tribe once signed exploration permits for strip-mining, and in the end, over 70 percent of the reservation land was leased out.[31] Filing a petition to the Secretary of the Interior and working at congressional levels, the tribe managed to cancel all the leases as of 1980.[32] Sweet Medicine, who foresaw the challenges that his people would face in the future, left an apocalyptic prophecy, and today the people on the reservation try to prevent the prophecy from manifesting itself.

Expressions of the Collective Memory in Self-narratives

By interpreting the Exodus as an ancestral sacrifice, people make meaning out of this event that was so relevant to their lives, and reaffirm their tribal identity. The collective memory of the ancestral sacrifice gives strength to the tribal members in their struggles with contemporary issues, assisting them in embracing the complexity in their heritage as well as US citizenship. Here, I introduce the narratives of three individuals who grew up on the reservation in order to illuminate how the collective memory is expressed in individual narratives.[33]

Finding Strength

Frank is in his late sixties.[34] Until his recent retirement, he kept his job in the "outside world,"[35] where he had to deal with non-Indian people. Considering the high rate of unemployment on the reservation, it is quite remarkable that he had held his job and supported his family.

Frank joined the Navy before finishing high school. Three years later, he came back to the reservation and finished high school. Soon after graduation, he married. While he attempted to attend the university in Billings, the G.I. Bill—providing $135 a month—was his only source of income, and it could hardly sustain the couple. "We were about to starve to death," he recollects. They decided to make a living through the Relocation Program promoted by the Bureau of Indian Affairs.[36] Eventually, they moved to California, where Frank learned electronics and worked for a computer and electronics company. Neither Frank nor his wife enjoyed life in the big cities of California, and when he found work with the Federal Aviation Agency, they moved to Utah and later Nevada. In 1976, they moved back to the reservation with their children. Frank states, "I really wanted to come home for some reason. It's strange. My mother had already died."

With this unknown attraction, Frank returned to the reservation and tried to find work. He started all over again as an apprentice at a nearby power plant. Frank moved up the ladder to become a supervisor, dealing with "people with problems." At the time, racism against Native people was overt in his workplace. "It is easier to deal with machines," he laughs. Frank reflects upon his working days:

> There are two ways of life. Cheyenne traditional ways and white way are completely different. With traditional ways, you live with people around, and you help them. For white society, you work and you forget everybody else and make yourself rich, you know. That's what I got out of it. And I went that route, but I really didn't care for that. There were no rewards in that. There were no good feelings you get out of that.[37]

People on the reservation spoke of "traditional ways," which expresses the practice of a traditional value system, including codes of conduct at ceremonies and rituals as well as in daily life. Frank rediscovered the value of "traditional ways" through his recovery from alcoholism. In his narrative, he spoke of his battle against alcoholism which, he considers, had its roots in denial of the Cheyenne culture and language infused through "education." Frank went to a boarding school where punishment was a daily routine and there was nothing he could do right in the eyes of white teachers. At home, his mother's accelerated drinking problem left him with a sense of abandonment. After having lost his grandfather who cared for him, Frank could not find a place where he could "feel good," and it was just a matter of time before he would seek a cure in alcohol.

His denial of being alcoholic was so deep that when he finally accepted the fact, he broke down in tears. Going to meetings of Alcoholics Anonymous, he rediscovered how to pray, and was invited to sweat ceremonies.[38] He re-established himself in the rewoven tie with his community. The Cheyenne have an adoption system that strengthens kinship beyond blood ties, and through this adoption, Frank was invited to a new kinship where he was able to receive teachings of the Cheyenne ways of life. With guidance and support from his uncle, he underwent a fast through which he found his place in the world. He recollects the following:

> I was down on the ground, where all the different insects were. They come to bite you, you know. I could hear grasshoppers eating over my ear. This was something I got to know that I was a part of the earth. I don't own the earth. I am a part of these insects that came to bite me. [Laughter.] And I'm going through life, just like they are going through life. They have a right to live, just like I do. It's kind of taught me that I am not really alone. I am a part of the earth. I had to respect this earth because this earth is a living thing.

Finding connections with people and natural world, he began to facilitate his life in accordance with traditional ways of life. In doing so, he learned how to help others and found joy in it. He has been a member of one of the military societies of the tribe, and that often requires a demanding schedule. He speaks of the ancestral sacrifice in the following manner and places himself in the line of the heritage.

> They came from Oklahoma and Fort Robinson . . . They finally came back here. And this is where we are now. They made a lot of sacrifices to come up. A lot of different stories about those who made sacrifices . . . I guess, you can think of those, and that gives you strength to go on. There was someone who really made sacrifices for you . . . And I guess now it's my turn. I cannot do much physical work, just advice. I don't know, sometimes, I don't feel like I have wisdom that grandfathers are supposed to

have. I am still learning each day, different things, new things. But I came a little way where I learn how to feel the way life is.

Frank speaks of the Exodus not just as a historical incident that needs to be explained to the interviewer. Using the word "sacrifice," Frank conveys the connections he felt to his ancestors.

Frank's narrative expresses a sharp contrast between Cheyenne ways and the ways of the outside world. His narrative communicates how he has lived through issues of alcoholism rooted in the conflicting worldviews, and how he has found a sense of home in his life. Frank is a quiet man who is humble in speaking of traditional ways of life. Since, he says, he was not raised in a traditional manner, he may not feel confident in speaking of "tradition" in detail. The "ancestral sacrifice" could be an accessible cultural resource for an individual like Frank who had once lost sight of the traditional value system but later returned to it and reclaimed his Cheyenne identity.

Embracing Complexity in Heritage

Nellie, in her mid-sixties, identifies herself as Cheyenne based on her sense of connection to the land. She states, "I've always loved our homeland and these red hills." She developed a sense of connection to the land and learned the ways of life through her grandparents. From her affectionate grandmother and protective grandfather, Nellie learned how to care for home and how to get along with people and respect elders. Her grandmother used to tell her, "You treat people good. If you don't gossip about others, then you give them no space to gossip about you because you're not carrying tales. Life is hard enough. You don't need to make it harder on yourself." Comparing the teachings from her grandparents with non-Indian ways, Nellie explains,

> You have to stop, and think about things, and don't jump into things. Take your time. That's one thing non-Indians have a hard time with. [They think] everything got to be done fast. But what I learned from my grandma is you do it right. It doesn't matter how long it takes. Just do a good job . . . You pray, and then you think it through, and then you decide. And that's usually the right way to go.[39]

Her grandparents lived in a remote area and worked hard from early in the morning till late in the evening. Nellie recalls, "They taught me so much just by living their lives." The place where she spent time with her grandparents has a special place in her heart. "It looks a lot different than it used to be . . . But it still just really touches my heart . . . When I came into different things, I think back to them. What would they do, you know?" For her, the red hills hold memory and the teachings of her grandparents.

In her narrative, Nellie calls herself "mongrel" and spells out her ancestry of Cheyenne, Oglala Sioux, Chippewa, Cree, French, English, and Irish. Growing up on the reservation, she was called "breed," "half-breed," and sometimes "white woman." In her youth, she already had a clear view of her marriage:

> I knew that I could not marry a non-Indian. I could not marry a full-blood. He would have to be a breed like I am . . . We would have more in common . . . Non-Indians, they don't go along with our beliefs. And if you marry a full-blood, then a lot of times, they or their family tend to look down on you because you're not a full-blood.

Another thing that she promised herself early on was not to marry a cowboy. She maintains, "I didn't want drinking in my life." Nellie's father was a cowboy and used to drink. Unlike her grandfather, many times he was not at home to be responsive to events in the life of his family. Unfortunately, in her own marriage, Nellie has had to deal with the alcohol problems of her husband and children. Dealing with her children's alcohol problem was especially hard on her. "I've seen too many lives messed up and lost because of alcohol. And it's just something you do not want your kids to have to go through," she asserts.

The children's alcohol problem left Nellie in deep self-doubt. "I must have failed somewhere along the line. I had a hard time with that one," she reflects. It was in this treacherous process that she rediscovered her faith. Together with her husband, she was invited to sweat ceremonies and began to appreciate them:

> All those years, there was always something in me . . . just a lonely, kind of empty feeling there. I always described it as "lonely" until I started going to sweats, getting involved in sweats and being around ceremonies . . . I wasn't taking care of myself as a Cheyenne woman. And then when I started doing it, it just felt right. It was good. I just got more strength from it.

With the regained faith, she went through some of the sacrificial rites when her family and friends were in need of prayer. One time when she and a friend fasted together, she had a series of dreams:

> It just poured rain [during the fasting], and we had to move our stuff back . . . I told [her friend], "It's just like my dream!" Just exactly! So many times, that happened. I don't know . . . I guess that you are on the right path when you have your dreams, and then they come true.

While the issues of alcohol at home had shattered her confidence as a mother, through traditional rites, she was able to place herself back on track.

Through the process of fasting, her Indian name was revealed, and the name happened to reflect her deep love for her homeland. "Whenever we are off the reservation and come back, I would see these red hills, and my heart would just get happy. So, I thought the name was appropriate." Nellie claims that her extended sense of connection to the land is supported by "people, memories, and stories." She addresses her connection to the land for which her ancestors gave their lives, in the following manner:

> We all grew up hearing the stories of how our people walked back from Oklahoma, what they sacrificed for our homeland. If our ancestors could go through that much, we can put up with what we have to and protect it . . . It's a precious place, and that's why we have to be respectful and take care of it. And then, all the people here, I might not feel comfortable around them, or trust them, or respect some, you know. But still, they're . . . a part of it [the tribe], and you just pray for them that they'll come to their senses someday.

The collective memory of the ancestral sacrifice helps her to see people on the reservation as one people with a common heritage.

Nellie's narrative defends her Cheyenne identity against antagonists within the community. Frequently, it is said that the mixed blood are for development while the full blood are for preservation. Nellie's narrative contradicts such a stereotype. Her narrative shows that an individual finds ways to affirm tribal identity, not just based on blood quantum but through love and affection for land that encompasses personal and collective memory.

Bridging the Two Worlds

Stone, in his mid-fifties, has been working at a power plant near the reservation for about twenty-five years. To hold a job in the "white man's world" for so long, he says, "takes pure motivation and discipline." His work is physically demanding. He considers the hardships of holding a job for one's family to be a part of Cheyenne male responsibility:

> As long as my body can hold up, I bring a check [home] every two weeks. I look at that as a similarity of bringing in a big fat buck or a big fat buffalo. Today, we pay for utilities. We pay for our home. We pay for our clothing and our transportation. But I look at that from that perspective . . . Sometimes, my son will say, "Hey, caveman," and I say, "Well, this caveman's going to bring money home that we're going to eat off . . ." Not in a way that someone's feelings are hurt, but in a way for him to understand that's what it takes nowadays to do things.[40]

For Stone, "bringing in a big fat buck" is not only an analogy. His father did a lot of hunting on horseback for his family, and Stone used to accompany him. In his narrative, Stone describes details of how his father facilitated hunting with prayers. Comparing hunting then with what it is today, he remarks, "Now, it is just like a sportsman thing . . . They get that trophy hanging in their living room. Just like a big beer party for the hunters, non-Indians and Indians alike. But the way I was taught, you got to respect that [animal]." Stone regrets that much of the cultural teachings of Cheyenne elders have been lost, thinking that perhaps there were reasons for the teachings to have been lost.

Stone's grandparents and parents considered the Cheyenne traditional ways of life and the ways of the mainstream society to be completely different, bearing no similarities. Unlike them, Stone has inhabited both worlds and believes that the Cheyenne way of life is still "workable" in the contemporary world. He speaks of "to adapt" and "to instill" as ways to deal with changes forced upon the tribe. "From generation to generation, the Cheyenne people had to adapt to each turn of the century or whatever came . . . At the same time, we always try to instill our [culture]," he explains. US Indian policy in the twentieth century swung back and forth between "assimilation/termination" and "self-determination," and each time that happened, tribes had to make the necessary adjustments.

Stone often mentions "Cheyenne male responsibility" in his narrative, and in doing so, he shows how he has adapted to changes and at the same time kept his heritage. He makes connections between his war engagement in Vietnam and the Cheyenne warriorship that has been highly honored in the community:

> When I volunteered to go into the military for three years, I chose to be in the Airborne Infantry. I knew that I was going into battle in Vietnam, and the Airborne Infantry, they're highly trained, disciplined men that are trained to live off nature, to be self-motivated, to be very sharp . . . It was instilled in us, like Cheyenne male roles and responsibility. You got a choice. You don't let somebody else do the thinking for you.

Emphasizing the difference between choosing to join the military and being drafted to be sent to war, he aligns himself with his Cheyenne heritage.

With the collective memory of "sacrifice," Stone establishes consistency in his narrative. He describes his war experiences from the perspective of "sacrifice" in the following manner:

> It's still in our blood to fight for freedom . . . Sure 58,000 plus died in Vietnam. . . . Generally speaking, I guess people don't really understand what freedom is . . . When

we went into battle there, we, young men, made the supreme sacrifice ... We made history because we made that determination to go in to assist to deal with Communists up front. Yeah, there was a change there [in Vietnam] ... I always feel that sacrifice that we made was worthwhile. Like a lot of anti-war protesters, they might say, "He's a crazy Vietnam veteran. He killed innocent people." But all goes to one point ... We accomplished what needed to accomplish there.

By using the word "sacrifice," Stone translates his war engagement as a "fight for freedom," and in doing so, he bridges his tribal identity and his citizenship in the United States, where "liberty" holds supreme importance.

Stone considers that his engagement in Vietnam was similar to what his ancestors had done for their future generations. Touching upon the collective memory of the ancestral sacrifice, he communicates his sense of connection to the land:

History tells us our people died for this land. They died. They made the sacrifices ... Everything is so beautiful here. So I could never live somewhere else. It wouldn't be home to me. It'd be a "rent" if I went some other place. When you look at history ... those sacrifices were made for us to be here, to live here, and we live here because we're bound with this land. There's a tie here. It's a real strong, ancestral bond.

On the surface, Stone's testimony as a freedom fighter seems successful in defending the righteousness of the United States in the Vietnam War. Yet, there exists an undeniably deep gulf between the two worlds:

Non-members come [to the reservation] from different parts of the United States. They don't have a clue about who they are. They don't have heritage. I always call them "instant leaders." Sometimes, they'll read a book about the Cheyenne people, and they try to direct people what to do ... They fractionalize our people. It's a genocidal attack to destroy our culture ... There are times in our history when the US government came to destroy the Cheyenne people. They destroyed our villages in the Sand Creek Massacre ... Just like what happened to Hiroshima and Nagasaki, and what is going on in Iraq.[41]

Here, Stone stands on the other side of the shore and accuses the United States. By mentioning Hiroshima and Nagasaki, Japanese cities where the United States dropped atomic bombs during World War II, along with Sand Creek where the massacre of the Cheyenne people took place, Stone tries to convey his point to the researcher, who is Japanese.

Toward the end of the interview, Stone reveals that he is suffering from post-traumatic stress disorder (PTSD) due to his experiences in Vietnam. The sight of blood still troubles him, so he cannot take his son hunting like his father did him. He uses "sacrifice" to make sense of his suffering. "I'm a disabled American veteran, and when I die, there is something for my family . . . That's my compensation because I made that sacrifice," he states. He concludes by saying, "I learned how to accept that [PTSD] because I chose the path. I wanted to be in the military. I wanted to go to the war. I didn't have to go to war, but I volunteered to go to combat duty." At the same time, he does not forget to mention that he does not want his son or daughters to be in the military "because you suffer a lot." While the traditional Cheyenne male responsibility and the suffering of Cheyenne men in the contemporary world might not easily find a meeting ground, the collective memory of "sacrifice" provides Stone a context in which he can spell out his experiences of PTSD.

Stone's narrative consists of conflicting elements. However, that should not be treated as a lack of integrity in his personhood. Instead, this should be understood as an indication of the irreconcilability he faces when honoring his Cheyenne heritage and at the same time, presenting himself as a citizen of the United States. In addition, narrating his experiences to an interviewer who was neither a member of the tribe nor an American citizen made him feel compelled to explain both the cultural context of his Cheyenne heritage and the mainstream value system of the United States. Perhaps it is more appropriate to see the opposing "pulls" expressed in his narrative as an indication of the uninhabitable gap that lies between the two worlds.

Frank, Nellie, and Stone, who grew up on the reservation, express their connection to the land in their narratives. They grew up with elders' stories. Frank notes that there are many stories, but he, like the other two, chooses to mention the Exodus from Oklahoma. Details of that historical event are not elaborated in their narratives; rather, their efforts are focused mostly on communicating their personal connections to the land to which their ancestors gave their lives. The Exodus from Indian Territory could be seen as one of the most telling stories that represents who the Northern Cheyenne people are today to non-members. In the case of the Northern Cheyenne, the succession of the tribal identity and the transmission of collective memory go hand in hand, and in the process, the individual members' sense of connection to the land plays an important role.

The "ancestral sacrifice" is a sophisticated code that evokes memories of particular historical events among the tribal members, and at the same time, has deep roots in the cultural value system. The "sacrifice" has its place in traditional ways. In the end, sacrifice is not a consequence, but an act; offering oneself and enduring physical challenge is essential to the ceremonial way, as in the Sun Dance and fasting. In the "traditional ways of life" to which all three refer, "history," "land," and "cultural practices" are one. Perhaps those of us who are non-Native might be able to gain some understanding of the value system in such a land-based culture through the concept of "tradition." However, "tradition" is often perceived as collections of still pictures of the preserved past.[42] This static view of tradition keeps Native peoples as a people of the past, preventing us from seeing the ever-evolving reality of tribal communities that seek to solve the contemporary issues that arise when confronted with larger societies. Frank, Nellie, and Stone successfully narrate their life stories without being trapped by such biased views toward Native peoples. By using collective memory of the ancestral sacrifice, they simultaneously touch upon the tribe's historical bond with the land and the cultural teachings that have supported this tie.

The narratives of these three individuals show how the collective memory of the tribe remains alive in its people's daily consciousness. By the very act of narrating their lives and recalling the historical past, the narrators test the relevance of the collective memory in the contemporary world. Despite the loss of traditional ways of life and the wisdom of elders, as the elders pass away, issues of "blood quantum," and the increase of pain and suffering at the interface of the two worlds, the three interviewees successfully define themselves as Northern Cheyenne. Through the prism of collective memory, they convey their points to the non-Native interviewer.

Conclusion

The Northern Cheyenne narratives make visible how collective memory works at a cross-section between history and memory. By using a discourse based on the collective memory of the ancestral sacrifice, the tribe's counter-history testifies against the national history of the United States. The Exodus from Indian Territory is given precedence over events from the relatively recent past, and by employing the discourse of the "ancestral sacrifice," the tribe's testimonial narrative bridges history and legend. While the tribe's communal past, composed in this manner, can hold relevance to its members' ways of life, it fluently communicates the tribal tie with the land to non-members.

These three individuals' narratives show how the "personal" is supported by the "communal." Olick differentiates "socially framed individual memories" and "collective commemorative representations and mnemonic traces," pointing to the necessity of examining the relations between the two.[43] In the case of the Northern Cheyenne, the two are congruous and, so far, in harmony. The collective memory in spontaneous individual recollections of the past is made possible by ongoing practices of ceremonial rites and contemporary efforts to preserve the reservation land through the tribal governance. Among the Northern Cheyenne, collective memory of individual members and that of tribal community are compatible, since collective memory resides not in commemorative representations but in lasting relationships between the land and the people.

At the moment, the Exodus from Indian Territory is an episode that signifies the tribe's commitment to its homeland, and the discourse of the ancestral sacrifice functions as the backbone of tribal identity. In early reservation time, the tribe used the "Miles' promise" (see earlier in this article) in its efforts to defend their entitlement to land. At best, the discourse of the "Miles' promise" can translate to imply "promised land," but almost certainly not "homeland." Through the discourse of the "ancestral sacrifice," the tribe can declare that the reservation is more than just a federal land in trust; it is their home. The ways in which focus of the tribe's testimonial narrative had shifted from the "Miles' promise" to the "ancestral sacrifice" have not been scrutinized. However, the shift indicates that expressions of collective memory would evolve in accordance with the needs of a community and its members.

In sum, the following can be concluded regarding the Northern Cheyenne narratives:

(1) In the contemporary world, the tribe's testimonial narrative has gained ground by reaching wider audiences through tribal governance and public exhibits. Internally, the collective memory of the tribe has been rejuvenated by the people's act of narrating their personal lives along with the recollection of communal past.

(2) Through the use of collective memory, the tribe and its members communicate their interpretation of their historical past to non-members in an agreeable manner. The conviction of the narrative is achieved by its consistency with cultural tradition of the tribe as well as its coherence expressed as a plot that "history" is expected to possess.

(3) The tribal testimonial narrative defends both the integrity of people and their sovereignty. The discourse based on the collective memory works as a cultural resource by which people in the community can establish a common understanding of the tribal identity, despite their diverse interests and complex heritage. It assists people to speak with one voice so that they can firmly assert their right to live on their homeland.

Notes

1. I would like to express my deep gratitude for the generosity of the Northern Cheyenne people who have kindly offered their time and shared their stories and wisdom with me. My gratitude extends to Dr. Richard Littlebear who provided me invaluable comments on the manuscript. This work was supported by JSPS Grant-in-Aid for Challenging Exploratory Research, KAKENHI 21652064, Nanzan University Pache Research Subsidy I-A-1 for the 2009 academic year, and I-A-2 for the 2010 academic year.
2. On the Cheyenne Exodus from Indian Territory, see Mari Sandoz, *Cheyenne Autumn* (New York: McGraw-Hill, 1953); John H. Monnett, *Tell Them We Are Going Home: The Odyssey of the Northern Cheyennes* (Norman, OK: University of Oklahoma Press, 2001); and Peter J. Powell, *People of the Sacred Mountain: A History of the Northern Cheyenne Chiefs and Warrior Societies, 1830–1879, With an Epilogue 1969–1974*, Volume II (San Francisco: Harper & Row, Publishers, 1981), 1153–1262.
3. Based on the interview research conducted by Kawaura (2009, 2008, 2007, 2006).
4. The language, the cultural customs and rituals, the land, and the reservation itself make the Cheyenne identity today. The Exodus from Indian Territory (1878) is one of the iconic instants in Cheyenne history that support today's Cheyenne identity.
5. Maurice Halbwachs, *On Collective Memory* (Chicago: University of Chicago Press, 1992), 46–83.
6. There is variation in spelling of the two peoples. This paper chooses to employ "Tsetsėhestȧhase and the So'taeo'o" as in the tribal council-approved writing system. It was approved by unanimous vote in 1996. (Comment from Dr. Richard Littlebear, president of Chief Dull Knife College.)
7. Tom Weist, *A History of the Cheyenne People* (Billings, MT: Montana Council for Indian Education, 1977), 9–24.
8. Ibid., 29–32.
9. Ibid., 47, 55–73.
10. The military system consists of Kit Fox, Elk Horn Scraper, Red Shield, and Dog Soldiers Society.
11. John Stands In Timber and Margot Liberty, *Cheyenne Memories*, 2nd edition (New Haven, CT: Yale University Press, 1998), 27–41; Peter J. Powell, *Sweet Medicine: The Continuing Role of the Sacred Arrows, the Sun Dance, and the Sacred Buffalo Hat in Northern Cheyenne History* (Norman, OK: University of Oklahoma Press, 1998), xxiii, 4–5, 70–71, 444–445, 460–471.
12. http://www.cheyennenation.com/ 2011.12.26.
13. The Constitution and Bylaws of the Northern Cheyenne Tribe on the Northern Cheyenne Indian Reservation was adopted in 1935 and amended in 1960 and 1996.
14. David E. Wilkins, *American Indian Politics and the American Political System*, 2nd edition (Lanham, MD: Rowman & Littlefield Publishers, Inc., 2007), 21, 26, 35.
15. Orlan J. Svingen, *The Northern Cheyenne Indian Reservation, 1877–1900* (Niwot, CO: University Press of Colorado, 1993), 3–7.
16. Ibid., 19–21; Monnett, 25–43; Chief Dull Knife College, *We, the Northern Cheyenne People: Our Land, Our History, Our Culture* (Lame Deer, MT: Chief Dull Knife College, 2008), 26–28.
17. Chief Dull Knife and Chief Little Wolf have a special place in the hearts of tribal members. The tribal college is named after Chief Dull Knife, and the tribe's government building after Chief Little Wolf.
18. Regarding the Sand Creek Massacre, see Jerome A. Greene and Douglas D. Scott, *Finding Sand Creek: History, Archeology, and the 1864 Massacre Site* (Norman,

OK: University of Oklahoma Press, 2004); Thom Hatch, *Black Kettle: The Cheyenne Chief Who Sought Peace but Found War* (Hoboken, NJ: John Wiley & Sons, Inc., 2004); Donald J. Berthrong, *The Southern Cheyennes* (Norman, OK: University of Oklahoma Press, 1963); and Stan Hoig, *The Sand Creek Massacre*, (Norman, OK: University of Oklahoma Press, 1961).

19. Crazy Dog Society organized and carried out the project.
20. Regarding changing views on the Battle of the Little Bighorn, see Charles E. Rankin, ed., *Legacy: New Perspectives on the Battle of the Little Bighorn* (Helena, MT: Montana Historical Society Press, 1996).
21. The aim of the project is to preserve tribal histories and cultures. Former Senator Conrad Burns of Montana endorsed the project by getting a $1,000,000 Department of the Interior appropriation. The important point in this project is that the tribal project team, not museum curators, chose the theme and designed the exhibit. The Crow tribe also produced an exhibit called "Parading through History: The Apsaalooke Nation."
22. Western Heritage Center, *American Indian Tribal Histories Project* (Aberdeen, SD: Coyote Publishing & Printing, Inc., 2005), NC-2.
23. In 1889, 138 ranchers and settlers signed a petition for the revocation of the Tongue River Indian Reservation, and 70 prominent citizens of Miles City filed a similar petition. Meanwhile *The Yellowstone Journal*, a local newspaper, promoted "A United Movement by Custer County for the Extinction of the Cheyenne Reservation." Svingen, 71.
24. Ibid., 69–72.
25. Corresponding to a letter from Indian Agent Upshaw dated in 1889, Miles explained about the Northern Cheyenne's scouting efforts, with which he successfully tracked down the Nez Perce under Chief Joseph. He argued, "They have fulfilled their part of the compact and it would be but justice for the Government to allow them to remain where it has placed them during the past years" (Ibid., 169–170).
26. For instance, the Southern Cheyenne and Arapaho in Oklahoma lost over 80% of their lands due to the General Allotment Act. The allotments could not be sold for 25 years. In this period, a Native individual was expected to be a "civilized farmer." After the period, heavy pressure was on the allottees to sell their lands. Wilkins, 117.
27. Resolution No. 108 declared the end of the trust relationship between the US government and tribes, ending federal benefits and support services to Native peoples. Over one hundred Native communities and in total 11,000 Native people lost their status as "recognized" and sovereign nations Ibid., 25.
28. Although the tribe tried to buy back the lost land soon after, the process of their loan was purposefully delayed by the regional BIA office.
29. John Wooden Legs, "Back on the War Ponies," *Indian Affairs*, 37 (June 1960): 3–4.
30. http://www.cheyennenation.com/ 2010.12.7.
31. Alvin J. Ziontz, *A Lawyer in Indian Country, a Memoir*, (Seattle & London: University of Washington Press, 2009), 148. The deal the tribe had gotten was as low as one-hundredth of the similar mining leases elsewhere. Stephen Hendricks, "Small Wonder: Northern Cheyenne Lawyer Defends Her Nation," *Sierra* (January/February 2004): 18.
32. In 1980, Congress passed the Northern Cheyenne Lease Cancellation Act. (Ziontz, 151–156, 163). James J. Lopach, Margery Hunter Brown, and Richmond L. Clow, *Tribal Government Today: Politics on Montana Indian Reservations*, revised edition (Boulder, CO: University Press of Colorado, 1998), 100-101.
33. The interviews were conducted in 2005 and 2008. In order to preserve the privacy of the interviewees, I use fictitious names.

34. Age at the time of the interview.
35. The direct citations from the interview transcripts are shown with quotation marks. All the interviews were conducted in English. The cited words respect the original verbiage of the interviewees.
36. The program was designed to make tribal members move out of their reservations and assimilate into larger cities.
37. The interview with Frank is dated Aug. 19, 2005, in Busby, MT.
38. The sweat ceremony could be seen as a purification ceremony. Inside the darkened, heated lodge, participants offer prayers under the guidance of an individual who is delegated to lead the ceremony.
39. The interviews with Nellie are dated Aug. 19, 2005, in Busby, MT, and May 3, 2008, in Lame Deer, MT.
40. The interview with Stone is dated Aug. 21, 2005, in Busby, MT.
41. By the time of the interview, the number of civilian casualties in Iraq came to approximately 25,000 since the US-led invasion in March, 2003. http://www.iraqbodycount.org/analysis/reference/press-release/12/ 2011.5.25.
42. Tradition, of course, has supreme importance to tribal communities. However, the traditional ways of life in land-based culture could not be adequately captured by the contemporary usage of the word "tradition," which regards culture as a solely human creation and disregards people's ongoing relationships with their land.
43. Jeffrey K. Olick, "Collective Memory: The Two Cultures," *Sociological Theory*, 17, 3 (November 1999): 333–348.

9

Voices behind the Mic: Sports Broadcasters, Autobiography, and Competing Narratives of the Past

Richard Haynes

"Know what I'm going to do tomorrow?" I said to Mrs Allison on Friday night in January 1927.
Mrs Allison did not know.
"I'm going to broadcast a football match."
"Don't be ridiculous, George" she said. "Whoever heard of anyone broadcasting a football match?"
—George F. Allison, the BBC's first commentator.[1]

Introduction

In contrast to the recollection above from the autobiography of the BBC's first television sports commentator, George Allison, televised sports now hold a significant place in the contemporary culture and economy of broadcasting—driving technological advances and the global reach of dominant media corporations. Although our understanding of how broadcasting has changed the structure and commercial presence of sports in society is well documented by historians, sociologists, and economists, our knowledge of exactly how broadcasting engaged with sports and transformed them as a cultural form is less clear.[2] Analysis of sports commentary by Crissel[3] and Tolson reveals the complexities of radio and television commentary and how sports broadcasting positions the audience—listener or viewer—as a "virtual member of the crowd."[4]

Such innovative studies help our understanding of how the utterances of sports commentators structure the viewing and listening experience and communicate the "meaning of the game." But while close readings of the commentators discourse are highly revealing—particularly regarding the constraining effect of broadcast technology in delivering an event to an "absent" audience—what they do not reveal is where the techniques of commentary come from or the story of how these techniques are learned by their exponents. The experience of being a sports commentator and the human engagement with the practices and institutions of broadcasting are largely ignored by such studies, which are more interested in the ideological and discursive structures of the broadcasts themselves. Narratives of an experiential kind do, however, abound in the memories of sports broadcasters themselves, many sharing their knowledge, experiences, and opinions on the subject through published autobiography. In this context, and as a primer to understanding the practices and careers of sports broadcasters, this chapter raises some epistemological questions regarding the historical method and interpretation of broadcasting history, in particular, an analysis of the historical and theoretical usefulness of autobiography in understanding the past.

The focus for thinking about such issues is the cultural and oral history of sports broadcasting by the British Broadcasting Corporation with a specific focus on the codes and practice of running commentary. BBC Television's outside broadcasts from sports have a unique and particular place within the history of public service broadcasting in the UK, and the basis for making some wider critical points on how narrative and memory works in autobiographical texts is a specific investigation into the human story of this organization and the people who worked in it.

By retracing the Corporation's coverage of sporting events, it is possible to analyze the institutionalized processes of sports commentary and its role in fulfilling part of the BBC's "cultural mission." From radio into television, the experiences, feelings, and interpretations of individuals who have worked, and are working, in BBC Sport—producers, editors, presenters, and commentators—have been recorded in a range of autobiographical texts to provide a rich testimony and unique history of a much-lauded, but largely under-researched, aspect of British popular culture.

This investigation of autobiography and written memories is part of a much broader research project that aims to produce a unique and definitive history of BBC sports broadcasting and commentary through oral testimony by the people who made it, in conjunction with evidence from the BBC's written archives. Although other histories of BBC sports coverage exist, they largely form a smaller part of other, more extensive projects, such as the history of the BBC in general or of the cultural transformation of sports by broadcasting.[5] Unlike other areas of BBC programming, there is no definitive study of sports commentary in existence, and the aim of this piece is to address this neglected field in academic literature.

Approaching the History of Broadcast Sports

Media history is a burgeoning area of enquiry within the field of media studies, and it influences the ways in which we think about contemporary transformations in media, society, and culture. Radical changes in media technology, distribution, and consumption have encouraged media scholars and social theorists to reappraise media histories in order to understand particular processes and actions in the present.[6] The history of sports broadcasting demands renewed research for various reasons. At an economic and political level, it plays a significant role in shaping the contemporary landscape of the broadcast ecology. Sports broadcasts have undergone dramatic change since the early 1990s, and the BBC's preeminence in sports production has been undermined by new competitors and new production practices. The connection of sports programming to the BBC's public purpose or the more abstract notion of "cultural citizenship" is a critical issue. There remains in British popular culture a sense that particular sporting events continue to have a "national resonance" with a significant proportion of the population. Throughout its history, the BBC has done much to foster this culture around major events like the Grand National, Wimbledon, or the FA Cup Final. The decision to combine autobiographical accounts with other forms of empirical evidence is, therefore, a way of gaining access to more tacit knowledge of the place of sports broadcasting in society, of how sports broadcasting works, and of the characteristics of the people who made it. Of interest here is just how autobiography, as a form of documentary evidence based on individual memory, informs, connects with, and forms part of the history of sports broadcasting.

The Uses of Autobiography

Individual memory is a universal experience, and as psychologists have informed us, there are temporal differences in how it operates (short-term versus long-term), and also differences in how memories are retained. More explicit memories clearly inform and shape the process of written autobiographies, which combine with wider social memories to form a narrative of the past. As Geoffrey Cubitt has argued, "personal memory is also part of the mental equipment that allows human beings to function in social settings,"[7] and we can take from this that the memories and experiences of sports broadcasters have a social use in that context and also contribute to a broader knowledge and understanding of the social practices of radio or television production. The process of remembering through autobiography also links selfhood with a narrative of the past, and again, successive autobiographies by sports commentators position themselves subjectively in a broader narrative history of broadcasting, sports, and the world of entertainment more broadly.

However, as Cubitt and others warn, autobiography and memoir, as tools for historical research, raise crucial questions regarding the honesty, truthfulness, and justifications for knowledge about a given subject. They raise questions as to how memory is constructed, how memoir accommodates or competes with other discourses for public recognition, and essentially how history and memory are connected to each other and to the present. These questions have become increasingly pertinent in the history of sports broadcasting, not least because many first- and second-generation broadcasters have now retired or reached the twilight of their careers and frequently feel compelled to place on record their intimate experiences, memories, and feelings on their lives as prominent public figures in popular culture. Over the past decade, sports broadcasters have produced more than twenty autobiographies, many providing a rich seam of information—albeit encoded in the institutional, social, and cultural circumstances in which they were written. How autobiography might be used, in conjunction with other methods of historical inquiry, including oral testament and archive material, to understand continuities and changes in sports broadcasting and the institutionalized techniques of practices like commentary within the culture of sports broadcasting is central to the argument I want to make here. Autobiography, then, provides entrée not only to understanding the careers and experiences of sports broadcasters but also to studying how the central "art" of commentary, as a form of communication, has evolved over time by a specialized elite of broadcasting professionals, and how they subjectively position themselves within this specialist field. However, before moving on to investigate the empirical evidence, it is important to establish some of the conceptual issues raised by autobiography and its usefulness in historical and memory research in terms of social experience, historical evidence, and as literary texts.

Social Experience

Sociology has increasingly used forms of biographical writing and materials in life studies and histories, particularly influenced by feminist interventions in the field.[8] This turn to biographical methods in the social sciences has opened up potential ways of understanding the connections between the individual and society.[9] Again, the autobiographies of commentators enable a way for us to understand how the genre of sports broadcasting evolved, how it was shaped by social, organizational, and economic forces, and what impact this had on the individuals involved as they forged the modern practices of sports commentary in radio and then television. There exists a broad range of work across various disciplines using biographical research or "life stories." As with the literary and historical approaches to autobiography, those working in the social sciences have addressed the epistemological concerns raised by the use of self-written accounts of people's lives.[10] As a methodology, biographical research has fostered a commitment to interdisciplinary work from various fields, and as Roberts suggests, the "intent of biographical research in its various guises is to collect and interpret the lives of others as part of human experience."[11] One can immediately see the value of this approach in analyzing the autobiographies of commentators and what they can tell us about the institutionalization of sports broadcasting and the emergence of commentary as a specialist occupation. Previous histories of broadcasting have made great use of biographical writing to understand the decisions and motives of key individuals at important junctures in the development of the medium. In particular, in writing the first volume of the history of broadcasting in Britain, Asa Briggs made extensive use of John Reith's book *Into the Wind*, published in 1949—part memoir, part visionary treatise on broadcasting and its role in society.[12] In the autobiographies of the BBC's formative commentators, the voice of the pioneer and innovator can also be heard.

As with any organization, the stories of the individuals within it can differ remarkably from the "official" history of the organization itself. Where the voices of practitioners may be subordinated in traditional histories of broadcasting, autobiographies reinstate these voices. This is especially so when an individual is no longer under the tutelage of a broadcasting organization and can reflect on the good and the bad times in their lives as broadcasters, often challenging more widely "received" interpretations and fostering of myths that center on particular events. Such moments of conflict and tension are, of course, the essence of popular autobiography and provide necessary narrative hooks by which the author can draw the reader into the intrigue in his life. Stories of arguments and fallouts between individuals can also be connected to wider sociohistorical contexts of key decisions, strategy, and politics. Of more significance are the ways in which autobiographies pull together individual and social lives. Crucially, autobiography can reveal the individual as a social being, or as Roberts puts it, "individuals as acting, experiencing, but within social contexts and structures."[13] Again, a noticeable feature in the biographical writing of commentators is the importance of social networks and acquaintances. For instance, how commentators begin their careers in broadcasting makes fascinating reading and reveals all manner of things about social structures, in particular class and gender, two of the most important social distinctions in shaping the early coverage of sports by the BBC.

The Human Side of History

A second analytical approach is to use autobiography as an historical record of the past. It is, in a very straightforward sense, an individual's testimony of what happened. Here, the interpretation of an individual's life, their place in events, and their relations with others is a crucial aspect of autobiographical writing and historiography. Autobiography, much like history, is an exploration of the past, and some of the analytical frames of enquiry are clearly similar, although the empirical approach to an accurate reflection of the past may be quite different. My interest in autobiographies of sports commentators was born of a desire to understand the history of sports broadcasting from within, by those that were there and are, in effect, providing an "insider" account of their daily working lives. A key aspect of autobiographical writing, then, is the interpretation of events from the perspective of the individual. The value of this approach to the past is that autobiography puts some flesh on the bones of key events, enlivened by human experience rather than dry, institutional, broad-brush strokes of history. Through a filtered narrative of the past we can therefore share intimate moments and feelings of what it was like to be at the BBC's first-ever sports broadcast[14] or be part of the team behind the coverage of the 1966 World Cup Finals.[15] The use of autobiography with respect to providing a human face and existential emphasis on the past does, however, require some careful consideration. There are two sides to every story (and sometimes many more), and the authenticity, credibility, and sincerity of any autobiographical story needs to be scrutinized carefully and corroborated by other empirical evidence where possible. There is also the need to take account of the fact that written autobiography is a retelling, or renarration, of memories that in most cases have been previously told in conversations, interviews, or speeches, and have been reshaped to fit the genre of biographical writing required by a publisher. Memories are therefore part of a longer narrative process, possibly narrativized many times before in different forms, but nevertheless recounted in autobiography as a highly polished version of a particular memory.[16]

Biography clearly has a place in historical research. The history of kings and queens, statesmen, and explorers accounts for a significant proportion of work in the field. But this particular brand of historiography—often referred to as the "great men of history" approach—has rightfully come under sustained attack for its narrow discourse on the past, which is biased in terms of its representation of class, gender, and ethnicity, as well as for suffering from a lack of reflexivity about the process of "doing history." Similarly, the claims to historical accuracy and authenticity that attach themselves to memoir and autobiography have been critiqued for the ways in which they claim authority for the explanation of the social world through the self. Here, poststructuralist critiques of the author suggest that all autobiography is a process of mediation, of the individual and the environment in which they live.[17] Crucially, autobiography is a process of remembering, which is refracted through memory, an activity that for most people is at best patchy and is always interpreted through a particular point of view. The personal narrative of memoir is always discursive and structured by the ideologies that inform the writer's thoughts at the moment of reflection and interpretation. It is a way of structuring or organizing time, and it establishes causality and continuity. The autobiographical narrative is also structured as much by what is forgotten as by what is remembered. Narrativizing memory also entails the use of literary conventions and devices, many of which are drawn from fiction and the creative drive to tell a good story of one's life. This is especially apparent when autobiographers expand on personal experience to represent the universal characteristics of social and cultural life. As Gunnthorunn Gudmunsdottir has noted:

> As the individual autobiographer writes on universal experiences, such as mother-daughter relationships, experiences of crossing cultures, or the death of a parent, he or she has to deal with the universal structure of these experiences. Universal structures necessarily contain a component deriving from conventions of representation, so they are in some sense always already 'made-up.'[18]

This point has resonance when autobiographies of broadcasters reflect on the institutional history of broadcasting or, in some cases, the evolution of a genre. Many of the works published by broadcasters between the 1940s and the 1960s were written prior to any systematic research into or academic theory about broadcasting and would not have benefited from critical analytical thought on the role and place of broadcasting in society.

Understanding the pioneering years of broadcasting in the 1930s, '40s, and '50s demands investigation of the complex ways in which the institutional aspects of broadcasting formalized new and innovative ways of communicating with an audience that, at the same time, had a wider bearing on the role of broadcasting in British popular culture and everyday life. As has been well theorized and empirically researched, the audience plays as much a role in our understanding of broadcast communication as does our analysis of the structure of broadcasting and the messages it delivers. The underlying aim of contemporary audience research is to understand the meaning of media representations to the audience; how their perceptions are associated with key media signifiers, and how they connect these representations with their lives. In the context of broadcast sports, audiences play a key social role in making sense of audio-visual representations of sports, and crucially, through prolonged exposure to the genre, develop a vernacular to critically examine its quality. In relation to the institutional memories of commentators, how might one possibly get an historical perspective on this process from an autobiography?

One answer is to review what commentators say about the audience when explaining their work. For example, it is well documented that during the early years of radio outside broadcasts from sports, the commentator gained assistance from some unlikely sources—namely a blind man sitting next to him as he addressed the audience. Such techniques were refined over time to allow the commentator to frame the broadcast for the audience, bringing them to the action, positioning them at the scene.[19] A longitudinal analysis of autobiographies provides some insight into how such practices evolved and, through trial and error, gained institutional status.

Autobiography as Literature

Finally, autobiography and biography can be viewed as literary works. As a literary pursuit, the writing of autobiography has particular traits and generic conventions, and the texts of sports commentators are no different in this respect. As long as autobiographies remain popular with an audience, they will continue to be written, and in terms of sports biography, the market is significant. The connection between writer and audience is therefore paramount, and any analysis of the sports commentator's autobiography needs to focus on this dynamic in order to understand why an autobiography is written and how a text is understood by its readership. The industrial process of producing autobiographies of well-known sports broadcasters certainly frames the form narrativized memories take. Indeed, the public notoriety or even celebrity status of a sports commentator is the *raison d'être* for publishing interest in the first place.

Any browse through the best-seller lists or Main Street bookstore reveals that autobiographies are enormously popular and occupy an important place in the publishing industry. There is even a niche television channel in the UK dedicated to biography, and a large part of historical documentary has a biographical focus (e.g., in 2010, BBC4 broadcast a documentary dedicated to the life of Rugby League commentator Eddie Waring). Autobiographies and biographies of sports commentators occupy an unusually privileged positioned on the bookstore shelves, alongside the biographies of sports stars, rather than the main biographical section or even the shelves earmarked for media and television. As an exercise in genre categorization, commentators' biographies sit uncomfortably alongside the biographies of the stars they are most likely to have commentated on. This is peculiar, as many commentators would view themselves as broadcasters and/or journalists rather than sports celebrities, yet their affiliation with sports is so overwhelming that their natural home is among the biographies of David Beckham or Wayne Rooney rather than celebrated BBC broadcast journalists like Jonathan Dimbleby or Jeremy Paxman. Of course, many commentators are increasingly ex-professional sportsmen (they are almost exclusively male) themselves, which may account for this categorization, but the majority are known to sports fans for their voice behind contemporary sports rather than the hazy days of their sporting past.

One possible outcome of such market categorization might be a suggestion that the autobiographical work of commentators is somehow "dumbed down" by the company they keep. Sports autobiography has a particular place as a sub-genre of biographical writing, with its own distinctive characteristics. Many sports autobiographies are ghostwritten, their subject matter is often inane and sensationalist, and they are clearly marketed at a predominantly male, nonliterary audience. The first of five planned autobiographical journeys by Wayne Rooney reflects this highly commercialized form of biographical sportswriting—dull for the most part, with a couple of sensationalistic "exclusives" for the serialized version in the tabloids. This kind of sportswriting might be more correctly named "hackiography" and has little literary merit. As the sportswriter and broadcaster John Arlott once remarked as he railed against the profusion of bland biographies often included in the "cricket library" of a friend and cricketing acquaintance:

> Again and again the 'library' consists of 'ghosted', so-called autobiographies of famous players, books so distressingly alike in matter, illustration and style that, merely by changing 'I' to 'he' and vice versa, whole chapters could be interchanged between them without anyone noticing the difference, for almost invariably they have been collected from identical news reports and reference books.[20]

In contradistinction, autobiographies of sports commentators are not ghostwritten, as many commentators are also seasoned journalists or writers, do not carry kiss-and-tell sensationalism, and tend to be more reflexive in their approach to both the individual's life story and their position in the worlds of broadcasting and sports—two related but wholly distinctive realms of experience. In this respect the reflections of commentators follow the dominant literary rhetoric of memoir—of the naked and transparent presentation of self. This process, of itself, suggests an egotistical motivation for writing an autobiography, a self-indulgence to tell the world just how interesting their lives have been. While this latter point may well be true in some cases, most autobiographies by sports broadcasters gain their purchase on the interest of the sports fan through their proximity to the stars, matches, and events they cover, and not necessarily because they move behind the scenes to reveal the practice of commentary itself. Commentators, then, tend to write their memoirs in the male autobiographical tradition—so redolent in sports culture per se.

One exception to this rule occurs when commentators, who also happen to be writers or journalists, use autobiography in different ways. In his semiautobiographical exposé of the snooker world, *Black Farce and Cue Ball Wizards*, former player, journalist, and commentator Clive Everton lambasted the greedy and entertainment-focused nature of the game, which came to be more about power and politics than the sport itself.[21] As longstanding editor of the magazine *Snooker Scene*, Everton places himself in the middle of snooker politics, and his autoethnographic history of post–World War II snooker captures a powerful sense of power struggles and corruption at the heart of the sport.

John Arlott's autobiography, *Basingstoke Boy*, is written in the third person, thereby producing a sense of distance from himself as the object of his attention. The use of the third person gives the book a degree of the fictional—explaining a person's life as if it were not his, the writing of the past dislocated from, but informed by, lived experience. Arguably many novels are autobiographical, and in this instance the autobiography uses literary devices of fiction to conjure up an image of the past. Arlott's reflections on life and his career as a journalist and broadcaster reveal much of the style and craft for which he is renowned. Among other things, Arlott was a poet before succeeding George Orwell as the BBC's literary producer. He counted Dylan Thomas and John Betjeman as close friends—and his movement in literary circles clearly influenced his writing and commentary on sports, skills he put to evocative use in his autobiography. In this sense his autobiography poetically mirrors the poetic visions he conjured up during his commentaries. *Basingstoke Boy* carries with it a trace of Arlott's "creative impulse" as well as a description of the content of his life, confessed and interpreted in Arlott's inimitable voice. Typically, Arlott's own introduction to his autobiography ponders on the process of writing it, a rare and conscious effort at self-reflexivity:

> This is an introduction to an attempt to look at the life of a man who, in general, enjoyed it, through his own eyes, but in the third person. Perhaps, too much reading of autobiographies, and other 'personal' writings, fostered a dislike of the use of the first person. Far too much writing appeared to suffer from the intrusive 'I'; which seemed often to infect it with conceit, self-satisfaction or, far more rarely, an almost equally unhappy mock modesty. That produced a personal resolution, some twenty or more years ago, to discontinue its use completely.[22]

Apparently, various sub-editors had replaced the first person, but Arlott remained resolute against the judgment of literary friends to continue with writing about himself in the third person, instead referring to himself as J.A. throughout the book.

The question of why a commentator writes an autobiography is partly answered through its commercial potential but also with a desire to show the "man" behind the microphone, to regard their careers as stories worth telling. Autobiographical narratives of commentators configure the protonarratives of their personal and professional lives—unifying their lived experience. Characteristically, most commentators choose to plot their lives both in connection with a series of key life changes—from school to university to first job to career in broadcasting, etc.—and also with key affective moments that provide emotional landmarks in their story. These may include personal feelings of success or failure in commentary or, commonly, reactions to great sporting moments or achievements they have witnessed. For some, it may also reflect on personal trauma that has shaped their working lives. In the context of understanding the history of broadcasting, these reflections on the emotional charge of sports and commentary are important. They are valuable because emotional autobiographical narratives convey possible truths that connect the "fictive" process of writing biography with the ontological being of lived experience and consciousness. Although postmodern critiques of autobiography emphasize the collapse of referential and fictional discourse in the narrative that is spun to recall a person's life, we can nevertheless draw some grounded historical findings from within the pages of a commentator's memoir.

Of course, these three analytical frames should not be viewed separately. They are connected in various empirical and theoretical ways. Literary approaches to autobiography that try to open up and interpret the text clearly have connections with the historiographic methods of interpretation, particularly in relation to understanding the experiential aspects of biographical writing and what they actually mean. Similarly, the epistemological understanding of autobiography in both history and sociology share a sense that we can never fully know an individual's past and his or her social environment, but in using biographical research we can at least be reflexive enough to accept its power to inform us about the past and an individual's sense of self, as well as guarding us against its limitations. In this way we can inform our understanding of the history of sports broadcasting from an interdisciplinary base.

Knowing the World of Broadcast Sports

I now want to apply this critical understanding of the usefulness of some specific autobiographical accounts of working in broadcast sports to its broader social history. For the audience, entry into this world of sports broadcasting works on a couple of populist levels. The first, common to most people who listen to sports on the radio or watch it on television, is the self-referential discourse broadcasting frequently uses to retell the history of sports itself. Sports broadcasting is often the leading exponent of revealing its past, reveling in the great sporting occasions of the past, glorious memories of leading sports stars, and even eulogizing the special moments of commentary by sports commentators who are often referred to as "household names." Whether it be Kenneth Wolstenholme's climactic comments to the 1966 World Cup Final or David Coleman's high-pitched crescendo at the end of the famous races between Sebastian Coe and Steve Ovett during the 1980 Olympic Games, television's version of the history of sports is in fact the history of televised sports itself. As Garry Whannel points out regarding televised sports more generally, the histories of sports—and the biographies of sports stars that form the cast of characters in great sporting events—are constantly retold in the present.[23]

This self-referentiality of televised sports is important for our understanding of how the history of sports is told and how it positions the audience to understand what the most important events of the nation's sporting past actually are. The "great moments of sports" also have a profound impact on the narratives of sports commentators. In some cases, like that of Wolstenholme, the commentary becomes the epitaph of their careers; reference to his commentary is used in the title of his own autobiography, and a whole chapter is given over to the event and his role in it.[24] Such episodes can take on their own wider resonance in popular culture; for example, a British 1990s sports game show also took Wolstenholme's immortalized lines from the 1966 Final, "They think it's all over," for its title. The second connection the audience has with the history of sports broadcasting is through the autobiographies of the commentators themselves as a particular breed of celebrity. Arguably, sports commentators are not celebrities at all. But since the 1990s, as a number of the more high-profile sports broadcasters have retired, or in some cases died, their stories as individuals within broadcasting and sports have caught the interest of the public in whose eyes (or, more correctly, ears) they are synonymous with their dominant consumption of sports—via television. Indeed a roll call of recent autobiographical works by British commentators is enough to suggest that sports broadcasting memoirs are a sub-genre all their own: Dan Maskell from tennis, Murray Walker from car racing, Bill McLaren from rugby union, Archie MacPherson, Brian Moore, Kenneth Wolstenholme, Alan Green, Barry Davies, and John Motson from football (soccer), Peter Alliss from golf, Brian Johnston, Richie Benaud, Henry Blofeld, and Peter Baxter from cricket, Michael O'Hehir from horse racing and Gaelic sports, Sid Waddell from darts, and Des Lynam, the former BBC and ITV sports anchorman.[25] When one adds recent autobiographies of former professional sports stars who have reflected on their new careers in broadcasting as pundits and analysts—including former soccer players Andy Gray and Alan Hansen, former managers Jimmy Armfield and Ron Atkinson, former England cricket captains Mike Atherton and Nasser Hussain, and former athlete Roger Black, to name but a few—the amount of biographical material on sports broadcasters is significant.[26] This spate of autobiographies is not without cause—most of the household names listed above (with the exception of Blofeld and Green, who emerged in radio during the 1980s) began their careers in the 1950s and '60s when, in its infancy, televised sports first found its feet. The longevity of their careers is testament to the particular professional culture of broadcast sports and the manner in which each exponent of the "dark art" (as Brian Johnston once called it) became synonymous with the sport they covered. There is poignancy in the timing of their broadcasting memoirs: the 1990s augured in a new era of broadcast sports, where subscription channels came to dominate the rights to major sporting events, particularly soccer, and the opportunities for older voices of sports to speak began to dwindle as their traditional home in terrestrial televised sports capitulated to market forces. The retirement of key names such as McLaren, Benaud, and Walker brought with them gushing plaudits from within broadcasting and the sporting press, and their autobiographies topped the nonfiction charts.

How the two popular narratives of sports broadcasting connect, inform, and conflict with each other—in other words, the linkage between the individual and the collective narratives of sports broadcasting histories—is the challenge ahead in thinking both conceptually and empirically about historical narratives and memory. I want to provide some brief examples of this, first by asking the question, how do people become sports commentators, and who are they? And secondly, what evidence is there for recognizing continuities and transformations in sports broadcasting and its practices?

Early Careers in BBC Sports

Careers in sports broadcasting hold a particular fascination because so few people hold such positions, and yet many more feel they could do a better job. In recognition of wider public envy of a career watching sports, numerous commentators readily acknowledge their professional good fortune, leading one of the most celebrated "voices of sport," cricket commentator John Arlott, to admit, "Not one of us, I am sure, would change his job for any other."[27] This raises questions of how commentators and presenters get into the industry and what skills and training are required. Moreover, once established, how are such careers developed and sustained, and how do they come to an end? What follows is a brief snapshot of key career moments from the autobiographies of some of the earliest to most recent commentators and sports presenters at the BBC. My selection focuses on experiences of recruitment into the industry and the nervous first broadcast.

Captain H. B. T. Wakelam gave the first running sports commentary for the BBC. By any reckoning, he is a true pioneer of outside broadcasting in this respect. His autobiography, *Half-Time: The Mike and Me*, is divided into two halves, much like the game of rugby union he principally covered between 1927 and 1939. In its schematic divide, prebroadcasting and during his broadcasting career, the book is organized as a metaphor for how he saw this change in his life and how it affected the way he thought about himself. His story before 1927 is one of middle-class upbringing in London, then preparatory boarding school before being educated at Marlborough and finally Cambridge, where he got his "blue" in rugby and cricket. The remainder of the first "half" of the book is given over to Wakelam's career in the army, but even here many of the anecdotes are given over to sporting achievements or acquaintances. The memories of school friends and masters, fellow soldiers, and acquaintances are typical of Edwardian and post-Edwardian middle-class male life. It was the kind of life that built up networks and contacts that meant something in terms of culture and stature. And it was Wakelam's standing as a well-known amateur rugby player with Harlequins and his authoritative position as a captain and First World War veteran that attracted the producer Lance Sieveking to phone him in January 1927, just more than one week before the BBC's first OB (outside broadcast) from sports—the international between England and Wales at Twickenham.

This route into commentary, from being a former player or professional and considered a known authority on a sport is a familiar pattern throughout the history of sports broadcasting. The tension between being an expert in broadcasting or an expert in sports has long been a topic of debate among BBC producers. Former sports performers or officials turned commentators such as Wakelam (rugby union), George Allison (soccer), Harold Abrahams (athletics), or W. Barrington Dalby (boxing) in the 1930s, through to Peter O'Sullivan (horse racing), Peter Alliss (golf), Richie Benaud (cricket), or Ted Lowe (snooker) through the 1950s and 1960s onward, or a whole host of contemporary sports commentators, presenters, and pundits, illustrates one particular route into broadcasting, born of expertise in sports and application to broadcasting. On the other hand, a long line of post–World War II BBC commentators such as Rex Alston, Raymond Glendenning, Brian Johnston, Max Robertson, Kenneth Wolstenholme, David Coleman, Harry Carpenter, Barry Davies, and many more, had backgrounds in journalism and applied the professional ideologies of reporting to sports broadcasting, with all of them applying their generic techniques to a range of sports rather than just one.

Underlying this tension of entry into sports broadcasting is the criticism that ex-sports stars become mere "cheerleaders" for a sport. They are perceived as lacking journalistic instinct for a good story.[28] There is also the sense that the cult of celebrity has much to do with who is employed in televised sports. In a mini-autobiography, *Life's New Hurdles*, giving an account of his movement from retirement from elite sports to a new career in broadcasting, former athlete and hurdling World Champion, Colin Jackson reveals some of the jealousy he felt on joining the BBC:

> Some people thought I was getting work in television because of my name, not what I had achieved. But I have worked hard to get where I am and I have worked hard to establish my name. So if my name now opens doors, there is nothing wrong with that. That's the way of the world. I'm not going to be embarrassed about it.[29]

Jackson's determination to make his new career work led him to seek intense training on broadcast techniques, even down to instruction on what clothes to wear in front of the camera. But his comments also reveal something about a closeted world of contemporary employment in sports broadcasting, where access to prestigious jobs are heavily guarded and available only to a select few, most with ready-made star status from their sporting careers. This contrasts with the formative era of sports commentary, where other networks and criteria seemed to apply.

For those not fortunate enough to draw on former careers in sports, social networks, opportunism, and chance were significant reasons for entry into the industry. With growing public demand for outside broadcasts from sports and the reintroduction of the BBC's television service in 1948, there were opportunities for new recruits to get a foothold in broadcasting. Many of the producers and commentators who joined the BBC after the Second World War were ex-servicemen looking for a new career. Kenneth Wolstenholme recounts in his autobiography that he had served in the RAF Bomber Command, but a chance meeting with a wartime colleague at Villa Park football ground set in train an assignment as a sports journalist, swiftly followed by an invitation to record a talk on cricket for the BBC in Manchester, which precipitated an opportunity to take a commentary test, and by 1949 he became the principal voice of televised football (soccer), a role he kept until 1971.[30] Peter West, who went on to become a versatile BBC commentator and presenter of sports, as a young sports journalist, was given an introduction to BBC management by the famous Edwardian amateur sportsman C. B. Fry after sitting next to him in a press box. According to West, Fry, a highly respected figure in both sports and British media, "had spent much of his life giving young men a push up the ladder."[31] His luck in sitting next to Fry that day kick-started a forty-year career in sports broadcasting. In the context of developing a career in television, both stories serve to illustrate the fortuity of being in the right place at the right time, as well as the perspicacity to grab an opportunity when presented. The autobiographical reflections on these lucky twists of fate are also delivered generously toward those who intervened, as life could have been so different if such events had not taken place.

Perhaps because of the unconventional nature of entry into the industry and the lack of formal qualifications for doing such a job, many commentators recount the stress and nausea brought on by early commentaries and performances. Wakelam talks of a "most remarkable internal reactive flood" due to his unease at broadcasting to an "unseen and unheard" audience. His explanation for the stress: "you can never tell how many of those who started in to hear you out are now fast asleep and possibly snoring."[32] Rex Alston, who joined the BBC in 1942, described his first solo cricket commentary as "extremely nervous," again due to the stress of his imagined audience which, after the first day's play, kept him awake "tossing and turning throughout the night" and causing him to turn to a sedative for the remainder of his first week as a commentator to ensure a good night's sleep. The anecdote, Alston reports, is used "merely to illustrate the acute tension which a Commentator undergoes, especially in the early days."[33] Indeed, the admission of a sense of stress and nervousness aroused through live sports broadcasting is apparent in most autobiographies. Long-time BBC rugby commentator Bill McLaren admitted he never lost that sense of anxiety: "I was always quaking until I heard the producer say, 'Cue Bill', but as soon as I opened my mouth, I was fine.."[34] The threat of nerves continues to have an impact on new broadcasters, even on those used to being in front of the camera. Colin Jackson's first role as the BBC's roving reporter during the London Marathon in 2004 left him feeling "petrified": "I have no idea what I said or if it made sense. I must have spoken three thousand words in ten seconds because I was so wound up."[35] The continuities of emotional experience of sports commentators are interesting to note, especially given the proliferation of media in contemporary culture, where sports coverage is commonplace and the technologies more complex.

Commentary Technique

Technological transformations in the coverage of sports have certainly changed the relationships between sports and broadcasting, and one might also expect techniques of commentary to differ from the pioneering era of the inter-War period through to the latter half of the twentieth century as the media–sport relationship matured. However, evidence from autobiography suggests that some techniques and considerations of the pioneers have longevity. Wakelam describes how the producer Lance Sieveking used a deaf war veteran who sat in front of the commentator's box so that he could explain the game directly to him. This engendered a conversational style in the commentator's mode of address, a characteristic that cast the listener as "companion" to the commentator as the narration of play unfolded.[36] Contemporary radio commentary is arguably more sophisticated in its use of language, but as Tolson suggests in his analysis of contemporary football broadcasts, "radio offers its listeners an imaginary identification with ideal spectators."[37] From its very humble and rudimentary beginnings, commentators clearly understood this problem and found innovative techniques to achieve this effect.

Similar accounts of the impact of either technological change or developments in the "art of commentary" can be found in most of the autobiographies. Henry Longhurst—heralded as one of the pioneers of television commentary—retraces the early years of televising golf and, in the following two anecdotes, manages to impress how arrangements for the commentator changed as it was realized that for the commentator the view from the monitor was of far more value than the view of the course:

> In 1955, when the art itself was making progress but before the days when commentators were held to be human, we were struck up on a tall and precarious tower behind the 17th, open to all the elements. The wind howled, the rain lashed across the links, our scant piece of waterproof protection was whisked off and fetched up in Meols Drive, and the score-keeping apparatus, already mottled with running ink of ball-point pens, eventually became so sodden that when you tried to turn the page it simply peeled off.[38]

However, as the BBC began to position more cameras with greater economy, focusing on the inward holes, and thereby ensuring that none of the leading competitors were missed, the role of the commentator changed. Longhurst continues:

> It was also realised, as was really known all along, that the commentator need not be able to see what he was talking about, since his first task is to watch the monitor, the cardinal sin being to talk about something the viewer cannot see, thus driving the latter into absolute frenzies of frustration. Thus at last we began to be pitched nearer the clubhouse rather than miles out on the course, and up only one ladder, and the hand of civilisation was extended towards us in the shape of little glass boxes to sit in.[39]

All golf commentary is now done "off-tube" in this way. Longhurst's brief narrative of how this came about reveals the way in which enhancing the role of the commentator became a matter of trial and error, but based around some core principles. Being able to present the listener or viewer with an accurate—"realist"—representation of events has long been a powerful professional ideology of sports broadcasting. The autobiographical memories of sports broadcasters reconfirm this process, albeit in more anecdotal and witty discourse.

Conclusion

Memoirs of a life in broadcasting therefore tell us a specific story, a personalized point of view. They are selective and often nostalgic. They usually follow a preconditioned narrative path from childhood to manhood—in this sense, writing a narrowly focused his-story. In the context of sports commentators, they are often boastful of sporting acquaintances and myopic in their recognition that although they may have been the voice behind a particular sport, how their words formed part of an institutionalized discourse—mediated through the work of technicians, producers, and editors—and how a commentator's words are received by the audience, are rarely acknowledged.

In this chapter I have simply wanted to suggest that autobiographies of broadcasting elites—like commentators—can be used sympathetically toward empirically informed histories of broadcasting. By "histories" I am recognizing the argument that biographical accounts give a particular view of the past—some may corroborate with other data, and others do not. Nevertheless, they should be recognized as being based on experience through the refracted lens of memory and nostalgia. There are words of warning, however. Using autobiography for historical research demands several analytical filters. I have suggested three, which I think are central: social theory, critical historiography, and literary theory. There may be others not mentioned here, but I think these are the most important.

In using autobiography in this way, the analysis is bound to become biographical itself. In other words, researchers must use their interpretative skills to make sense of the autobiographical text and then make a biography or biographies themselves—creating a new narrative from existing narratives. Arguably, the autobiography of a sports commentator reflects the era in which it was written. As the biographical genre changes over time, so the discursive frame in which autobiographical work is written also guides its hand. Therefore, autobiographies of Wakelam, Allison, and Glendenning, written in the 1930s to 1950s, have a similar voice—assuredness brought by Oxbridge education and matter-of-factness brought by regimentation in the armed forces and the Corinthean values of sport, untainted by the rise of heavy commercialization in the 1960s. On the other hand, contemporary autobiographies of Alliss, Benaud, and Walker are more nostalgic for a Corinthian age, while at the same time imbued with the need for high entertainment values, a necessary aspect of biographical work in the competitive environs of contemporary publishing. Autobiographies therefore present some complex methodological issues, our understanding of which can be illuminated by theories of life writing and other probing questions of truth posed by historiography. Nevertheless, in searching for a way of understanding how the generic form of sports broadcasting has been culturally transformed, autobiography does provide a rich seam of information, albeit encoded in the institutional, social, and cultural circumstances in which they are written.

Notes

1. George Allison, *Allison Calling: A Galaxy of Football and Other Memories* (London: Staples Press, 1948), 37.
2. Garry Whannel, *Field in Vision: Televised Sport and Cultural Transformation* (London: Routledge, 1991); David Rowe, *Sport, Culture and the Media* (Milton Keynes: Open University Press, Second Edition, 2003); and Raymond Boyle and Richard Haynes, *Power Play: Sport, the Media and Popular Culture* (Edinburgh: Edinburgh University Press, Second Edition, 2009).
3. Andrew Crissell, *Understanding Radio* (London: Routledge, 1994).
4. Andrew Tolson, *Media Talk: Discourse on TV and Radio* (Edinburgh: Edinburgh University Press, 2004), 111.
5. For a general history, see Asa Briggs, *The History of Broadcasting in the United Kingdom: Volume IV: Sound and Vision* (Oxford: Oxford University Press, 1978); for specific analysis of televised sports see Stephen Barnett, *Games and Sets: The Changing Face of Sport on Television* (London: BFI Publishing, 1990), and Whannel, *Fields in Vision*.
6. Michael Bailey, ed., *Narrating Media History* (London: Routledge, 2008).
7. Geoffrey Cubitt, *History and Memory* (Manchester: Manchester University Press, 2007), 14.
8. Liz Stanley, *The Auto/Biographical I: Theory and Practice in Feminist Auto/Biography* (Manchester: Manchester University Press, 1992).
9. Prue Chamberlayne, Joanna Bornat, and Tom Wengraf, eds., *The Turn to Biographical Methods in Social Science Comparative Issues and Examples* (New York: Routledge, 2000).
10. Brian Roberts, *Biographical Research* (Milton Keynes: Open University Press, 2001).
11. Ibid., 15.
12. Asa Briggs, *The History of Broadcasting in the United Kingdom: Volume I: The Birth of Broadcasting* (Oxford: Oxford University Press, 1961).
13. Roberts, *Biographical Research*, 88.
14. H. B. T. Wakelam, *Half Time! The Mike and Me* (London: Thomas Nelson, 1938).
15. Alec Weeks, *Under Auntie's Skirts: The Life and Times of a BBC Sports Producer* (Brighton: Guild Publishing, 2006).
16. Cubit, *History and Memory*, 16.
17. Julia Swindells, ed., *The Uses of Autobiography* (London: Taylor and Francis, 1995).

18. Gunnthorunn Gudmundsdóttir, ed., *Borderlines: Autobiography and Fiction in Postmodern Life Writing* (Amsterdam: Rodopi, 2003), 6.
19. Tolson, *Media Talk*.
20. John Arlott, cited in David Rayvern Allen, ed., *The Essential John Arlott: Forty Years of Classic Cricket Writing* (Brighton: Guild Publishing, 1989), 266.
21. Clive Everton, *Black Balls and Cue Ball Wizards: The Inside Story of the Snooker World* (Edinburgh: Mainstream Publishing, 2007).
22. John Arlott, *Basingstoke Boy: The Autobiography* (London: Willow Books, 1990), ix.
23. Garry Whannel, *Media Sports Stars: Masculinities and Moralities* (London: Routledge, 2001).
24. Kenneth Wolstonholme, *50 Years . . . And It's Still Not All Over* (London: Robson Books, 1999).
25. Dan Maskell, *Oh I Say!* (London: Fontana Press, 1989); Murray Walker, *Murray Walker: Unless I'm Very Much Mistaken* (London: Willow, 2002); Bill McLaren, *My Autobiography: The Voice of Rugby* (London: Bantam, 2004); Archie MacPherson, *Action Replays* (Edinburgh: Chapman Publishing, 1991); Archie MacPherson, *A Game of Two Halves: The Autobiography* (London: Black and White Publishing, 2009); Brian Moore, *The Final Score: The Autobiography of the Voice of Football* (London: Hodder and Staunton, 1999); Alan Green, *The Green Line: Views From Sport's Most Outspoken Commentator* (London: Headline, 2000); Barry Davies, *Interesting, Very Interesting: The Autobiography* (London: Headline, 2007); John Motson, *Motty: Forty Years in the Commentary Box* (London: Virgin Books, 2009); Peter Alliss, *Peter Alliss: My Life* (London: Hodder, 2004); Brian Johnston, *Another Slice of Johnners*, ed. Barry Johnston (London: Virgin, 2002); Richie Benaud, *My Spin on Cricket* (London: Hodder and Staunton, 2005); Henry Blofeld, *A Thirst For Life: With the Accent on Cricket* (London: Coronet, 2001); Peter Baxter, *Inside the Box: My Life With Test Match Special* (London: Aurum, 2009); Michael O'Hehir, *Life and Times of Michael O'Hehir* (Dublin: Blackwood Press, 1996); Sid Waddell, *Bellies and Bullseyes: The Outrageous Story of Darts* (London: Ebury, 2007); and Desmond Lynam, *I Should Have Been At Work* (Edinburgh: HarperCollins, 2003).
26. Andy Gray, *Gray Matters: The Autobiography* (London: Macmillan, 2004); Alan Hansen, *A Matter of Opinion* (London: Partridge Press, 1999); Jimmy Armfield, *Jimmy Armfield, The Autobiography: Right Back at the Beginning* (London: Headline, 2004); Ron Atkinson, *Big Ron: A Different Ball Game* (London: Andre Deutsch, 1998); Mike Atherton, *Opening Up: My Autobiography* (London: Coronet, 2003); Nasser Hussain, *Playing With Fire: The Autobiography* (London: Michael Joseph, 2004); and Roger Black, *How Long's The Course?* (London: Andre Deutsch, 1998).
27. John Arlott, "Televised Cricket," in Brian Johnston, ed., *Armchair Cricket 1968* (London: BBC, 1968), 25.
28. Raymond Boyle, *Sports Journalism: Context and Issues* (London: Sage, 2006).
29. Colin Jackson, *Life's New Hurdles* (London: Accent, 2008), 39.
30. Wolstonholme, *50 years . . .*, 78.
31. Peter West, *Flannelled Fool and Muddied Oaf: An Autobiography* (London: Star, 1987), 44.
32. Wakelam, *Half Time*, 204.
33. Rex Alston, *Taking the Air* (London: Stanley Paul, 1951), 51.
34. McLaren, *My Autobiography*, 207.
35. Jackson, *Life's New Hurdles*, 42.
36. Crissell, *Understanding Radio*.
37. Tolson, *Media Talk*, 112.
38. Henry Longhurst, *My Life and Soft Times* (Edinburgh: HarperCollins, 1983), 258.
39. Ibid., 259.

III

Claims Based on Narratives versus Official History

10

The "Book of Us": Will and Community in South African Land Restitution

Christiaan Beyers

Charmaine: If I could write a book, of my own life! (. . .)

Teresa: You don't need to write a book, Charmaine, you just . . . you just rewind the cassette.

How to represent traumatic experiences of dispossession is a question not just for anthropologists, oral historians, or other expert researchers; it is first posed in the testimonies they collect and study. For people[1] who were forcibly displaced by the apartheid and colonial regimes, "community" is central to answering this question, especially as they currently lay claim to land in post-apartheid South African restitution. The Commission for the Restitution of Land Rights explicitly prioritizes claims where there is strong evidence of the existence of a unified and mobilized "community," and considers oral testimony admissible evidence for the process of mounting legal claims. The idea of doing justice in land restitution is thus strongly associated with narratives that invoke an emotionally charged sense of "community" as a basis for claiming rights. Of course such narratives extend far beyond legal parameters, and underscore wider notions of group identity, moral entitlement, and social citizenship. In highly publicized cases such as District Six—the focus of the present chapter—a

---

* I am grateful to Gabrielle S. MacIntire for comments on an earlier version of this chapter.

substantial body of literature has emerged, which interrelates dialogically with ongoing oral testimony to create a rich discursive context for narrating and contesting collective identity and entitlement.

Located in the center of Cape Town on the slopes of Devil's Peak and overlooking the harbor, District Six has become an infamous symbol of the injustice of apartheid. The majority of its estimated 60,000 residents were forcibly removed between 1968 and 1982, as its buildings were gradually demolished. Its residents were scattered all over the Cape Flats—a vast peripheral area of the city—thus breaking up social networks, friendships, and families. Most did not see much of their former neighbors again until the land restitution meetings. Restitution thus involved a coming together after a long period of absence. It also meant bringing forth latent suffering. In particular, testimonials sought to bring largely private, internalized experiences of loss and pain into public spaces, before the eyes of officials, politicians, lawyers, journalists, and researchers like myself—all with privileged access to the means of representation. Furthermore, former residents shared their testimonials with others who had been forcibly displaced in Cape Town, and even when speaking in their absence, often addressed them. This suggests a basic hypothesis: Community, as a collective project of memory and restitution, is morally constituted through co-testimony.

This chapter focuses on the intersubjective and dialogical aspects of testimonial narratives in the context of collective projects aimed at achieving restitution. How do testimonial interviews work to posit a commonality of experience and feeling in the face of a historical rupture of a life-together, and thereby frame collective entitlement to public space? I attempt to move beyond constructivist approaches to identity, focusing instead on how individual will comes to be expressed as collective form in narrative. I contend that testimonial narratives by victims of forced removals are most fundamentally about restoring agency, which is understood as the ability to exercise volition in the sphere of speaking and narrating trauma and, more generally, in determining the course of one's life. I also suggest that understanding how will and volition determine narrative form is central to the analysis of how "constructions" such as community arise within testimonial interviews. A sense of community is not merely a preconstituted object of a discourse of identity, as it is commonly treated in social constructivist approaches; it also arises from the way in which, in the words of Marc Bloch, "we incorporate the experience of a multitude of others along with our own"[2] when "we" produce eyewitness accounts of the past. Solidarity is thus performed as the expanded remit of an utterance; it is about exercising will and intention in the way in which we arrange remembered occurrences into a more or less coherent narrative, enlisting the company of some and not of others. Unlike the factual evidence ushered by legal truth-claims, the testimonial narratives studied here invoke connectedness, belonging, and dialogue itself—"evidence" of a moral kind, if you will.

This chapter will focus on a conversation occurring in a group interview with four former residents of District Six. This enables an analysis of the co-production of meaning and identity within immediate person-to-person dialogue. Moreover, I study how the conversation calls upon and refers to absent others to address not only myself as interviewer within the active role that I play in the discussion, but also a wider public. The conversation eventually comes to center upon an autobiographical text from District Six, thus explicitly widening the dialogical frame of reference. This brings the process of co-testimony to a point of collective self-reflection, as interviewees consider how most justly to represent their remembered experiences of community life. I suggest that their very line of interrogation of the limits of autobiographical form is itself highly revealing of dilemmas inherent in the practice of oral testimony in the case of land restitution; in particular, it poses questions of how to represent what happened to "community" in the wake of its violent disintegration, and how to do so from a domain of socioeconomic marginality and from within the generally disenfranchised realm of oral cultural expression.

District Six

District Six has long been celebrated for its social heterogeneity, urbanity, and nonracial and egalitarian ethos before it was declared a "white group area" in 1966. It has become a preeminent space of remembrance since 1994, after the inauguration of the post-apartheid land restitution program for victims of forced removals, which promised vindication in the struggle for justice. As elsewhere in South Africa,[3] land restitution has been occasioned by a narrative of the loss of "community." Restitution is widely seen as affecting District Six's resurrection, not only in the redevelopment and resettlement of vacant land in the area, but in the form of a "collective project" around reviving something of the social fabric that is thought to have characterized the former area.

The broader project of restitution involves a field of cultural production that is firmly grounded in testimonials about the former District Six. District Six claims a substantial body of literature—much of it autobiographical—as well as academic histories and ethnographies that serve to archive testimonies, and artwork, theater, and music that depict life in the former neighborhood. Positioned at the center this field of cultural production is the well-known District Six Museum, founded just before the fall of apartheid. It is located on the edge of the now-demolished former neighborhood and has become a landmark among ex-residents and others in the city supporting their cause. Museum intellectuals have quite self-consciously sought to establish the museum as a gatekeeper for tourism, educational initiatives, and testimonial-based research. Testimonies by ex-residents continue to be recorded, certified, accredited, and archived by researchers and cultural entrepreneurs directly associated with the museum, as well as outsider researchers and journalists. This has given rise to considerable struggles for cultural authority, intellectual property, and symbolic capital.[4]

Indeed, it is not an exaggeration to say that testimonies and related autobiographical representations are the foundation for the post-apartheid cultural construction of District Six. More concretely, testimony is a central aspect of constituting the claimant group as a sociopolitical entity. Some of the ex-residents' first steps in becoming legal claimants are often marked by giving testimony. Thus claims forms encouraged narrative responses, and most applicants responded in kind. To the questions "Please give the reason for your claim (If you need more space please attach a separate page)" and "Other evidence to substantiate you claim," the majority responded emotionally about the "peaceful and happy life" in District Six and the pain, suffering, and grief wrought by their displacement. A large number attach an extended written narrative of several pages that resembles a brief life story.

More significantly, before and after the submission of claims forms, the restitution process has involved a series of meetings or reunions by former residents at which long-separated friends, acquaintances, and relatives find one another after many years of separation and recount stories to one another. These meetings have served as a basis for generating or consolidating collective memories of the "good old days," and of subsequent losses and struggles. In short, land restitution has encouraged the production of testimonies amongst District Sixers, thus generating a symbolic interiority based on shared memories. The sensibility engendered by co-testimony, in turn, frames a conviction in collective moral entitlement to restitution.

Paul Ricoeur observed that the intense production of testimonies by numerous witnesses who engage with one another can, under certain conditions, give rise to a distinct public space.[5] We have mentioned the physical manifestations of such space in forms such as meetings, reunions, and the museum; it also has a symbolic manifestation, the basis of which is the sense among claimants, as a group of witnesses, that their experiences of life in the former District Six and their subsequent forced displacement are, in some essential aspect, the same, and that their many testimonies are mutually supportive and trustworthy. As Ricoeur argues, if the core statements of testimony are "I was there" and "Believe me," testimonies often carry a parallel assertion of "If you don't believe me, ask others." In such cases, memory can become an institution because of, in Ricoeur's words,

> the stability of the testimony ready to be reiterated, and next the contribution of the trustworthiness of each testimony to the security of the social bond inasmuch as this rests on confidence in what other people say . . . The credit granted to the word of others makes the social world a shared intersubjective world.[6]

There are important questions about who participates in this institution, given sharp social, economic, and cultural differences among claimants. Except in the most extreme cases, the question is not one of absolute difference, but of the differential incorporation of certain voices. Poorer District Sixers are less likely to have submitted claims or to be able to afford the supplementary costs of resettlement. Furthermore, due to the history of racial segregation, people classified as "African" were historically marginalized and culturally excluded, in line with policies of influx control and labor preference to "coloreds" in Cape Town and in the western Cape region. "Africans" thus had to maintain a low profile in the city, as their presence was legally restricted to temporary laborers in jobs that could not be filled by "whites" or "coloreds." Moreover, their forced removals occurred before the official declaration of District Six as a "white group area" in 1966, and they were cast further to the periphery or outside of the city, and with less compensation, than their "colored," "Indian," and "white" neighbors. Their resulting poverty, substandard education, and social exclusion affect the extent to which they can competently participate in legal and symbolic domains.[7]

Will and Community

Why does will offer a privileged entry point to testimonials in District Six? In the first place, because a person's "will to choose" the course of his or her own life was often seen by my interviewees as the most basic capacity that was denied by forced removals and as the object of land restitution. If "choosing" is understood as being able exercise one's agency in a basic way, it is of course the most fundamental "right," without which any of the other rights do not mean much. As sixty-two-year-old Irene Jansen—who, at the age of thirty-nine, was "told to move"—says, "my right is defined through where I can stay, my democratic right is I am free to choose."[8] Taken in a broad way, volition may be seen as the essential basis for what is commonly called "self-determination" in the discourse of human rights, and is thus inherently linked to the concept of dignity. Shamil[9], a fifty-eight-year-old Muslim man, captures this idea:

> I felt devastated—I was still young—being removed, being displaced to another environment without having to make a choice, because I mean, human beings have a choice in life, I mean that is a human right, isn't it? And not having recourse to that choice, I think this was very criminal, was very painful to the people, you see. If look at the older people, I mean when they heard the news of this area, you could have seen the fear, and everything just sank.[10]

Although choice is ultimately to be exercised by the individual, it is seen as inherently about the individual's relation to others. Shamil interprets the denial of his own agency in the context of the suffering of others, and addresses the substance of his assertion to me as a rhetorical question that invites response. One might say that he reflexively performs a certain dialogic ethos that existed in the former District Six.

This is also clearly evident in the remarks of Abdurahman, a sixty-five-year-old Muslim man currently living in a middle-class area, who thematizes a broader sense of responsiveness to others as a prescription for the future. I asked him whether it will be worth the effort to rebuild the neighborhood in District Six, and he replied:

> Yes, just to remind people, that uh, *in ander woorde, jy moet nie vir jouself wees nie, jy moet wees vir een die ander ene.* You see [translating the foregoing], you don't live [for] yourself, you must live for one another. To see to one another's needs also. And to look after one another, even if they're sick—that's what happened in those years in District Six.[11]

For Abdurahman, restitution is about being able to exercise moral agency, which consists of carrying forth the memory of a time when the predominant ethic was putatively one of mutual care and support. Remembering is an active agency, by which one takes a stance in the present and anticipates the future through an aspiration: redevelopment is not merely about erecting buildings; it is to assert the integrity of a remembered ethos as a moral imperative, so that the state of people's future lives will *remind* them of how they were in the past. Memory is thus conceived as being at the center of a project to regenerate a new civic ethics.

Abdurahman's perspective is typical amongst "colored" District Six interviewees in particular, since they constituted the majority of residents, and the district was widely seen as a "colored space,"[12] in keeping with their relative privilege vis-à-vis Africans mentioned earlier. They commonly evoke a sense of "the spirit of District Six" by describing the general positive traits of "community" life. Many would affirm "the magical" quality of that time and place, a quality that had to be experienced to be fully understood. Rosemary Ridd, who did fieldwork in District Six in 1976 and 1978, remarked that "local people impressed upon me that the District Six area possessed a spirit which outsiders could not grasp. They said that they could not *tell* me about it, but that I could only experience it for myself."[13] Paradoxically, however, testimony demands that this spirit be told about—that it be translated for outsiders like her and myself. Ex-residents would seem to be saying that "the spirit" consists of a particular ethos of mutual support and mutual cultural enrichment, which is experienced as a social bond by those who share testimonials of it, and which may, to a certain extent, be experienced vicariously by outsiders. After Fatima—a thirty-three-year-old woman who was a child when her family moved—brought up the spirit of District Six in our interview, and I asked her whether it was still alive, she explained:

> Because you see, the spirit is not only in the place, it's in the people. And the people who left there have their memories, have their . . . Children were born, people got married. That will always be in their hearts and memories, you know. So I mean, the spirit will be back where the people are. You know, a house without people is nothing but a house. A house with people has spirit, has everything. You know. So I'm sure the spirit will still be there. Definitely.[14]

In a space characterized by the co-production of testimonials, appropriate witness is seen to consist of expressing something of how one was infused with the spirit that others are also bearing witness to, even after the physical manifestation of the neighborhood (or "house") was destroyed. Moreover, as an object of representation, community figures not merely as something of the past but as a meaningful horizon for an emerging future, in which personal struggles are socially and politically embodied in a project. Reference to the spirit thus manifests a principle of common faith and commitment. Testimony facilitates this simultaneously retrospective and projective process, because it is not just addressed to the immediate listener but also to a wider range of future listeners in the public domain.

These brief excerpts can be fruitfully employed to raise a further set of issues, which may be framed by setting up a dichotomy in terms of "evidence." Not surprisingly, land restitution law prefers clear-cut factual evidence that is legally documented, such as property deeds or other documented sources attesting to one's former residence in the District. In the absence of such documentation, oral testimony is allowed in tandem with affidavits from former neighbors, school teachers, church leaders, and so on, attesting to the fact that one resided in the District.[15] To the extent that the claimant's memory is relied upon, it is to extract factual data where the reliability of recall can be determined by cross-referencing it with the accounts of others or with other documentary evidence. The claimant's will and connection to others in community thus are of consequence only in the sense that they are instrumental to the production of valid evidentiary statements; the question is simply whether the claimant has decided to tell the truth. The influence of the evidentiary paradigm among claimants is revealed by interviewees frequently and spontaneously volunteering information such as the precise street address or addresses where they used to live, and the kind of documentation that they have to prove it.

One might, however, speak of another kind of "evidence" that corresponds to a different kind of truth-claim, which predominates in and structures the interviews, namely one's historical place in the city as a kind of moral and political right. This kind of evidence is properly narrative rather than factual in form, and attests to a sense of belonging or membership rather than ownership or residency. The individual's claim is seen as part of a broader claim of a community's right to exist. More precisely, such evidence invokes a property of relatedness, of having known such-and-such persons and been an integral part of their lives. Testimony is seen to consist not merely of the recall of an aggregate of isolated events or information; rather, it invokes an integral past where place and identity are mutually constitutive. Methodologically, such evidence relies on interpretive description of events and subjective experiences and is thus more episodic in nature—that is, it concerns phenomena that are defined by a time period and a context of relationships, histories, and emotional attachments and aversions. It is thus essential to the very production of such evidence that it is an interpretive act in which will is manifested relationally.

To be sure, these two kinds of evidence can overlap and interrelate in testimony and related popular discourse. This is illustrated by a man from District Six, well versed in its street culture—a member of the family that I lived with over many years of research—who on several occasions, and outside of the context of an interview, urged me to ask anyone who tells me that they are from District Six whether they knew of a certain well-known personality, a particular hangout spot, or what a certain colloquialism meant. If they did not know, he claimed, they were not from District Six. To be sure, this kind of "factual" information could not have been shared by all District Sixers; for example, some of the wealthier claimants that I interviewed, who had lived higher up on the mountain slope, saw the street culture as unrespectable—as pertaining to *skollies*(ruffians). But in a sense this is precisely the point: for my friend, being in the know attested to being a real District Sixer, that is, sharing in its majority street culture and social fabric.

Group Interview

I now turn to three moments of a group interview carried out in 2002 in order to flesh out the volitional and relational aspects of dialogical narrative form in the testimonial interview. The interview began as a prearranged meeting with a single respondent, whom we shall call Nweti. It took place where she lived in Guguletu, a township on the outskirts of Cape Town where most "African" District Sixers were relocated. Brayton, a friend who drove me to the location of the interview, and who has close family from District Six, accompanied me for the interview. When I arrived, Nweti decided to call her neighbors from the same street, who were also relocated from District Six. A second respondent arrived after about twenty minutes of interviewing Nweti, and thereafter two more arrived: Charmaine, Nomsa, and Teresa. The interview includes discussion of the autobiography *Sala Kahle, District Six: An African Woman's Perspective*,[16] to which we turn in the third moment. Here "justice" is framed not primarily in terms of obtaining restitution through a collective project of community restoration but rather in terms of a prior self-reflexive question: what a "book" that purports to speak for such a community ought to look like—i.e., what sort of representational form is capable of *doing justice to* the community in its quest for historical justice.

Building upon the theme of dialogue, my analysis of the interview below draws on the work of Mikhail Bakhtin, for whom dialogue—rather than individual consciousness as such—is always in the beginning; selves and others do not actually exist in any meaningful way except through dialogue with one another.[17] His work is useful because of his analysis of how speech, will, and a communal orientation play out in utterances within ongoing dialogue. Utterances express the subject's will as a decision manifesting a comprehensive value orientation in relation to the values of others—one that is emotional-volitional, rather than rational. Speech acts are thus born of "value-positing consciousness" within the "answerable" context of community norms; in other words, they bring cultural norms into play in a singular and unique address by a self to an other. Whenever one endeavors to say something, one begins by conceiving what one wishes to convey and how one will do it, thus determining the bounds of the utterance. But the utterance is not necessarily executed to its finality, as if by an original blueprint; the intonation and generic composition, as well as the content, may be creatively altered in the utterance's dialogic unfolding. In other words, the utterance's "addressivity"—its anticipation of an active response from a listener—helps to constitute it, and this opens it to the possibility of responsive modification.[18] Unlike a sentence or a word as a grammatical or lexical unit in itself, the utterance is a "unit of speech communication," and even of *"speech communion."*[19]

For Bakhtin, the will is finally evident as the speaker's or author's intention—refracted through the intentions of others—in the materiality of the utterance, which exists on the boundary between two consciousnesses, and constitutes them as speaker and listener, or writer and reader. Indeed, for Bakhtin (at least in his later work), dialogue is not even something that occurs primarily between subjects, but rather between their utterances, which interact and mutually condition one another in a process often referred to as *dialogism*.[20] As one Bakhtin scholar puts it, "Dialogism might be defined as the process of dialogue which is installed within the very semantics of discourse, organizing the word's meaning and performing its 'creative work on its referent'."[21] The concept's usefulness is in its ability to describe the responsive inter-relation between very diverse kinds of utterances, texts, languages, and discourses. In contrast to the concept of "intertextuality," as used in post-structuralist and semiotic analyses, Bakhtin's dialogism retains a concept of will at the center of the analysis. My study of the group interview aims to demonstrate how dialogue and dialogism in co-testimony produce a sense of collective agency, that is, invoke a group identity or sense of community by channeling will into the direction of a collective project of memory.

First Moment: Individual Testimony

The oral genre of the testimonial interview is closely related to the "life story" in its orientation toward remembering past events and arranging them within a narrative so as to create a sense of moral order and meaning. If a genre may be understood in terms of "patterned expectancy"— that is, "an agreement between writer or speaker and reader or listener on what sort of interpretation is to be made"[22]—the testimonial genre in the context of land restitution is essentially characterized by commemoration. A past "golden era" is thus thrown into sharp relief by the suffering and loss occasioned by forced removals, which are seen as effecting a catastrophic fall from grace and innocence. The joy and fullness in community is contrasted with suffering and emptiness following its dissolution, and memories that mark this contrast are invoked to articulate a sense of entitlement to some form of redress.

Unprompted, Nweti began her interview with me in the usual way of life histories, by telling me about her birth and school years in Cape Town. It was not long before she uttered the refrain that "there's no apartheid" in the old District Six, reflecting a widespread perception among District Sixers that relative to the world outside of the neighborhood, District Six was characterized by a remarkable degree of conviviality across color lines. I was concerned that putting forth this image of harmony merely reflected Nweti's anticipation of what she thought I wanted to hear, so I proceeded to "test" her account by asking about schools, which were segregated by law, as in the rest of South Africa. Nweti conceded that as someone classified as "African," she went to a different school than her "colored" neighbors, but also insisted that this ultimately did not matter in her characterization of life in the former District Six:

> Out of school! . . .we's used to go to Y Hall, we mix and mix, mix! Hello, we mix! You come to my house for tea, there's no apartheid, I go to your house to sleep one [night, or for] afternoon tea. We had . . . we had lovely times, good times. We had . . . you know when it's hot, when it's warm, where . . . we sleep on the *stoep* [balcony]. We couldn't close the doors because it was hot, and we're not scared. When the car—there was no garages—the car was parked outside, you find your car there, not scared that there were somebody come and steal. If there . . . there were *skollies* [ruffians], but they didn't interfere with us. They were gangsters. They were gangsters. If they know you, and all of us, all of us go *bioscope* [cinema] to, they don't worry.

In support of her claim about a former benevolent community, Nweti responds to me by invoking an ethos of conviviality where people from diverse walks of life "mixed," without fear of crime. The image is sharpened by an implicit contrast with the condition of life in Guguletu during the long present since removals, characterized by high levels of criminal and gangster violence, alienation, and spatial segregation.

My primary interest here is the respondent's will in fashioning community as the basis for truth within a testimonial narrative—even counterfactually. "Evidence" for Nweti's claim about District Six is moral in the first instance. In spite of acknowledging the existence of segregation in schools—a very significant part of her life as a child—she decides to represent this as insignificant. What counts for Nweti is her experience of what happened after school, when a feeling of connection across color lines existed as an antidote to apartheid. Faithful interpretation, and hence veracity, is grounded in the quality of ethical relatedness. Nonetheless, several aspects of Nweti's testimony reveal the extent to which apartheid penetrated life in the district. For example, she recounted how friends and family classified as "African" "must have permit, otherwise you must hide them under the bed!" At my prompting, Nweti also told of having to call people working in shops within District Six *baas* (boss). Later, Africans were not allowed inside the shops and had to stand at the shop door to ask for something if they wanted to buy it. When I pointed out the apparent contradiction of those memories with her claim of egalitarianism, Nweti insisted that no such discrimination ever applied amongst neighbors belonging to different racialized groups. At another point, however, she describes the kindness of her Muslim neighbors when they give *sadaka*, in terms that minimally suggest a degree of inequality:

> They're so kind! I don't know what day, I forgot now, but . . . then they were to stand outside when you were kids and . . . they throw the money and you go and pick up the money . . . *ja!* That's what the Muslims used to do.

Despite my critical line of questioning, my approach was sympathetic, in keeping with the expected disposition of the "witness to the witness"[23] within a testimonial interview. To be sure, the interviewer plays an active and integral part in the course of the interview, not only by his or her verbal interventions but by responsive gestures. However, in some group interviews where respondents know each other well, respondents can at various points come to address each other directly, to the point where the importance of the interviewer recedes. This would eventually lead discussion to stretch the boundaries of the typical commemorative structure characterizing the genre, as we shall see.

Second Moment: The Course of Group Testimony

A second respondent, Charmaine, appeared after about twenty minutes. Shortly thereafter, two more respondents joined the interview, Nomsa and Teresa. Charmaine and Teresa self-identified as "colored" women, and had been moved to Guguletu because they were married to two late Mozambiquen men classified as "Africans." The other two Xhosa women's husbands had also passed away. All were neighbors and friends living on a short street on the outskirts of the township. When

Charmaine arrived, she corroborated Nweti's positive characterization of life in the district: "[We] Mixed a lot here, so where we grow up, there was Jews, there was Muslims, there was Indians, all nations! And we grow up together." However, she continued, everything changed with her relocation to Guguletu, where race-consciousness took over. In Charmaine's words, "the attitude change of the people, to race. It was only to race!" She felt herself regarded as an outsider in Guguletu not only because of her racial ascription as "colored", but also because of having married a foreigner: "Because number one it's my husband he's a different . . . nation of this people. You understand? [CB: Yes.] And we couldn't fit him in! And I couldn't fit me in!"

Nomsa then arrived, and the discussion proceeded on the theme of their forced displacement. Nomsa stated that "My mother died, because of . . . ill treatment; when we came here we didn't find . . . anything in the houses, the houses they had no windows," and Charmaine concurred that the house that they were resettled in was "like a stable." About three or four minutes later, the last interviewee, Teresa, arrived and chimed in on the theme of removals: "We were like a person coming into the desert!" Teresa and Charmaine made common cause with their Xhosa neighbors, Nomsa and Nweti, in terms of their shared origins in District Six and their common values, their memory of a previous life comparatively free of problems of discrimination and hardship, and the traumatic experience of rupture through their forcible relocation. In District Six, they claimed their Mozambiquen husbands were accepted as insiders; however, beyond the district they faced discrimination from all sides. In keeping with the prohibitions of the Mixed Marriages Act, Teresa recounted that her marriage to a Mozambiquen man was deemed illegitimate and immoral: "finding a nice man, a decent man, that knows how to communicate with a young girl, it was [considered] a sin!" Moreover, her husband did not have South African citizenship, which meant that he was reluctant to register their two children: "Now, you can't . . . you can't register them Xhosa because they not Xhosa! Or Zulu or Sotho. Now what must we do?" The children were eventually registered as "South African." Charmaine and Teresa's experience of discrimination as "colored" women in Guguletu carries through to the present. As Teresa put it, "Racism is alive even amongst black people!"

Thus idealizations of a past community find their antithesis in both the racialism of the apartheid world outside of the neighborhood and in the separation characterizing present township life. However, the posited commonality of experience was then revealed to have its source in a more threatening adversary altogether: the present-day violence and crime with which residents are regularly confronted in the township, and to which District Six is dramatically counterposed. The women's conversation came to focus on the sexualized violence that has come to define township life, with the raping, maiming, and murdering of women. As Charmaine put it, "you safe nowhere." Nomsa gravely interjected, "No, no." "You're not even safe in church," Charmaine added. They discussed a litany of cases occurring in their immediate neighborhood—the brutal and often gruesome details need not be repeated here—and agreed that "it happened . . . in the time when the children started to rule." After the Sharpeville massacre of 1976, and especially during the 1980s with the intensified township violence directed at "collaborators" with the apartheid regime, youth were often pitted against their own parents. According to Nweti, "It . . . it was the riot thing made the children wild!." The women concurred that "it's getting worse," and that it is exacerbated by the "rough movies" the children watch on television and the lack of strong legal sanctions for crimes committed. Conversation on this subject had the effect of spiraling on without any intervention from myself as interviewer, until finally Charmaine arrested the movement with "What is this interview about anyways?" We then brought the conversation back to the intended primary focus of the interview: District Six, forced removals, and land restitution.

It is important to pause to consider how testimony catapulted into a different direction than initially intended. The generic expectations of the genre were superseded in a way that revealed the core impetus for positing a commonality of experience, and thus a sense of *past-oriented* community, to exist in the anxieties about the abject horrors of intergenerational and sexual violence occasioned by *present* township life. The latter is directly attributed to the dramatic rupture and destruction of a previous comparatively peaceful existence in District Six. Restitution, which officially means compensating for past wrongs, thus gains its most salient social meaning in the context of present, ongoing wrongs which are much more immediate. Something of this tendency is also evident in many of the one-on-one interviews that I conducted. However, these latter interviews usually subsume present injustice and suffering within a larger narrative about forced removals. Some of the primary advocates for restitution also emphasize that the present-day injustices in the townships are a direct result of the legacy of forced removals.[24] However, as becomes much clearer in this group interview, present sexual violence, in particular, comes to represent an independent, more overwhelming injustice or trauma.

We have been observing the process by which community surfaces as an object of volition in the flow of a semi-structured conversation within a group interview. This process is culminated in the excerpts in the next section.

Third Moment: "The Book of Us"

After Charmaine recounts the trials of her and her family's removal and resettlement, she concludes:

> <u>Charmaine</u>: If I could write I could write a book, of my own life!
>
> <u>Nomsa</u>: Exactly.
>
> <u>Charmaine</u>: I couldn't go out to look to write, I could just write a book of myself, how was life. But unfortunately I haven't got the money, to write that book! And I should write that book of my own life!

At this point Teresa rejoins, "You don't need to write a book, Charmaine, you just . . . you just rewind the cassette." She thus effectively tells Charmaine that she is being too self-concerned, and that others have been through just as much as she has. Furthermore, Teresa reflects this statement back onto the very performance in which all present are engaged—a recorded testimonial interview that strives to arrive at a consensus, the substance of which comes to be represented as the content of *collective* experience. Moreover, Teresa judges Charmaine's proposition inadequate not only because of its content (that it is about the individual rather than the community) but also because of its form (that it is to consist of a written individual monologue rather than oral testimonial dialogue).

Conversation then briefly moved on to a different matter, as I asked whether they will feel that justice will have been served upon receiving compensation. I directed the question to Nweti and Nomsa, as legal claimants, for Charmaine and Teresa had both failed to submit claims in time for the 1998 national deadline. After Nweti and Charmaine in turn expressed how monetary compensation could never make up for the suffering that they had been through, I asked, "if this money can't make the past right, what would be able to? . . .what is needed in order to get one beyond this suffering?." Teresa then seized the initiative—in spite of my question not being directed to her—and responded "I would say, if I may say. Our children, and our grandchildren, they must respect, what, the freedom fighters were fighting for us. They . . . they mustn't let them down, to do what they're doing at the moment, killing, and staying like hooligans!" It is noteworthy that in spite of not being a claimant, she articulates a sense of moral entitlement. She went further to emphasize the commonality of all of the women in facing a corrupted and violent youth, thus again evoking present township violence as the source of nostalgic commemoration. Everyone could, of course, agree that "children must know where they come from!"

At this stage, Nweti decided to take up Teresa's earlier point about the book. The focus of the dialogue shifted, as Nweti referred to Nomvuyo Ngcelwane's autobiographical *Sala Kahle, District Six*:

> Nweti: You see in this book, but now, there, Nomvuyo, huh? She doesn't talk the way I think she should write it. Because she wrote it more . . . about her family . . .
>
> Teresa and Nomsa: *Ja.*
>
> Nwetu: You understand? It's more about her family! It's not more about. . .
>
> Brayton: District Six.
>
> Nweti: District Six.
>
> Teresa: It's a community.
>
> Nomsa: *Ja*, it's a . . . it's a community.
>
> Chris (author): Mmm.
>
> Nweti: Understand? If somebody could write a book, come District Six, not about my family.
>
> Nomsa: *Ja*, for . . . for everybody.
>
> Nweti: For everybody!
>
> Nomsa: District Six is their home.
>
> Charmaine: And they grow up.

The interviewees then proceeded to reminisce about the good times in District Six, and contrast these with their difficult lives in Guguletu.

The conversation takes the form of a widening dialogical circle that refers to ever more interlocutors. The first exchanges between Charmaine and Nomsa are relatively contained, referring to a book that Charmaine would like to write to capture her life for public consumption. This statement in itself is not unusual; what is interesting is how it is taken up by other participants in the interview. After a brief digression following my question to Nomsa and Nweti, the frame of reference of Charmaine's statement is expanded. This is prompted by Teresa's emphatic interjection, which has the effect of transporting our minds to the worlds of children today. This, in turn, sets the stage for Nweti to bring up *Sala Kahle, District Six*, which has the effect of dialogically opening the discussion beyond itself toward another complex textual utterance. Teresa and Nweti thus reframe the discussion from the evidently individual focus of Charmaine's original comments (with Nomsa's agreement) about writing an autobiography, and instead talk about *somebody* writing about District Six—a true autobiography of community. The book's story would be appropriate only insofar as it adequately represents the stories of a collectivity—one which consists not just of all four women present, but of an undefined number of District Sixers who are not present, and does so in an appropriate form and style—that "talk the way I think she should write it." The meaning of the word "book" thus changes; moreover, the domain in which its meaning is derived shifts. While the question would seem to be who should best author this book, it is more importantly about what form the book should take as the embodiment of the story of community, and thus about the character of that community and its relation to representation.

Discussion

Rather than treating community as a discursive product that is traded in various altered forms after the fact of its genesis, my analysis of the group interview locates a prior will toward community in the very relay of discourse. Before community is a "construction," it is a potentiality—for confluence of purpose, intent, or intentionality—which is mobilized as emotional connection, commitment, and decision, through speech acts. In fact, its reification as a more or less stable construction or image amounts to a kind of abstraction from the living process in which "it" is performed as an emergent potentiality within language. To be sure, when Teresa uses the term "community," she appropriates it from a wider context in part defined by Ngcelwane's usage but also by many others. However, as is clear from the flow of conversation, each speaker uses the word in a way that anticipates the response of others. To the extent that the speaker thus renders the word amenable to her own intended significations, these are themselves inflected with her (anticipated) positionality vis-à-vis others. Will thus never exists in a pure and isolated form; it is summoned forth by the utterances and acts of others, and its expression is refracted through the intentions of others.

Dialogue consists in transfiguring the domain in which words or memories come to mean something and *not* something else, and this process should not be seen primarily as a rational outcome, but as an emotional-volitional one, since it is first and foremost an expression of a disposition towards others in a determinate use of language. The dialogical circle expands by means of the surfacing of new motivations and attitudes toward others and others' utterances. After Nweti, Teresa, and Brayton reframe the discussion, Nomsa joins the cause, while Charmaine finally comes on board at the end of the excerpt. Support is thus effectively mobilized for the new interpretation of "book," and this gives rise not just to the arrival of a kind of agreement, but to what might be called a *collectivizing intentionality*. The "speech wills" of the various speakers are, in the process of conversation, directed toward a point where self transcends itself toward other. But what is the shape of this self-transcending, collectivizing movement of dialogue?

Charmaine's initial wish to write an autobiography is marshaled, in the process of discourse, into a form that is not only addressed, but self-consciously *answerable*, to a set of values and norms that she encounters through other speakers and an author, others who—after some disagreement—agree that they have experienced *essentially the same thing*. This occurs in a narrative typical of the genre in question, which has been sketched here in the broadest terms as a progression from an original state of harmony, solidarity, and meaning, to a dramatic rupture and fall from grace, to a long present consisting of conflict, anomie, and meaninglessness, and finally to some kind of (incomplete) restitution for the loss of the original. "Community" is thus invoked, after Nweti's intervention, as a symbolic rubric through which voices can most legitimately express themselves in their individuality, the appropriate grounds from which to speak about experiences (in this case, of displacement and resettlement), which are thereby construed as properly belonging in a common domain. Clearly, then, we have here a struggle not only for voice but also for narrative context. At stake is not just whether a statement is true or false, or accurate or not, but the internal persuasiveness of statements that attest to the collective moral truths of original harmony, suffering and struggle, and entitlement.

The figure of a book can be fruitfully used to raise further questions that are not explicitly raised by the interviewees. In evoking the true likeness of the community "from the inside," the ideal book would presumably be of value to outsiders such as myself—as it is, of course, well known that interviewers come around in the interest of writing articles or books. The discussion carries a tacit message: outsiders cannot presume to write the book of community, to bespeak a collective identity, and the purpose of any effort of my own must be analytical in the first instance. But could any insider actually write the book? What would such a book look like? Two apparent paradoxes spring to mind. First, if the book is to be an autobiography, as at least Charmaine and Nweti wish, it is to embody community in the life of one person, the autobiographer. The story of District Six must, in this sense, be personified. The autobiography requires of the author that she objectify herself, thus making the self into an other, and the implicit demand is that this must in turn happen in a way that is representative of the community in which the self is situated. As can be read by Teresa's call, community exceeds the self, but it is nevertheless critically about the self—about the creation of new selves, "that know where they come from!" And yet it would seem from Nweti's further assertion that *Sala Kahle, District Six*—(and by implication, Charmaine's proposed book)—was *merely* a book about her family and her own life that the problem is precisely that no individual can write this book. What kind of register would be appropriate to such a project? The legal evidential paradigm would be inadequate by its very nature. What would seem to be required is a work of interpretation, one which—notwithstanding the desire for closure on the matter—is always imperfect, unfinished.

A further paradox arises from the fact that the story of community is to be written by those who, in some sense, are least "empowered" to write it. In the excerpt above, community figures as a thread linking generations and as a kind of call for justice, something which stands against a historical wrong. These ends, it is assumed, are ultimately best achieved through writing the kind of book that Ngcelwane has tried to write—a narrative of a life, in which writing imitates lay speech, with photo illustrations from the family album to further bring the words to life. Thus Nweti's comment on Nomvuyo, "She doesn't *talk* the way I think she should *write* it," judges her effort unsuccessful. As we have seen, it was explicitly judged to have failed because it took the experience of one to stand in for others. More tacitly, however, might one not conjecture that *Sala Kahle, District Six* could not but have failed on Nomsa's terms because, as published word, it participates in the realm of money and power, outside of the domain of community? The discussion began, after all, with Charmaine's desire to write a book if only she had the money, which in turn we can see as a metaphor for her socioeconomically marginal position. Moreover, as we saw earlier, the lives of the subaltern are here defined not only by a lack of economic wherewithal but by being confronted by high levels of violence on a daily basis. If, as I have suggested, this latter issue is a driving impetus for the commemoration of community, the desire to capture precisely such a remembered community in writing—a form of representation associated with privilege—comes to appear as fundamentally ambivalent.

These points may well overextend the intentions of the interviewees, and make too much of reflexive issues of representation. However, they do seem to me to be useful in raising the general question of the relationship between the process of forming collective identity in the relay of conversation among those who are largely excluded from the means of representation and the various forms of proxy representation by which an identity is ascribed on their behalf. In spite of the seemingly overwhelming power of written discourse in modern societies to name reality and thereby condition truth-claims made in spoken discourse, the interviews presented demonstrate an ongoing struggle to reclaim agency—here under the auspices of community—in oral testimony.

Conclusion

This chapter has emphasized the intersubjective and dialogical dimensions of testimony. Its concern has not been with extreme cases of trauma often privileged in recent academic writing on testimony, characterized by the loss of "the mental synthesis that constitutes reflective will and belief,"[25] wherein memory is characterized by fragmentation, isolation, and the unbearable weight of the "unspeakable." Instead, its concern has been with narrative memory and the ways in which individuals incorporate experiences within the framework of a broader story of community in testimony. Will is present both in the act of claiming restitution as such, and in the way in which a speaker shapes narrative of belonging and entitlement in her address to others—not only outsiders but insiders within community, many of whom are also engaged in providing testimony. Community is both an object of discourse, a *thing out there* that people talk about, and *a way of speaking*. This becomes clear in analyzing the dialogic aspects of a group interview as live co-testimony.

As interlocutors of discourse, we exercise agency not merely by manipulating received discursive elements to construct identities for ourselves. Volition is exercised in a deeper way in creating a sense of commonality out of putatively collective experience. A sense of community arises from the way in which we enlist the experience of others in narrating the past, since memories themselves involve contexts within which we relate to others, and where we identify our experience with others. In some sense I am doing this as I write by generating a "we" out of the imaginary "discussion" in this chapter. But there is, of course, more to the shaping of communal identity. As discussed in relation to the group interview cited here, the sense of an "us"—what we have in common—is consciously produced, in this case in a process of actual dialogue, which actively summons the wills of others toward a collective object or name. This is most clearly evident in the final moment of the group interview, where one person's wish for a "book" to represent her individual experience is contested in favor of a book of "us." The imaginary book is to provide an account of collective life, which insiders can agree is a just one. Moreover, as a kind of metaphor for community, the book lives not only among verbal utterances such as those in the interview, but among other books. One might say that the consciousness of an "us" becomes more explicitly dialogical.

Insofar as "community" figures here as presupposed object of discourse, it is not just as the substantive claims that can presumably be made about it, but as a horizon of meaning to be disclosed by just representation. In its deeper significance, community is therefore not so much a fixed starting point or end point, but a symbolic domain, a potentiality, through which individual wills are summoned in dialogue—something in the name of which will is responsively brought into actualization. In the kind of testimony considered here, individuals' experiences, meanings, and values are committed to narrative by being attributed to a particular collective form, a "we," which thus serves as the interpretive rubric for moral truth-claims. The process by which community is thus mobilized occurs responsively, by speakers who will themselves into its hearth and home in the very way in which they tell the story of their own and others' lives. In some sense the primary audience is not the future public to which the telling is addressed—in accordance with the structure of the genre—for this public is in need of translation (and of something which in some sense is "untranslatable"), and can at best only experience the spirit of community partially and vicariously. Testimony is first addressed to other insiders, with whom a sense of belonging is putatively shared. For it is in dialogue with these fellow community members—present and absent, real and imagined—that a frame of reference for morally persuasive "evidentiary" statements is continually being defined, even as the matter of their ultimate referent is taken to be, in essence, settled. As long as such statements are occasioned by their conscious, volitional, and performative invocation of moral relationship as counterweight to ever present assertions of monologic principle, re-productions of reified "construct," or requirements to produce verifiable data, the conversation will be very much alive.

Notes

1. Restitution aimed to provide redress for removals on the basis of racially based laws. The vast majority of victims were black – in other words, classified as "colored," "Indian," and "African," but not "white".
2. Marc Bloch, in Elizabeth Tonkin, *Narrating Our Past: The Social Construction of Oral History* (Cambridge: Cambridge University Press, 1994), 41.
3. Deborah James, *Gaining Ground? "Rights" and "Property" in South African Land Reform* (London: Routledge, 2007); Cherryl Walker, *Landmarked: Land Claims and Land Restitution in South Africa* (Athens: OhioUniversity Press, 2008).
4. Christiaan Beyers, "The Cultural Politics of 'Community' and Citizenship in the District Six Museum, Cape Town," *Anthropologica, Special Issue—Citizenship, Politics and Locality: Anthropological Perspectives*, ed. Catherine Neveu, 50, 2 (June 2008): 359–73.
5. *Memory, History, Forgetting*, trans. Kathleen Blamey and David Pellauer (Chicago: University of Chicago Press, 2004), 164.
6. Ibid, 165.
7. Christiaan Beyers, "The will-to-community: Between loss and reclamation in Cape Town," in *"Restoring what was ours": The Rights and Wrongs of Land Restitution*, ed., Derick Fay and Deborah James (London: Routledge/Glasshouse Books, 2008).
8. Personal interview, May 21, 2001.
9. All interviewees in this chapter are referred to by pseudonyms in order preserve anonymity, as requested.
10. Personal interview, May 25, 2001.
11. Personal interview, May 30, 2001.
12. Crain Soudien, "District Six and its uses in the discussion about non-racialism," in *Coloured by History, Shaped by Place: New Perspectives on Coloured Identities in Cape Town*, ed., Zimitri Erasmus (Cape Town: Kwela Books, 2001), 117.
13. Rosemary E. Ridd, *Position and Identity in a Divided Community: Colour and Religion in the District Six, Walmer Estate, Woodstock Area of Cape Town* (PhD dissertation, Wolfson College, Oxford University, 1981), 82.
14. Personal interview, Cape Town, May 28, 2001.
15. In addition to former property owners, the Restitution Act allows for claims from former tenants who had resided in the area for at least ten years. In District Six, the majority of former residents were tenants.
16. Nomvuyo Ngcelwane, *Sala Kahle, District Six: An African Woman's Perspective* (Cape Town: Kwela Books, 1999).
17. Mikhail Bakhtin, *Toward a Philosophy of the Act*, ed.Vadim Liapunov and Michael Holquist, trans. Vadim Liapunov (Austin: University of Texas Press, 1993).
18. Bakhtin, "The Problem of Speech Genres," in *Speech Genres and Other Late Essays*, ed. Carol Emerson and Michael Holquist, trans. Vern W. McGee (Texas: University of Texas Press, 1986).
19. Ibid, 73 and 67.
20. Bakhtin, *The Dialogic Imagination: Four Essays by Mikhail Bakhtin*, ed. Michael Holquist, trans. Carol Emerson and Michael Holquist (Austin: University of Texas Press, 1994).
21. Graham Pechey, *Mikhail Bakhtin: The Word in the World* (London: Routledge, 2007), 66.
22. Tonkin, *Narrating Our Past*, 51.
23. Michael G. Levine, *The Belated Witness: Literature, Testimony, and the Question of Holocaust Survival* (Stanford: Stanford University Press, 2006).
24. Personal interview, Cape Town, Anwah Nagia, June 14, 2002.
25. Pierre Janet, cited in Bessel van der Kolk and Onno van der Hart, "The Intrusive Past: The Flexibility of Memory and the Engraving of Trauma," in *Trauma: Explorations in Memory*, ed. Cathy Caruth (Baltimore: Johns Hopkins Press, 1995), 175.

11

"What May or May Not Have Happened in the Past": Truth, Lies, and the Refusal to Witness Indigenous Australian Testimony

Kelly Butler

Throughout the twentieth century, and intensively from the mid-1980s, Australian Indigenous people have given testimony in a variety of forms and contexts: from poetry and life writing to legal evidence for land rights cases.[1] Indigenous testimony has been most audible since the 1997 release of *Bringing Them Home,* the Report of the Human Rights and Equal Opportunity Commission into the Separation of Aboriginal and Torres Strait Islander Children from their Families (1997). The report collated the testimonies of Indigenous Australians who had suffered under the past government practice of removing Indigenous children from their families—a group that came to be known as the "stolen generations"— and was met by an extraordinary outpouring of public emotion. During this time many non-Indigenous Australians acted as "secondary witnesses" to Indigenous peoples and affirmed the truth of their testimony in a variety of ways. These included reconciliation marches and campaigns for a national apology, which was finally achieved in 2008 by incumbent Labor Prime Minister Kevin Rudd. Some Australians, however, refused the role of secondary witness and sought to discredit Indigenous testimony to past injustice. This was particularly true of the conservative media and of the former Liberal government led by Prime Minister John Howard (1996–2007). Many media commentators, including popular journalists Andrew Bolt and Piers Akerman, refused to witness to *Bringing Them Home* and wrote derisively of its "lies." Similarly, Howard repeatedly voiced his skepticism about Indigenous testimony and dismissed its present implications by urging Australians to stop "navel-gazing" about "what may or may not have happened in the past."[2]

As numerous theorists of testimony have outlined, the role of the secondary witness is crucial to the testimonial exchange.[3] Testimonial truth is produced dialogically through the interaction of two witnesses: the words of the eyewitness or testifier are accepted as truthful by the secondary witness. The presence of this "second person" is so fundamental to the exchange that, in Dori Laub's terms, "the absence of an empathic listener . . . an other who can hear the anguish of one's memories and thus affirm and recognize their realness, annihilates the story."[4] Accordingly, this chapter considers what it means to refuse to witness, and examines how this refusal affects both the truth value of testimony and its broader cultural and political work as a method of claiming justice in relation to past events. Using conservative media responses to Australian Indigenous testimony, this chapter analyzes the way that refusal disrupts the circuit between testimony, truth, and justice. In particular, this chapter examines the ramifications of the refusal to witness through a focus on three key events in the public circulation of Indigenous Australian testimony: the controversy surrounding whether or not Indigenous leader Lowitja O'Donoghue was a "stolen" child (2001); the legal failure of the so-called stolen generations' "test case" *Cubillo v Commonwealth* (2000); and the long-running clash over the construction of the Hindmarsh Island Bridge that centered on a dispute over "secret" Indigenous knowledge (1994–2001).

An examination of the public life and media reception of Indigenous Australian testimony serves as a rich case study for a consideration of the cultural and political work performed by witnessing. The refusal by many prominent Australians to witness to Indigenous testimony produced a climate of doubt in which, for many, Indigenous life stories were always already under suspicion. Crucially, the sustained refusal to witness and the conservative branding of Indigenous peoples as "liars" revealed the extent to which the cultural politics of witnessing was oriented to the needs of (white) non-Indigenous Australians. While testimony remains an important tool for Indigenous Australians in their campaigns for justice and recognition—as it does for other marginalized groups around the globe—it is highly vulnerable to shifting standards of "truth" and dependent on the benevolence of sympathetic witnesses.

Witnessing Australian Indigenous Peoples

Although Australian Indigenous Peoples have a long history of providing testimony to non-Indigenous governments, missionaries, and researchers, it was not until the release of *Bringing Them Home* that their testimony became central to public debates about justice, historical responsibility, and the nation.[5] *Bringing Them Home* drew on the testimony of more than one thousand Indigenous people to argue that during the period between 1910 and 1970 "between one in three and one in ten" Indigenous children were removed from their families by the state in an act that constituted a form of genocide.[6] The report urged non-Indigenous Australians to accept this history and recommended that the federal government deliver an official apology to promote reconciliation between Indigenous and non-Indigenous Australians. While *Bringing Them Home* acknowledged that the quasi-judicial nature of the HREOC Inquiry limited its ability to "test" Indigenous peoples' evidence, it nevertheless asserted the truth value of Indigenous testimony by drawing upon it as the primary evidence used to sustain its findings.[7] Crucially, *Bringing Them Home* employed Indigenous testimony in a way that foregrounded the role of non-Indigenous Australians as secondary witnesses. For Ronald Wilson and Mick Dodson, the lead commissioners of the inquiry, the "devastation" of Aboriginal Australians "cannot be addressed unless the whole community listens with an open heart and mind to the stories of what has happened in the past and, having listened and understood, commits itself to reconciliation."[8] But as Felman and Laub have suggested, the witnessing exchange not only requires the secondary witness to acknowledge the trauma of the testifying subject, but is "at the same time a witness . . . to himself."[9] In relation to the stolen generation testimonies, non-Indigenous Australians were drawn to consider their own implication in the dispossession of Aboriginal peoples, in both the past and the present. As Gillian Whitlock has argued, this process was experienced as shaming by many secondary witnesses who came to realize "how ruthlessly and completely race" had shaped the experiences of the stolen generations.[10] In this way *Bringing Them Home* inaugurated a process of witnessing to both Indigenous peoples and their experiences *and* the complicity of non-Indigenous Australians with practices of settler colonialism.[11] Crucial to this witnessing was committing oneself to ameliorating past injustice through participation in the process of reconciliation.

Bringing Them Home became the center of a popular discourse on reconciliation that figured witnessing and an apology as key to the nation's future.[12] While reconciliation had been an official government-managed process since the promulgation of the Council for Aboriginal Reconciliation in 1991, the release of *Bringing Them Home* galvanized the public and, for the first time, the concept of reconciliation "entered everyday discourse."[13] Though the concept of reconciliation has been widely criticized for its vagueness, it described the desire of many who believed that coming to terms with Australia's history of Indigenous dispossession was vital to "moving forward" into the future.[14] Many non-Indigenous Australians, including prominent public intellectuals, politicians, and writers, sought to participate in the reconciliation process by acting as secondary witnesses to Indigenous peoples; thousands attended protest marches and signed so-called "sorry books" in order to lend their support to an official apology.[15]

Yet despite the fact that many non-Indigenous Australians supported the testimonial claims of the stolen generations, this group remained a vocal minority.[16] In fact, in the decade between the release of *Bringing Them Home* and Rudd's apology to Australia's Indigenous peoples, the need to listen to the testimony of Aboriginal people was repeatedly and vehemently rejected by the Howard government. Instead of accepting the intergenerational responsibility of non-Indigenous Australians for past government wrongdoing, Howard promoted "practical" reconciliation aimed at encouraging Indigenous Australians to improve their own lives. More generally, Howard and his supporters in the conservative media were alarmed by the prevalence of what they dubbed the "black-armband view of Australian history": history that sought to emphasize the "guilt" of non-Indigenous Australians *vis-à-vis* the colonial past and the present social disadvantage of Aboriginal peoples.[17] Howard urged Australians to feel "relaxed and comfortable" about the past and minimized the violent aspects of Australian history that were foregrounded by testimony.[18] Howard's unwillingness to engage with notions of collective responsibility was not simply a denial of aspects of Australian history, it constituted a refusal to witness and acknowledge the validity of Indigenous testimony as a form of truthful evidence about the past. This inability to listen to testimony and take up the role of witness was perhaps most stark in his now-infamous opening address to the 1997 Reconciliation Convention. Timed to coincide with the tabling of *Bringing Them Home* in parliament, the Reconciliation Convention brought together Indigenous and non-Indigenous politicians, historians, and activists to discuss the future of reconciliation in the wider community.

In his opening speech Howard expressed his "deep sorrow for those of my fellow Australians who suffered injustices under the practices of past generations towards indigenous people."[19] However, he refused to extend this personal regret to a formal apology and was jeered by Convention participants, many of whom turned their backs on the Prime Minister. In response Howard acknowledged that there were some "blemishes" on Australia's past, but criticized those who portrayed the nation's history as a "disgraceful record of imperialism, exploitation and racism."[20] Howard's resistance to an official apology was also related to the legal implications it might raise, with an admission of culpability leaving the government open to potential claims for compensation. Indeed, when Prime Minister Rudd finally issued an apology in 2008 he explicitly rejected the issue of compensation— something for which Indigenous activists and scholars continue to fight. Thus, despite the willingness of many Indigenous Australians to share their testimony—and the desire of many non-Indigenous Australians to respond and take up the challenge of witnessing—the conservative Howard government promoted a turn-of-the-century political and cultural climate unwilling to consider the implications of testimony.

Refusing to Witness

It is now commonplace to assert the fundamental role of testimony to human rights campaigns and processes of transitional justice.[21] There has, however, been little discussion of the refusal to witness and the effect that this refusal can have on the humanitarian causes advanced by the circulation of victim testimonies.[22] That is, if the testimonial exchange is dependent on the willingness of the secondary witness to empathetically engage with testimony, how does the refusal to witness disrupt the circuit between testimony, truth, and social justice? As I have suggested in relation to the Australian context, practices of witnessing may exist within an overarching climate of hostility and skepticism. Crucial to the development of this climate is the specter of the false witness—the fear of being "taken in" by false testimony. To consider this fear is to appreciate the extent to which testimony exists within a spectrum of life writing that has, at times, been vulnerable to identity hoaxes and false eyewitnesses.

False witnesses puncture what Philippe Lejeune has termed "the autobiographical pact": the implicit agreement between reader and author that affirms the fidelity of the relationship between an autobiographical text and a real, verifiable individual.[23] In Australia, a number of "false" Indigenous life narratives circulated during the 1990s, perhaps most famously Wanda Koolmatrie's *My Own Sweet Time* (1997), a false stolen-generation narrative written by a non-Indigenous man, Leon Carmen.[24] Alongside the hoaxing of Indigenous identity, a number of other identity frauds targeted so-called "minority" identities, including Helen Demidenko/Darville's *The Hand that Signed the Paper* (1994), an anti-Semitic novelization of her family's supposed experiences in the Ukraine.[25] Though by no means restricted to Australia, Maggie Nolan and Carrie Dawson have argued that the debates that have surrounded ethnic identity hoaxes, such as that of Koolmatrie and Demidenko, "tell us about the desire for authenticity in multicultural Australia."[26] In this sense, instances of hoaxing and imposture that involve "minority" ethnic identities have been particularly damaging. In demonstrating the thirst of the Anglo-Australian reading public for true representations of minority and ethnic experience, hoaxes reveal the extent to which the transmission of testimonial life narrative is dependent on the benevolence of Anglo-Australians—a benevolence that is attracted to the very markers of affective "ethnic" identity mimicked by hoax narratives.

The perceived correlation between life narratives and actual lives has been crucial to the success of contemporary autobiography and testimony.[27] Thus, the fracturing of the pact between readers/listeners and life narratives not only impacts the trust of the audience but casts doubt on the social and political causes founded on the circulation of "true" life stories. As Whitlock has written in relation to another antipodean hoax—the Norma Khouri affair—"the hoax testimony is a parasite. This means two things: it travels on a dominant testimonial current, and it saps the power of that current by drawing all testimonial narrative into disrepute."[28] In this way, to take seriously the implications of false testimony for individual listeners is to acknowledge the vulnerability of testimony as a vehicle for social, cultural, and political change, and to consider how easily the truthful foundation of testimony may be shaken by imposture and doubt.

The remainder of this chapter will examine how some Australians, particularly key members of the federal government and conservative media, promoted an attitude of skepticism toward Indigenous testimony during the late 1990s by mobilizing the fear of false witnessing. To be clear, I do not consider the cases under examination to be instances of identity hoaxing or imposture. However, I do seek to demonstrate how the refusal to witness and a cultural climate of skepticism is produced by exploiting the vulnerability of the secondary witness.

Doubting "Stolen" Children

As we have seen, from the mid-1990s a broad discourse on reconciliation developed in Australian public culture that saw many non-Indigenous Australians act as witnesses to the testimony of the stolen generations. At the same time, the federal government, conservative public intellectuals, and media commentators sought to discredit the truth value of testimony, often relying on the fear of the false witness to do so. Conservative suspicion of Indigenous testimony coalesced around several prominent events, including the Hindmarsh Island Bridge Royal Commission; the *Cubillo-Gunner* stolen generation "test case"; and, within the context of the release of *Bringing Them Home*, with a series of "revelations" about the private lives of prominent Aboriginal leaders, including Lowitja O'Donoghue. Several conservative columnists have been especially interested in probing the "truth" of stolen generation testimony, in particular the Melbourne *Herald Sun*'s Andrew Bolt and the Sydney *Daily Telegraph*'s Piers Akerman. The work of Bolt and Akerman was augmented by the semi-academic commentary of writers in the journal *Quadrant*, though Bolt and Akerman and their colleagues in the popular press—Michael Duffy, Frank Devine, and Christopher Pearson—were the most visible proponents of an anti-testimony discourse within Australian public culture. Bolt and Akerman focused on the perceived unreliability of some testimonies as evidence of a broader "invention" of a stolen generation "myth."[29] Any perceived weaknesses in Aboriginal oral testimony, particularly discrepancies associated with the fallibility of memory, were discounted as evidence of "lying" and an indication that only (non-Indigenous) documentary sources should be used to understand the nation's past.

Conservative criticism of the stolen generations has often focused on the life histories of specific Indigenous people as a way of casting doubt on the value of *Bringing Them Home* as a whole. In 2001 Andrew Bolt reported that, contrary to popular belief, Lowitja O'Donoghue had not been stolen from her family; rather, "she was given away" by her father.[30] O'Donoghue, then patron of the National Sorry Day Committee and former chairperson of the Indigenous representative body the Aboriginal and Torres Strait Islander Commission (ATSIC), became the center of a media storm focusing on her childhood and the circumstances of her separation from her mother. Drawing on interviews with relatives and communications with O'Donoghue herself, Bolt claimed that O'Donoghue had been voluntarily sent to the missionary-run children's institution

Colebrook Home in South Australia. Crucially, Bolt claimed that O'Donoghue had "misled Australians" and quoted her as saying, "I don't like the word stolen and it's perhaps true that I've used the word loosely at times."[31] In the face of intense media pressure O'Donoghue eventually conceded that she was "a removed child, and not necessarily stolen."[32]

Mining the specificities of O'Donoghue's life history, Bolt went on to suggest that his revelation had broader implications for other stolen children and their claims for legal redress and, moreover, for questions of a national apology. It would, he argued, "come as a blow to supporters of the 'stolen generation'."[33] Accordingly, Bolt argued that the "stolen generations" was a mythic structure promoted by "sanctimonious liberal humanists" and underwritten by the unreliable testimony of Indigenous people, many of whom suffered "false memory syndrome."[34] The accusation that stolen children were the victims of false memory syndrome was argued strongly in the pages of conservative journal *Quadrant,* where P. P. McGuinness "likened the testimony of the separated children to invented tales of childhood sexual abuse, Satanic possession or alien abduction."[35] The comments of Bolt and others sparked a media controversy and even drew a response from Prime Minister Howard, who suggested that Australians cease "this navel-gazing about the past":

> It's time we stopped this business about who was to blame for what may or may not have happened in the past. It's time we stopped using excessive . . . outrageous words like genocide and it's time we focused on making things better in the future.[36]

Here, Howard leveraged doubt about the specificities of O'Donoghue's separation from her family to cast aspersions on the concept of a stolen generation as a whole. Moreover, he used anxiety about "what may or may not have happened in the past" as justification for eschewing consideration of settler responsibility for violence committed against Indigenous peoples. Drawing upon the life story of only one prominent Indigenous person, both Bolt and Howard sought to extend suspicion of O'Donoghue's testimony to that of *all* Aboriginal people.

Conservative critics of the stolen generations have typically couched their objection to testimony in "commonsense" understandings of truth and morality. Responding to criticism of his exposé of O'Donoghue, Bolt lamented hyperbolically that "yesterday I learned that telling the truth is a crime against morality in Australia."[37] Similarly, Akerman suggested that "if the Aboriginal industry cannot deal honestly with the issue of the so-called stolen generation then there cannot be any genuine reconciliation."[38] For both Bolt and Akerman an inability to understand the "truth" about the stolen generation was due not only to the duplicity of Indigenous people, but to the machinations of what Bolt has termed "a moral mafia": a cabal of self-hating white liberals devoted to a "black armband view" of Australia's past.[39]

In order to overcome these forces, commentators suggested that the emotive or affective dimension of Aboriginal stories needed to be overlooked in favor of a "sober investigation of what did happen."[40] Repeatedly, conservative discussion of the stolen generations has encouraged readers to disengage from the emotive qualities of testimony in order to perceive the facts contained in documentary (colonial) "evidence." Somewhat perversely, the dismissal of testimony has been figured as a way of ascertaining the "real" facts and thus helping to "ease the pain" of those Indigenous people who were separated from their families.[41]

The role of affect in the testimonial exchange has been highly contentious within critical discussions on witnessing, with some critics suggesting that life narrative actually gains its power not from any formal or referential quality, but from its production and transmission of affect. Writing in the wake of the Wilkomirski controversy, Phillip Gourevitch has linked the popularity of the hoax testimony *Fragments* to its affect or emotive power.[42] That is, Gourevitch argued that testimony is read—and valued as authoritative and authentic—because of its ability to transfer different affects to the reader to engage their empathetic capacities. Binjamin Wilkomirski's memoir *Fragments,* published in German in 1995, presented itself as the recollections of a child Holocaust survivor before being exposed by journalists as a fabrication.[43] Such was the popularity of *Fragments* that many Holocaust scholars sought to rehabilitate the text as valuable due to the vicarious trauma or "prosthetic" memory that it allowed secondary witnesses to experience.[44] This process of witnessing was deemed to be so valuable, and productive of a profound, experiential relation to the Holocaust among non-survivors, that in some discussions affect was privileged over authenticity. It is a position that has been implicitly supported by the dominant theorizations of testimony within Holocaust studies, particularly in the work of Felman and Laub, who have figured testimony as an inchoate expression of trauma, rather than as a representation of actual events.[45]

Despite the fact that the dialogic and constructed nature of testimonial truth is now well-accepted by scholars working on testimony and life writing, the strength of testimony as a vehicle for the recognition of injustice in the public sphere rests on its relationship to actual events as a form of truthful evidence. In their analysis of the critical response to the

Wilkomirski hoax, Andrew Gross and Michael Hoffman have argued that *Fragments* remains a troubling text precisely because it demonstrates that "affect is no guarantee of accuracy."[46] While a hoax testimony may indeed be moving, they have argued that the personal and cultural power of life writing is diminished through a dismissal of referentiality as a marker of authenticity. What is at stake here is not simply that demonstrably false testimony "fails" to match a verifiable reality, but that it is testimony's affective pull that draws secondary witnesses to consider the truth of testimony in the first place. The aura of emotive authenticity has underwritten numerous cultural and political claims anchored by first-person stories of injustice, trauma, and suffering. When the tenuous connection between affect and actuality is disrupted, it inhibits the ability of minority voices to speak their stories within the very public culture that demands of their stories a particular emotive intensity and affective appeal. In this way Bolt and others could urge their readers to doubt stolen-generations testimony because of its particular generic qualities—not its relationship to histories of dispossession.

Testimony on Trial

Though published life narratives—and the testimonies recorded as part of truth and reconciliation commissions—have not been customarily subjected to juridical standards of evidence, conservative commentators have been concerned to track the progress of stolen-generation testimony through the courts. Much criticism of *Bringing Them Home* focused on its failure to judge testimony according to "the rules of evidence" and, as such, conservatives have fetishized court cases involving Indigenous litigants as true tests of authenticity.[47] For some, the court provided the most appropriate space to ascertain the truth of the claims of Indigenous people; conversely, for a range of Aboriginal claimants, the courts served as a forum not to "prove" themselves, but to achieve a tangible form of justice.

By far the most high-profile legal "test" of Indigenous testimony came during *Cubillo v Commonwealth*.[48] Promoted as a stolen-generation "test case" in the media, and noted as highly symbolic by the court itself, the case was brought in 1999 by the North Australian Aboriginal Legal Aid Service on behalf of Lorna Cubillo and Peter Gunner. Both Cubillo and Gunner had been removed from their Aboriginal families as children, under powers granted by the *Aboriginals Ordinance 1918* (NT). Cubillo was eight in 1947 when she was removed to the Retta Dixon Home in Darwin, while Gunner was seven when, in 1956, he was taken from Utopia

Station to St Mary's Hostel, near Alice Springs. Their action sought to prove that the government was "vicariously liable" for their removal as children and their subsequent detention and abuse while in care.[49]

Ultimately Justice O'Loughlin found against Cubillo and Gunner, deciding that the Commonwealth was not liable for any injury they sustained while in care. Controversially, he also argued on the basis of a thumbprint made by Peter Gunner's mother that she had consented to his removal. The case hinged on O'Loughlin's interpretation of evidence—both oral and documentary—which he ultimately found to be "incomplete."[50] With reference to Cubillo, O'Loughlin accepted her oral evidence regarding the circumstances of her removal, but claimed that there was a "huge void" with respect to the reasons why she was removed.[51] In particular, O'Loughlin felt that the absence of documentary evidence inhibited his ability to rule on the reasons for her removal; he claimed this in spite of the voluminous material offered by the litigants and their consultant historian, Ann McGrath, who provided a thorough reading of contemporary child removal policies. Here, O'Loughlin underscored the court's preference for "official" documentation over both Indigenous testimony and the historical interpretation of professional historians. For Ann Curthoys, Ann Genovese, and Alexander Reilly, "the court's preference for official documentary evidence stands at complete odds with the notion that Indigenous peoples can 'prove' their own history in the face of a dominant language, and law."[52] As Trish Luker has concurred, "Lorna Cubillo failed in her claim because she did not meet the law's impossible burden of proof."[53]

For historians and legal scholars *Cubillo* has demonstrated the incommensurability of the public discourse on reconciliation and redemption, and the evidentiary demands of the Australian legal system. As Jennifer Clarke has argued, the legal process exposed deficiencies in stolen-generation evidence that were not apparent, nor especially important, in the broader public process of "telling our stories" inaugurated by *Bringing Them Home*.[54] Accordingly, Luker has argued that O'Loughlin's failure to witness to the trauma of Cubillo and Gunner, as demonstrated by their testimony and "in documents which trace a history of policies intended to erase Indigenous peoples," affirmed "the law's power to control the way we make sense of traumatic histories and memories."[55]

As a "test case" *Cubillo* underscored the complexities of seeking justice within the courts and traced the limits of testimony within this context. It did not, however, serve to disprove the existence of a stolen generation, and in the case of Cubillo herself, it actually affirmed the horrific circumstances of her removal.[56] Nevertheless, for conservative commentators *Cubillo* was highly significant and cast doubt on *all* forms of Indigenous testimony.[57] In response to their "failure" Bolt concluded that "the 'stolen generation' can no longer expect us to believe them without question."[58] For Bolt, *Cubillo* was the latest in a long line of supposedly false stolen-generation testimony, which included activist Charles Perkins, Olympic athlete Cathy Freeman's grandmother, and Lowitja O'Donoghue as false "stolen" children. In this way conservative critics underscored the authority of the (colonial) law to adjudicate Indigenous testimony and reified the legal process as the *only* assurance of its truthfulness. In doing so they eroded the discursive space available for the sympathetic dissemination and reception of stolen-generation testimony.

"Secrets" and "Lies"

If the controversies surrounding *Cubillo* and O'Donoghue linked "faulty" Aboriginal testimony to the truthfulness of the stolen generations as an historical process, the earlier "Hindmarsh Island Affair" highlighted tensions between testimony and the law in the context of land rights and heritage protection. During the 1990s, Ngarrindjeri women rose to national prominence as a result of their efforts to prevent the construction of a bridge connecting *Kumarangk* (Hindmarsh Island) in the lower Murray River, with Goolwa on mainland South Australia, areas they considered to be of crucial spiritual importance. Within a broader post-*Mabo* political milieu preoccupied with the meanings of Aboriginal stories and their implications for land rights, the Hindmarsh controversy captivated the Australian media's imagination and became a conservative *cause célèbre*.[59] The long-running "affair" began in 1994 and centered on a group of Ngarrindjeri women clustered around Doreen Kartinyeri, who argued that the *Kumarangk* area was significant in terms of their fertility.[60] They claimed that because the significance of the Coorong was classified as restricted knowledge within their culture, they could not elaborate publicly as to the area's importance. At its core, the "affair" hinged on a dispute between two groups of Ngarrindjeri women; those allied with Kartinyeri and a group of self-described "dissident" women who questioned the existence of restricted knowledge about the Coorong.[61] The subsequent Hindmarsh Island Royal Commission found that several Ngarrindjeri women had colluded in the "fabrication" of secret knowledge, and ruled that construction could proceed.[62] The Ngarrindjeri women involved were branded "liars"—despite the fact that they had refused to provide evidence to the Commission—and the phrase "secret women's business" became a conservative byword for lying Aborigines.[63]

In 2001 Tom and Wendy Chapman, the couple behind the bridge development, brought action against a range of parties whom they believed had contributed to costly delays in the construction of the bridge. While Justice von Doussa found against the Chapmans, he crucially re-assessed the genuineness of Ngarrindjeri belief regarding the area covered by the bridge, exonerating the women.[64] Though Kartinyeri lived to hear von Doussa's verdict, the affair had already succeeded in mocking Indigenous relationship to country, as well as working to discredit testimony. Accordingly, Irene Watson has suggested that when the Ngarrindjeri women presented "another way of knowing the world that threatened 'white privilege', 'white truth' prevailed."[65] Within the context of subsequent land rights campaigns, the event set a precedent for the dismissal of applications to heritage protection based on cultural knowledge not freely available to settlers. It also, in a post-*Mabo* climate, worked to destabilize Indigenous being-in-place and refigure Anglo-Australians as superior guardians of normative relations to the country. This was particularly demonstrated in the affair's reliance on white anthropological expertise and its use by the law.[66] In this way, Hindmarsh Island set the scene for the development of a popular culture of denial of Indigenous testimony, which, as we have seen, took on renewed force in the late 1990s in response to the challenge of *Bringing Them Home*.

Conclusion: Failed Witnesses

Popular commentary about the truthfulness of Indigenous testimony produced a climate of doubt in which the words of Aboriginal people were continually under suspicion. With respect to the stolen generations, Bolt and Howard both used cases of alleged fabrication to cast doubt on *all* testimony to child removal. On this foundation, they built the case that stolen-generation testimony had inappropriately maligned the nation's history, smearing "too much dirt on our past."[67] Here, conservatives not only doubted the "truth" of the testimony of individuals but the broader role that Indigenous testimony had played in intervening in public memory about Australian history.

Speculating on why conservative skepticism had been so fierce in the 1990s, public intellectual Robert Manne positioned these writers as failed witnesses. "Some," he argued, "have so little capacity for empathy that they genuinely cannot imagine the harm inflicted on a child taken from the warmth of a family to a loveless institution where their skin colour is regarded as a cause for shame."[68] Here, Manne drew attention to the centrality of affect in the reception of testimony and the necessity for secondary witnesses to empathize with marginalized subjects. In refusing to respond affectively to testimony, conservative writers failed to understand testimony as a mode of speech dependent upon the existence of a willing witness to activate its truth.

As theorists of testimony have affirmed, the "truth" of testimony is confirmed only through the exchange of witnessing. This is not to argue that authenticity or referentiality is not important in assessing the truth-value of testimony, but to emphasize the extent to which testimony is dependent upon the willingness of a listener to engage. Truth, then, in autobiographical and testimonial terms, is contingent: on the vagaries of memory and the complexities of subjective experiences and, most crucially, on the capacity of the secondary witness to engage in dialogue.

Testimony cannot perform its cultural and political work without secondary witnesses. The refusal to witness, then, is, in the first instance, to do violence to an individual or group, to deny the truth of their experiences of suffering or injustice, to fail to recognize the mark of their survival. But to ignore testimony is also to elide the possibilities of witnessing as an active force for change: both symbolic and actual. It is to preclude what Deborah Bird Rose has understood as "a moral engagement of the past in the present," an approach that:

> resists closure, whether that closure aims to decree that the violence in the past (or even in the present) is finished, or whether it claims more specifically to outlaw or ridicule historians and others who seek to remember violence.[69]

Ultimately, conservative criticism of testimony as faulty evidence has worked to obscure a key value of testimony, which is its ability to activate the process of witnessing and serve as a starting place for a form of memory-work that opens the possibility of remaking the past in the present.

To be clear, I have not argued that concepts of referentiality are unimportant when considering life narrative and testimony, but I have complicated this through an analysis of the subject-position of the secondary witness. The secondary witness is vulnerable to false testimony and, as such, may often hold quite legitimate concerns about the meanings of life narratives. Yet this suspicion often exceeds the circumstances of a particular hoax, destabilizing the broader cultural work performed by testimony. Since the early 1990s, hoaxing, deliberate imposture and conservative skepticism combined to contribute to a climate of doubt in

Australian culture, in which the voices of minority subjects were always already under suspicion. And this is my chief concern: that the practice of witnessing, while initiated by the need of the testifier to speak, is actually oriented toward the secondary witness and dependent upon their benevolence and capacity for empathy. In an Australian context, this has positioned Anglo-Australians as arbiters of both individual truth and the national past. To accept the challenge—and risks—of a more ambivalent form of witnessing testimony is to work toward the ceding of this privilege to consider how *all* voices are worthy of considered attention. This will mean, in Kelly Oliver's terms, accepting the "response-ability" of witnessing: to respond to testimony "in a way that opens up rather than closes off the possibility of response by others."[70]

Notes

1. Australian Indigenous Peoples make up approximately 2.5 percent of the total Australian population and comprise two distinct groups: the people of the Torres Strait Islands between northern Queensland and Papua New Guinea, and the Aboriginal people of the Australian mainland and Tasmania. Though they are referred to collectively as "Indigenous peoples," Aboriginal Australians are marked by a wide diversity of language, experience, and culture.
2. John Howard, cited in Emma Macdonald, "Stolen Claim Backfires on O'Donoghue," *Canberra Times*, February 24, 2001, 1.
3. Shoshana Felman and Dori Laub, *Testimony: Crises of Witnessing in Literature, Psychoanalysis, and History* (New York: Routledge, 1992); Dominick LaCapra, *History and Memory after Auschwitz* (Ithaca: Cornell University Press, 1998); Kelly Oliver, *Witnessing: Beyond Recognition* (Minneapolis: University of Minnesota Press, 2001); Gillian Whitlock, "In the Second Person: Narrative Transactions in Stolen Generations Testimony," *Biography* 21, 1 (Winter 2001): 197–214; Rosanne Kennedy, "Stolen Generations Testimony: Trauma, Historiography, and the Question of 'Truth'," *Aboriginal History* 25 (2001): 116–31; Dora Apel, *Memory Effects: The Holocaust and the Art of Secondary Witnessing* (New Brunswick, NJ: Rutgers University Press, 2002).
4. Dori Laub, "Bearing Witness, or the Vicissitudes of Listening," in *Testimony: Crises of Witnessing in Literature, Psychoanalysis, and History*, ed. Shoshana Felman and Dori Laub (New York: Routledge, 1992), 68.
5. Penny van Toorn, *Writing Never Arrives Naked: Early Aboriginal Cultures of Writing in Australia* (Canberra: Aboriginal Studies Press, 2006).
6. Human Rights and Equal Opportunity Commission (HREOC), *Bringing Them Home: Report of the National Inquiry into the Separation of Aboriginal and Torres Strait Islander Children from Their Families* (Sydney: Human Rights and Equal Opportunity Commission, 1997), 37, 266. It is important to note that although *Bringing Them Home* described the practice of child removal as genocide, according to the United Nations' definition, the issue of whether or not the stolen generations were subjected to genocide was fiercely contested by commentators and academics both sympathetic and hostile to their claims.
7. Ibid., 20.
8. Ibid., 4.

9. Laub, "Bearing Witness, or the Vicissitudes of Listening," 58.
10. Whitlock, "In the Second Person," 199.
11. Fiona Probyn-Rapsey, "Complicity, Critique, and Methodology," *ARIEL: A Review of International English Literature* 38, 2 (2008): 65–82.
12. Michelle Grattan, ed. *Reconciliation: Essays on Australian Reconciliation* (Melbourne: Black Inc, 2000).
13. Angela Pratt, Catriona Elder, and Cath Ellis, "Papering over the Differences: Australian Nationhood and the Normative Discourse of Reconciliation," in *Reconciliation, Multiculturalism, Identities: Difficult Dialogues, Sensible Solutions*, ed. Mary Kalantzis and Bill Cope (Common Ground Publishing, 2001), 187.
14. Angela Pratt, *Practising Reconciliation?: The Politics of Reconciliation in the Australian Parliament, 1991–2000* (Canberra: Department of Parliamentary Services, 2005).
15. Maryrose Casey, "Referendums and Reconciliation Marches: What Bridges Are We Crossing?" *Journal of Australian Studies* 89 (2006): 137–52; Haydie Gooder and Jane M. Jacobs, "'On the Border of the Unsayable': The Apology in Postcolonizing Australia." *interventions* 2, no. 2 (2000): 229–47; Whitlock, "In the Second Person."
16. It is incredibly difficult to quantify support for an apology to the stolen generations, and even harder to assess the number of Australians who participated as "active" witnesses in reconciliation activities. Murray Goot and Tim Rowse have undertaken a comprehensive analysis of opinion polling on the issue of reconciliation. They found that an "examination of the data suggests that for Australians reconciliation was largely about non-Aboriginal Australians acknowledging the past and about Aboriginal Australians taking responsibility for their future." Their work has demonstrated that support for reconciliation fluctuated widely and that these shifts illustrated how non-Indigenous Australians were often "divided" internally over what reconciliation should mean for the nation (Murray Goot and Tim Rowse, *Divided Nation?: Indigenous Affairs and the Imagined Public* [Melbourne: Melbourne University Press, 2007], 150).
17. Stuart Macintyre and Anna Clark, *The History Wars* (Melbourne: Melbourne University Press, 2003), 128–33.
18. John Howard, cited in Liz Jackson, Interview with John Howard, 19 February 1996, *Four Corners,* ABC, [Transcript] available from: http://www.abc.net.au/4corners/content/2004/ s1212701.htm; accessed January 28, 2009.
19. John Howard, "Opening Address to the Australian Reconciliation Convention," Melbourne, 1997, *Australian Legal Information Institute,* available from: http://www.austlii.edu.au/ au/other/IndigLRes/car/1997/4/pmspoken.html; accessed January 25, 2009.
20. Ibid.
21. See especially Kay Schaffer and Sidonie Smith, *Human Rights and Narrated Lives: The Ethics of Recognition* (New York: Palgrave Macmillan, 2004).
22. The major exception is, of course, the phenomenon of Holocaust denial, although this work largely avoids a discussion of the mechanics of testimony to focus on refusal in the broader context of anti-Semitism. See, for example, Kenneth S. Stern, *Holocaust Denial* (New York: American Jewish Committee, 1993); Stephen E Atkins, *Holocaust Denial as an International Movement* (Westport, CN: Praeger, 2009).
23. Philippe Lejeune, *On Autobiography*, ed. Paul John Eakin, trans. Katherine Leary (Minneapolis: University of Minnesota Press, 1989).
24. On the history of hoaxes in Australian literary culture, see especially: Maggie Nolan, "In His Own Sweet Time: Carmen's Coming Out," *Australian Literary Studies* 21, no. 4 (2004): 134–48; David Carter, "O'Grady, John, *See* 'Culotta, Nino': Popular Authorship, Duplicity and Celebrity," *Australian Literary Studies* 21, no. 4 (2004):

56–73; Michael Heyward, *The Ern Malley Affair* (St. Lucia: University of Queensland Press, 1993); Simon Caterson, *Hoax Nation: Australian Fakes and Frauds, from Plato to Norma Khouri* (Melbourne: Arcade Publications, 2009).
25. On Helen Demidenko see especially Robert Manne, *The Culture of Forgetting: Helen Demidenko and the Holocaust* (Melbourne: Text Publishing Co., 1996).
26. Maggie Nolan and Carrie Dawson, "Who's Who? Mapping Hoaxes and Imposture in Australian Literary History," *Australian Literary Studies* 21, no. 4 (2004): vi.
27. On the continued reader association of the author with the subject of autobiography, see Kate Douglas, "'Blurbing' Autobiographical: Authorship and Autobiography," *Biography* 24, no. 4 (2001): 806–26.
28. Gillian Whitlock, "Tainted Testimony: The Khouri Affair." *Australian Literary Studies* 21, no. 4 (2004): 171.
29. *Herald Sun* columnist Andrew Bolt is particularly known for his characterization of the stolen generations as a "myth." See, for example Andrew Bolt, "Straight Talking Seen as a Crime," *Herald Sun*, 24 February 2001, 3; Andrew Bolt, "A Moral Mafia," *Herald Sun*, 13 April 2000, 18.
30. Bolt, "Straight Talking Seen as a Crime," 3.
31. Andrew Bolt, "Sorry, but I Wasn't 'Stolen'—Leader Admits She Lied," *Daily Telegraph*, February 23, 2001, 3.
32. Ibid.
33. Ibid.
34. Bolt, "A Moral Mafia," 18.
35. McGuinness, cited in Robert Manne, "In Denial: The Stolen Generations and the Right," in *Left Right Left: Political Essays 1977–2005* (Melbourne: Black Inc., 2005): 272.
36. John Howard, cited in Emma Macdonald, "Stolen Claim Backfires on O'Donoghue," *Canberra Times*, February 24, 2001, 1.
37. Bolt, "Straight Talking Seen as a Crime," 3.
38. Piers Akerman, "Sorry, It's the Truth," *Courier Mail*, March 2, 2001, 13.
39. Bolt, "A Moral Mafia," 18.
40. Editorial, "The Healing Value of the Truth," *Courier Mail*, February 24, 2001, 22.
41. Akerman, "Sorry, It's the Truth," 13. See also, Piers Akerman, "Embracing the Lie Prolongs the Pain," *Daily Telegraph*, April 6, 2000, 23.
42. Phillip Gourevitch, cited in Andrew S. Gross and Michael J. Hoffman, "Memory, Authority, and Identity: Holocaust Studies in Light of the Wilkomirski Debate," *Biography* 27, 1 (2004): 13.
43. Stefan Maechler, *The Wilkomirski Affair: A Study in Biographical Truth* (New York: Schocken, 2001).
44. See especially the invocation of the notion of "second-hand witnessing" in Michael Bernard-Donals, "Beyond the Question of Authenticity: Witness and Testimony in the *Fragments* Controversy," *PMLA* 116, 5 (2001): 1302–15. Compare with the concept of "prosthetic memory," a product of the transferential relationship between testifier and witness, in Alison Landsberg, "America, the Holocaust, and the Mass Culture of Memory: Toward a Radical Politics of Empathy," *New German Critique: An Interdisciplinary Journal of German Studies* 71 (Spring–Summer 1997): 63–87.
45. Felman and Laub, 5.
46. Gross and Hoffman, "Memory, Authority, and Identity," 35.
47. On criticism of *Bringing Them Home* for failing to cross-examine witnesses, see Ron Brunton, "Betraying the Victims: The 'Stolen Generations' Report," *IPA Backgrounder* 10, 1 (1998).
48. *Cubillo v Commonwealth*: (1999) 89 FCR 528; (2000) 103 FCR 1; (2001) 112 FCR 171. It is instructive, though beyond the scope of this chapter, to compare the "failure"

of Cubillo-Gunner and its treatment of Indigenous testimony to other cases, particularly the first stolen-generation case, *Kruger v The Commonwealth* (1997) 190 CLR 1; the land-rights case *Yorta Yorta Aboriginal Community v State of Victoria* [1998] 1606 FA; and the first successful stolen-generation compensation case, *Trevorrow v State of South Australia (No 5)* [2007] SASC 285. For a detailed analysis of these cases and their significance for the legal status of Aboriginal testimony, see Curthoys, Genovese, and Reilly, *Rights and Redemption: History, Law and Indigenous People* (Sydney: UNSW Press, 2008).

49. Ibid., 134.
50. O'Loughlin cited in Trish Luker, "'Postcolonising Amnesia' in the Discourse of Reconciliation: The Void in the Law's Response to the Stolen Generations," *Australian Feminist Law Journal* 22 (June 2005): 82.
51. Ibid.
52. Curthoys, Genovese, and Reilly, *Rights and Redemption*, 136.
53. Luker, "Postcolonising Amnesia," 85.
54. Jennifer Clarke, "Case Note: *Cubillo v The Commonwealth*," *Melbourne University Law Review* 25, (2001). Available from: http://www.austlii.edu.au/au/journals/MULR/2001/7.html#Heading68. Accessed on: 22 November 2009.
55. Luker, "Postcolonising Amnesia," 87.
56. Lorna Cubillo's testimony of her removal included descriptions of "a lot of people crying" and "hitting themselves with hunting sticks so that blood was pouring down their faces." Lorna Cubillo cited in Luker, "Postcolonising Amnesia," 85.
57. See, for example: Akerman, "Sorry, It's the Truth," 13; Mark Metherell and Debra Jopson, "Stolen Children Ruling Vindicates Stance: Pm," *Sydney Morning Herald*, August 12, 2000, 2; Michael Duffy, "Myths Perpetuate a Stake in Victimhood," *Daily Telegraph*, August 12, 2000, 23.
58. Andrew Bolt, "Confusing Emotion with Facts Won't Help the Aboriginal Cause," *Herald Sun*, August 14, 2000, 18.
59. On the historical significance of *Mabo*, see Bain Attwood, ed., *In the Age of Mabo: History, Aborigines and Australia* (Sydney: Allen & Unwin, 1996).
60. Though the planning process and application for the bridge began as early as 1989, the "affair" did not become public until 1994 when the Aboriginal Legal Rights Movement, acting on behalf of a group of Ngarrindjeri people, sought to protect the area under the Commonwealth's *Aboriginal and Torres Strait Islander Heritage Protection Act 1984*. For a summary of events, see Curthoys, Genovese, and Reilly, *Rights and Redemption*, 167–90. See also Margaret Simons, *The Meeting of the Waters: The Hindmarsh Island Affair* (Sydney: Hodder, 2003).
61. For an account of this dispute from Kartinyeri's perspective, see Doreen Kartinyeri and Sue Anderson, *Doreen Kartinyeri: My Ngarindjeri Calling* (Canberra: Aboriginal Studies Press, 2008).
62. Hindmarsh Island Bridge Royal Commission, *Report of the Hindmarsh Island Bridge Royal Commission* (Adelaide: The Royal Commission, 1995). The bridge was completed in 2001.
63. Bolt referred to the affair as a "nonsense case," while Akerman described the "secret women's business" as "ideological hogwash cooked up by feminist anthropologists." Bolt, "Confusing Emotion with Facts Won't Help the Aboriginal Cause," 18. Piers Akerman, "Truth and the Black Armband Brigade," *Daily Telegraph*, March 1, 2001, 19.
64. *Chapman v Luminis Pty Lt (No 4)* (2001) 123 FCR 62. See also Curthoys, Genovese, and Reilly, *Rights and Redemption*, 167–90.

65. Irene Watson, "Settled and Unsettled Spaces: Are We Free to Roam?," in *Sovereign Subjects: Indigenous Sovereignty Matters*, edited by Aileen Moreton-Robinson (Crows Nest: Allen & Unwin, 2007): 16.
66. Curthoys, Genovese, and Reilly, *Rights and Redemption*, 168.
67. Bolt, "Confusing Emotion with Facts Won't Help the Aboriginal Cause," 18.
68. Manne, "In Denial: The Stolen Generations and the Right," 303.
69. Deborah Bird Rose, *Reports from a Wild Country: Ethics for Decolonisation* (Sydney: UNSW Press, 2004), 14.
70. Oliver, *Witnessing*, 18.

12

Individual Desire or Social Duty? The Role of Testimony in a Restitution Procedure: An Inquiry into Social Practice

Nicole L. Immler[1]

Narratives of victimhood, or in a broader sense, life-story narratives, have gained an important role not only in historiography but also increasingly in the field of transitional justice and in the courtroom. The former is a result of the establishment of oral history and the "history from below" of the 1970s, and the latter emerged from truth commissions (e.g., in South Africa and Latin America) that asserted the usefulness of allowing the witness to speak during a reconciliation process.[2] Both cases are less about the specifics of the past than about the benefits of the storytelling for the individuals in the present; less about gathering evidence than about being an end in itself.[3] Additionally, the International Criminal Court (ICC) in The Hague established new procedures for increased victim participation in legal procedures, not just as witnesses, as was the case in the ad-hoc UN tribunals of the Former Yugoslavia and Rwanda, but also as victims, allowed (within limits) to tell their stories. The Rome Statute (1998) grants victims the right to participate in proceedings, the right to request reparation, and the right to legal representation. Such rights are often granted by national law, but were entirely new to international law.[4] This interest and belief in the participation of victims as a means of creating better preconditions for justice and future reconciliation is a phenomenon that has progressively developed since the 1960s. But to what extent does it favor the victims (with respect to empowerment or recognition), and what are the pitfalls? What are the implications of a legal framework on the narrative construction of the past?

A brief history of witnessing by victims of Nazism will highlight how testimony relates to the public discourse over time. I shall then examine the challenges of one testimony in a restitution procedure sixty years after the war, with regard both to evidence and to defining the role of a witness. This article will explore testifying as social practice by scrutinizing a hearing from a recent restitution claim in Austria about returning a house that was aryanized in 1938 in Vienna. It aims to reconsider the meanings of "testimony" in a restitution procedure and to show how the study of reparation procedures can make a critical contribution to the study of testimony and vice-versa. I will argue that in scholarly debates and institutional practice, the topic of compensation to victims of National Socialism has often become mired in historical and legal details, instead of focusing on the social practice and its ambivalent effects.

Life-Story Accounts of Victims of Nazism

In the first post-war decade, justice was carried out without a niche for the victim, who was thought to be too emotional for the juridical search for data and culpability. Moreover, the legal proceedings fashioned themselves as future- rather than past-oriented. This selective and collective forgetting as well as post-war myths of anti-fascism, resistance, and victimhood, facilitated Europe's astonishing post-war recovery.[5] In this atmosphere, high-ranking perpetrators of National Socialism were put on trial in the name of justice and future peace. The victims of National Socialism, however, were not encouraged to tell their stories. At the Nuremberg Military Tribunal (1945–46) the victims and their stories played a subordinate role in the courtroom, which was legitimized by the fact that the lawyers had full access to the extensive archives of the Nazis. They questioned only a few witnesses, mainly to confirm the documents.[6] Moreover, the testimonies were entirely constrained by the format of juridical interrogation, which is interactive but not dialogic, centers on the procedure and not the witness, and tends to conflate accuracy with sincerity.[7] This is also characteristic of subsequent trials, such as the Auschwitz trials in Frankfurt (1963–65), which broke the silence of the 1950s, but disappointed the victims. Next to all the difficulties of returning to Germany and being confronted with the perpetrators in the court, former victims had to defend their reliability as witnesses, and accept acquittals and sentences of detention they deemed too short.[8]

Similarly the reparation procedures had no place for the life stories of the victims. This is clearly expressed in the application forms for restitution at that time, which requested a quantification of all losses and provided categories for material goods but offered no space for relating personal experiences. Following Frank Bajohr, this "material reductionism" was enforced by the use of abstract language as well as by the separation of the procedures regarding damage to life and damage to property, excluding any non-material losses regarding lifestyle or education. Some people added lengthy reports of their story of persecution and inserted their life stories into the files anyway.[9] However, as we know from the history of the German *Wiedergutmachung*, the application form answers were often shaped in a way that did not reflect personal histories or suffering, but rather promised the greatest chances of recognition. Victims, often with the help of specialized lawyers, who translated life stories into juridical categories, modeled the data of their lives in accordance with compensation categories, tailored to what commissions would expect and approve.[10]

The files show how over the years, irrelevant facts began to disappear, and relevant descriptions of the persecution become more detailed; how language adjusted to the legal logic and the mindset of that time.[11] However, the official expectations and requirements changed over time. Under the Federal Compensation Act (BEG 1952), in the 1950s the authorities required survivors to show proof of damages due to persecution. Thus, the applicants focused on their forced presence in the ghetto, the poor living conditions, their daily struggle for survival, the loss of personal freedom and health. These narratives of persecution left little space for narratives of the everyday—describing, for example, the hours of labor inside or outside the camp; often the work was not even mentioned, because the BEG compensated the loss of personal freedom but not lost wages. At that time no one was interested in these questions, whereas forty years later, in order to receive a ghetto pension (2002), survivors were required to prove that the work they had done during their time in the concentration camp was like an employment relationship, based upon free will instead of forced labor. Now, in the context of social legislation, they emphasized the orderly working relationship they had had, while in the BEG applications, people reported that they had not had a choice. Those differences in the narratives caused the authorities to reject more than ninety percent of the applicants. As Constantin Goschler has pointed out, in their rejection, the authorities preferred to mistrust the applicants, instead of inferring that ghetto pension law was based on a "false fiction of normality" that did not correspond at all to the petitioners' experience of the ghetto.[12] Moreover, the pension law inverted the persecution narratives, as well as the logic of compensation. Those who had been relatively better off in the ghettos by holding jobs were most likely to receive a pension. This example illustrates how the public discourse on the Holocaust and its juridical categories shaped the applicants' self-perception as well as their self-presentation.

Directly after the war, many victims preferred not to talk about the past. They were confronted with a public that did not want to hear their stories, and they perceived themselves as survivors; they just wanted to start a new life. Later, when claims for compensation still had not been honored, despite decades of fighting for this, the lack of acknowledgement of their personal experiences was often experienced as traumatic. Because their suffering had gone unrecognized, they felt that their family history had not been officially legitimated.[13]

Only with the Eichmann trial in 1961 in Jerusalem did these personal memories begin to reach a wider public. When personal memories were used in court, survivor narratives came to the foreground, and over a hundred survivors spoke up in public. The figure of the witness (*Zeitzeuge*) was born.[14] The Eichmann trial turned the genocide into a series of individual experiences with which the public could identify. At the same time, those individual stories gained "semantic authority" by transcending individual testimony.[15] They were translated into a collective story of the suffering of the Jewish people, which evoked identification with the victims beyond the juridical framework. By contrast, during the Auschwitz trials in Frankfurt (1963–65), where "normal" members of the SS were charged for their daily routine of murder, the status of the more than two hundred witnesses was "only" that of legal, *eye* witness (*Augen-, Beweiszeuge*), as they were called upon to provide evidence against the perpetrators, not to act as witnesses (*Zeitzeuge*) tasked to remember.[16]

In the 1970s, the status of the witness slowly transformed from *Zeuge*, a witness asked only to confirm documents or to provide documentary evidence within a strict juridical framework, to *Zeitzeuge*, one who was asked to remember and recollect, to tell his or her story to help construct a collective history of what was only called the "Holocaust" in Germany after the airing of the TV series *Holocaust* (1979). This series (USA 1978, Austria 1979) crystallized the victims' experiences in the public's mind, and survivors started to talk more openly about themselves. However, the increasing mediality of the Holocaust changed the character of witnessing. While the classical *Zeuge*, in court or in the media, is an observer of events, the *Zeitzeuge* represents the past through storytelling, mediating the past through emotions rather than explanations. The "observer" became "representative," an embodiment of an authentic historical presentation by emotionally touching the audience—indicating, according to Judith Keilbach, a shift from a juridical to a historical discourse, from objectivity to emotionality.[17] This media interest in individual destinies was supported by a "psychological turn," which occurred first in the field of medicine and then in society.

When Post Traumatic Stress Disorder (PTSD) was discovered in the late 1970s, in close connection with the Vietnam War, and recognized by the American Psychiatric Association in 1980, a new awareness emerged of the long-term psychological dimensions of war trauma.[18] This new trauma discourse was a precondition for the acknowledgement and the calculation of belated damages for *Wiedergutmachung* (such as providing more specialized treatment). However, the diagnosis of "trauma" also often re-victimized the victims by, for example, undermining their authority, as in cases in which their reports as witnesses were not considered in legal proceedings as providing evidence because of their trauma, or cases in which perpetrators were acquitted because they had been traumatized.[19] While directly after the war the *Wiedergutmachung* represented a purely juridical procedure regarding material matters, it gained a symbolic dimension as "survivors" turned into "victims" and the juridical discourse transformed the discussion into an identity discourse. The "forgotten victims" of National Socialism (such as Roma and Sintis) were "(re)discovered" toward the end of the 1980s, while for some groups (such as forced laborers from Eastern Europe) compensation issues were only addressed in the late 1990s. When this topic (re-)emerged in the 1990s in Austria, how much of a role did life stories and testimonies play in the reparations procedures that took place sixty years after the war?

The Life-Story Approach in Austrian Reparation Procedures

Austria, like many European countries, developed a new policy[20] of public engagement with the legacy of the Holocaust in the wake of the fiftieth anniversaries of the 1990s. These anniversaries revitalized specific memories that focused on the annexation of Austria by Germany in 1938, the end of the war, the liberation, and the struggle for the state treaty. At the same time, the global discourse involving the "Swiss Nazi Gold Bank" affair, new attention to art theft (initiated by the confiscation of Schiele paintings in 1998 in New York) and, in particular, the class-action suits in the United States against German and Austrian firms, served to exert outside pressure on Austria. Consequently, the government of Austria initiated (among other things) a Historical Commission, an Art Restitution Law (both 1998) and two different Funds for victims of National Socialism.

The life-story approach served as the basis for the 1995 policy of the "National Fund of the Republic of Austria for Victims of National Socialism" (NF), in effect saying, "We are interested in your story." It acknowledged victims with the general gesture of a lump-sum payment, which was based upon a small questionnaire regarding some basic personal facts that could prove that this person had been forced to leave Austria in 1938. Life-story questions were asked on the final page in an open way, leaving space for the applicant to add extra information. In the letters, applicants were also invited to contact the Fund for additional help. Many survivors visited the Fund, and the employees listened to thousands of stories in application procedures. Later, some of these testimonies were published in the public reports of the Fund.[21] The employees also visited potential applicants in and near Vienna, who were either too old to come to the Fund office or were members of specific groups such as the Roma, who had often difficulties completing the applications. Outside of Austria, the Austrian embassies were tasked with this job, which generally took the form of a visit from the NF General Secretary to explain the procedures and personalize the restitution policy.

This approach changed in 2001, when the questionnaires of the "General Settlement Fund" (GSF) began to address heirs also and started to request many details. It was a very ambitious attempt to individualize victim stories, and to compensate for what had been stolen on an individual basis. This fact-finding mission was based upon a detailed twenty-eight-page questionnaire covering categories such as education, bank accounts, mortgages, stocks, bonds, businesses, insurance policies, real estate, and movable property. In addition to providing monetary compensation for those specific losses, the GSF returned property such as houses or pieces of art, but only if they were publicly owned by the Republic of Austria, the city of Vienna, or the federal states, on 17 January 2001, the date on which the "Washington Agreement" was signed between Austria and the United States. The Washington Agreement aimed to dismiss all pending class-action lawsuits against Austria and Austrian companies filed in US courts. In practice, this individualized approach paradoxically led to less attention to life stories and the communication process and more to a feverish search through the archives. It created a dynamic in which the scrupulously detailed questionnaire, supplemented by archival research, gave personal memories less critical importance in the process since they generally lack that kind of detail. Nevertheless, in some restitution cases, hearings were held if there was not enough historical evidence in the archives to determine a case. Then either the applicants or family members who witnessed the respective events were invited to recount what they knew about the historical situation. Below I will describe such a case, analyzing how the presentation of a life story and the argumentation attendant to its presentation changed during the claim process, and how the applicant reflected upon this process when later interviewed.

Ellis's Restitution Case[22]

Ellis, born in the early 1920s in Vienna, filed a restitution claim with the General Settlement Fund in 2004 for the restitution of a house in Vienna that had belonged to her mother's family in 1938; in 2001 it belonged to the city of Vienna. Filing the claim was not her own idea, as she repeated again and again in our 2009 interview in London. She emphasized that the Jewish community in Vienna had "begged" her to make this claim. The case "came to light" during the research of the Austrian Historical Commission. They documented property transfers between 1938 and 1945 in Austria and focused on the cases that involved public ownership in 2001. The Jewish Community would then examine the question of whether a restitution request had prospects of success. In Ellis's case they discovered that her maternal step-grandmother had been deported to a concentration camp, where she was murdered, and that her house in Vienna had been aryanized by a dressmaker with a tailor shop. He purchased the house for a pittance and sold it after the war to the city of Vienna for a large sum. Upon learning this story, Ellis concluded, "he profited twice."

This part of her family history was new to Ellis. Her mother had come from an upper-middle-class Jewish background, her father had worked as a watch repairman and goldsmith, and she had been raised in a social-democratic milieu. She and her parents had lost contact with the wealthier branch of the family after they lost everything in the depression in 1929. She described herself as part of the middle class who had already been plunged into poverty in those early years, so she was asking herself, "What shall I ask for?" In the interview Ellis emphasized that she herself refused to deal with those issues: "I wanted nothing to do with it, somehow I refused.. . .," just like her parents had done; she claims they had never thought about compensation. She quoted her father as saying, "I have survived, that is the most important. [. . .] Actually nothing happened to me." She went on to state that material losses meant nothing to her, as "we lost everything in life twice"; first, when she fled with her family to England in 1938, and second, when she again fled to England in 1968, this time with her husband, after having lived in Czechoslovakia as a confirmed socialist. "It [the restitution] came to me, it does not matter to us in life. Possession was not the most important; having property was not our main goal."

Ellis explained the fact that she had filled in various applications at different times as having been the result of collaboration with others: the first was initiated by a friend, a later application was facilitated by the help of a lawyer, and finally another was driven by the suggestion of the Jewish community in Vienna. This most recent application was formulated on the basis of the documents from the archives, which indicated that the sum paid for the house in 1938 was only a fraction of its value at the time, and that the lawyer who represented the claimants, Ellis's aunts, was known to have had a National Socialist past. As Ellis reported in the interview:

> I have seen the papers; they [the aunts] had a lawyer and the *Arisierer* had a lawyer too, both were ex-Nazis, and they made the deal, offering her a settlement of 600 Schillings. 600 Schillings [*it was in fact 6,000, N.I.*] for a whole house! Only a crazy person could agree to this.[23]

But the claim, submitted in December 2004, was rejected by the GSF Commission in February 2006 because there had already been a restitution procedure in 1953 that had been finalized in a settlement signed by Ellis's aunts.[24] Here the GSF law states that if a piece of real estate was the subject of a claim that had previously been decided upon by an Austrian administrative body, then restitution or compensation was not possible again, unless it could be proven that the former procedure had been "extremely unjust."[25] This meant that evidence was required of a significant difference between a property's value and the sale price (*Wertdifferenz*), but evidence was also needed of the restricted private autonomy of the individuals involved (*eingeschränkte Privatautonomie*) to act in their own interests. In this respect the Fund's rejection highlighted the fact that one of the applicants was living in Austria at the time of the deal and that they had an official representative, which indicated that they had had freedom of choice.

After the rejection, the Jewish community of Vienna approached Ellis again, insisting she make an appeal, as they considered it a test case for the definition of "extreme injustice." Winning the case would mean that other applicants could profit from it in the near future. Ellis was finally convinced by their argument that if she did not make the claim, she would be "harming or disadvantaging others." In December 2006 they made the appeal along new lines. Whereas her first claim had focused mainly on an unjust deal, this claim highlighted the assertion that her aunts had not been given the option to make a different decision or strike a better deal at that time. She argued that her aunts' autonomy had been restricted when they signed the settlement due to their difficult economic circumstances and psychological conditions. Ellis's claim detailed how one of her aunts, studying in London since 1936, was so traumatized by the London Blitz that she was severely psychologically damaged and had to spend some time in a psychiatric clinic. Ellis argued in her appeal that when her aunt was involved in the restitution process in September and October of 1950, she was still in poor psychological condition, worsened by the fact that she had just returned to Austria, was unemployed, and had no economic resources. Her autonomy in deciding whether to accept the restitution procedure had thus been rather limited. Later, her aunt did have work, but a week after signing the settlement in March 1953 she became ill and stayed home for the next two weeks. As Ellis argued, her illness indicated that her experience of the procedure had been very distressing and traumatizing, and that she was rendered unable to make a rational choice about whether to accept or reject the settlement.[26] Moreover, her aunt's sister, who had lost her only son in Auschwitz and was caring for a sick husband, was in a psychologically difficult and economically tense situation as well.

This line of argumentation in Ellis's application was partly questioned by the representatives of the city of Vienna, who doubted whether one could claim to have been experiencing trauma in the mid-1950s due to the bombing of London, especially since this person had continued to practice her profession and had decided to return to Austria. This, they thought, challenged the claim of mental distress or impairment. Moreover, they argued that it was inappropriate to call the lawyers "former Nazis" eight years after the war, because they had been appointed on "the legal basis of a democratic Austria."[27] This led the GSF restitution commission to invite Ellis for a hearing to gather more evidence.

The Hearing

The hearing before the commission officials in August 2007 in Vienna was aimed at getting to know more about the extent to which the aunts could have made an independent decision in the 1950s. Ellis repeated what she had written in the application, adding that after her aunt had been discharged from the psychiatric hospital, she had moved in with her mother. This living arrangement was so exhausting for her (she was pregnant at the time) that she soon left her parents' home. Later, in the new decision, the Arbitration Panel of the GSF referred to the description of her aunt's "traumatized condition"[28] that made it impossible for the protagonists to make a rational decision for or against the settlement. The new decision acknowledged that the economic and psychological conditions had restricted her aunts' autonomy and that the settlement had been inadequate. As a result, the Committee advised the city of Vienna to return the former family house, or rather to pay the heirs an equivalent sum for it since the property was being used as a school building when the decision was made in 2006. Ellis herself received a small share of three percent, because her mother had owned only a few shares of the house.

Strangely, this positive decision hardly features in the interview with Ellis; it is overlapped by other stories of worries. Ellis started to talk about her experience with the compensation only after she had told me her family's story and her own story, and only after we had had lunch together and a basis for trust had been established. After she had recalled the historical details of the case in matter-of-fact language, her husband interrupted, reminding her that she "should also say that it did not go through the first time." Ellis went on to explain that "In the first instance it was rejected as it was not unjust enough." Then she described how she "was asked" to get involved. Her husband interrupted again, rephrasing it: "They hired you," hinting at some instrumentalization. Then he went on to describe his concerns and fears that his wife might have been treated poorly in the procedure. For example, he described an informal meeting they had in Vienna with the various parties of the restitution claim, organized by the Jewish community who had invited Ellis, as well as representatives of the Austrian government, the city of Vienna and the GSF Restitution Commission. He reported in detail how they met a young lawyer there who was in charge of their case: "He approached me, saying he had many questions, and then only asking one—an irrelevant one." Ellis interjected, "I think he asked if I knew my grandmother or something like that." Her husband continued: "A completely trivial question. Then I realized, and Ellis as well, that it was a pure formality." His impression that the meeting was a farce was confirmed when the application was rejected. Some months later, after the appeal was made, and the case was taken up again, Ellis was invited to a formal hearing, this time by the Arbitration Panel of the Restitution Commission. Ellis, although unhappy with this invitation, admitted that she could not reject the pleas of the Jewish community to create a precedent case study. Based upon their former experience, her husband repeated his reservations about the meeting: "And then I said, she should not make a fool [*Kasperl*] of herself," emphasizing how much he worried that the second hearing would also become a "show," just a "pure formality" with trivial questions.

This example shows the delicateness of such encounters. While retelling the story, it becomes clear that because she was invited, she expected to be asked as a witness to give a detailed account about past events; she expected questions and engaged listeners, the formal features of a life story interview. However, it seemed to her that merely her appearance at the meeting was sufficient to sustain either her claim or that of the Jewish community. She felt uncertain about her role in the meeting because she had not been treated as a witness.

Despite all the caution, or maybe because of this caution, she described the second hearing as a similarly ambivalent experience. Even though it helped to alter the earlier decision of 2006, and was in this sense a success story, it was not so in other ways. The fact that she was confronted with an unknown and larger audience than she had expected caused some discomfort with the situation. She described it as "quite a show, and a public event." Her husband confirmed her view: "There was a show, as feared." However, a few moments later, they referred to the meeting as "quiet," "very polite," and "respectful." It seems they perceived this politeness as an affront: "the president—the chairman—went out of his way," and the representatives of the city of Vienna "of course were against" this measure. As an academic accustomed to acting in the public sphere, Ellis's discomfort seemed to extend beyond questions of space, publicity, and the audience. Rather, it was triggered by the awareness that one still had to demand justice: "Today, we only won in the second instance," was something she and her husband repeated during the interview, emphasizing that they had to be insistent to obtain justice.

Individual Desire or Social Duty?

Although Ellis's claim was successful, and her testimony helped to sway the decision in her favor, in the interview they focused on their uneasiness surrounding the claim. They mentioned the pressure from America as a "maker" of the GSF, the hostile administrative bureaucracy she encountered when she tried to get back her Austrian citizenship, and the suspiciousness of others that she was trying to obtain a pension by fraud.[29] All these side-stories indicate that she still experiences mistrust and even discomfort with her role as a witness. This demonstrates her emotional upheaval about the way she was treated, or rather, how she felt she had been treated. The first (informal) hearing had created the feeling that they had invited her less for her knowledge than to create the aura of legitimacy. The same suspicions were aroused by the second (formal) hearing, which she summarized with the following words: "I did not need to tell them that since there was archival proof. I said what I knew about Aunt Marta, and this was confirmed." She might have asked herself what value the hearing had for the Commission. Did they believe her only because they found the corresponding documents in the archives, or would they have reached the same decision only on the basis of her testimony?

This uncertainty might have triggered certain defensive and distancing narratives which she repeated during the interview, when saying it was all other people's idea, emphasizing that she was petitioning as a favor to others—family members, representatives and the larger community of victims. This narrative of "I was asked to fill in the forms" is typical of many applicants, as they rarely formulate the right to make a claim.[30] This is more common in the second generation, which is much more outspoken and demanding about compensation matters. They often criticize their parents' defensive behavior and want them to make a claim, because in their view, it signals emancipation and empowerment. But survivors like Ellis tended to react with reluctance. By distancing herself ("But I am really not trying," "I don't have to stand for that"), she minimizes the danger of getting hurt, but she also minimizes the likelihood of accepting what she has gained.

Ellis's ambivalence may also have had political reasons. Her remarks indicate that her orientation as a socialist prevented her from showing interest in "property/money-issues." Since this was not her "main goal in life," she associated compensation with a capitalistic endeavor that was foreign to her family, "one which she did not try very hard" to achieve. On the other hand she described herself as being involved in a tight social network that asked her to apply. When she told of how a colleague motivated her to find out more about the compensation procedures, it was more to relate the story of their friendship and the way information was exchanged among colleagues, than to represent the story of the compensation itself. This angle was more about the process than the product, more about her lifestyle than the specifics of compensation. The way she represented herself and framed her life—that of a left-wing academic who, until 1968, passionately believed in communist ideals and was active in the socialist movement (and afterward steadfastly maintained her beliefs)—leaves no place for material desires. That world consists of loyalties, friendships, academic relationships, mutual support, and intellectual passion. In this framework the compensation story is represented as being part of social relations and obligations. It represents not individual desire but social duty.

Conclusion

The narrative frame suggested above downplays any personal dimension and integrates the topic into Ellis's worldview instead of touching her on a personal level. One might ask, as Srila Roy has done, whether a transformation has taken place here, one of personal pain into social suffering. Roy describes how personal pain articulated as public testimony is often transformed into "social suffering," in the same way that storytelling creates a "we," a sense of belonging. "Testimony is, in the final instance, a speech act that draws its meaning from a collective, plural 'us' rather than the 'I' who is in pain."[31] Ellis spoke on behalf of her aunts and her parents, and on behalf of the Jewish community—expressing a mediated pain and victimhood. A typical "Zeitzeugen" rhetoric, in which it is one's duty to witness or report, can be detected here. But Ellis also stated that this urge to bear witness was imposed by others on her and went against her own desire to *not* become personally involved.

After having fought so hard to gain distance, authorship, and recognition in other fields, she did not like to perceive herself as dependent on the judgment of others. Moreover she associated reparation procedures as such with choosing a victim position, with being degraded to a mere petitioner, a role in which she definitely did not envision herself. She expressed an inner conflict between the role expected of her (the social duty to identify with the victims) and her own ideas about lessons she had learned from the past, such as the fleetingness of material possessions, the persistence of intellectual property, and the necessity of social networks. Distinguishing between individual desires and social duties might be one way out of this dilemma.

If we then adjust our perspective to hers, and do not look at the testimony in terms of evidence but view it in the performative dimension, what is revealed? As much as a testimony is about content, it is also about a formal setting: the supporters, the opponents, the judge, and the witness. Viewed from this perspective, it seems that Ellis reasoned she had been treated poorly because she "still" had to fight for justice, though only after having intervened and made an appeal was her case resumed. Only by emphasizing different elements of the story or history, was she able to persuade the Fund to look into the archives again, and to examine the previously available material in a different light. However, in the end, Ellis concluded that it was the archival evidence that brought about change, and not her testimony. Although her statement in itself was unemotional, her use of the passive voice shows that this left her feeling powerless, even though she won the case. Moreover, ultimately it was the acknowledgment of her aunt's trauma that altered the decision. Thus, a "shift" did take place—one from a discourse about justice to one about trauma; from a discourse about persecution and looting to one about private autonomy and individual conditions; from the promise of compensation to the reality of only partly calculated amounts.

Ellis's remarks can be construed as a critical comment on those judicial categories that were established to legitimize the committees' final decision, but that also determined her status as witness. In other words, she had to remodel her story and claim not simply *injustice*, but *extreme injustice*; she had to stress not hard facts, but psychological conditions. This was Ellis's criticism of the performative nature of the legal process and giving testimony—a game she nonetheless learned to play. However, she seemed disturbed that she had succeeded by following the rules, and not because of her story. When she pictured the hearing as "quite a show, a public affair," and when her husband spoke indirectly of a *Kasperltheater*, it meant she felt that her testimony had not so much been used to confirm the facts, or to acknowledge her as a witness, but rather to legitimize the procedure—and little more than that.

What can this specific case study teach us? Testimonies have gained an important role in the field of transitional justice, forming a crucial basis of so-called Human Rights regimes, such as the International Criminal Court. The participation of victims as a means of personal healing and of creating better conditions for justice and future reconciliation is often interpreted as a progressive development in national and international law, but this is not undisputed in the scholarly literature.[32] This case study has aimed to illustrate that even when a hearing seems to run smoothly and is part of a successful claim, difficulties and frustrations may nonetheless be associated with it. Because testifying in legal proceedings means mixing two distinct rationalities and concepts—one which looks for concrete truth and evidence, the other for a comprehending mind—the whole communication process itself is at least as important as the outcome of the proceedings.[33] In the study of telling life stories, it is precisely in this dialogical character and its performative dimension that reparation policies can learn the most. According to oral historian Luisa Passerini, one has to place emphasis on the interpreter: "All autobiographical memory is true: it is up to the interpreter to discover in which sense, where, and for what purpose."[34] This begs for more reflection on the reciprocity between telling a life story, witnessing, and reparation procedure.

Notes

1. This work was made possible with the financial support of the National Fund for Victims of National Socialism in Vienna.
2. Victim testimony also prominently featured in the community Gacaca ("grass-lawn") courts of Rwanda.
3. See Anne Fleckstein, "'Nothing but the truth.' Bezeugen in der südafrikanischen Wahrheitskommission," in *Politik der Zeugenschaft. Zur Kritik einer Wissenspraxis*, ed. Sibylle Schmidt, Sybille Krämer, and Ramon Voges (Bielefeld: Transcript, 2011) ['Nothing but the truth' Testifying in the South African Truth Commission, in *Politics of Witnessing. Critique of a Practice of Knowledge*], 311–329; Jose Brunner, "Trauma and Justice: The Moral Grammar of Trauma Discourse from Wilhelmine Germany to Post-Apartheid South Africa," in *Trauma and Memory: Reading, Healing, and Making Law*, ed. Austin Sarat, Nadav Davidovitch, and Michal Alberstein (Standford, CA: University Press, 2007), 97–118; Priscilla B. Hayner, *Unspeakable Truths. Transitional Justice and the Challenge of Truth Commissions (New York: Routledge, 2010)*.
4. Anne-Marie de Brouwer and Marc Groenhuijsen, "The role of victims in international criminal proceedings," in *International Criminal Procedure towards a Coherent Body of Law*, ed. Goran Sluiter and Sergey Vasiliev (London: Cameron May, 2009), 149–204; Jo-Anne Wemmers, "Victim reparation and the International Criminal Court," in *International Review of Victimology*, 16 (2009): 123–126, 124.
5. Tony Judt, *Postwar: A history of Europe since 1945* (London: Penguin Books, 2006). This is most evident in the fact that West German authorities have launched over 106,000 investigations since the end of the war, but these have resulted in only 6,500 convictions; leaving no doubt that covering up and obstructing justice were given priority. Cf. *Im Labyrinth der Schuld: Täter—Opfer—Ankläger*, ed. Fritz Bauer Institut, Irmtrud Wojak, and Susanne Meinl (Frankf.a.M.: Campus Verlag, 2003) [*In the labyrinth of guilt: perpetrators—victims—prosecutors*].
6. See Annette Wieviorka, "Die Entstehung des Zeugen in *Hannah Arendt Revisited*," *"Eichmann in Jerusalem" und die Folgen*, ed. Gary Smith (Frankf.a.M.: Suhrkamp, 2000) ["The Formation of the Witness in *Hannah Arendt Revisited*," *"Eichmann in Jerusalem" and its Impact*], 136–159; for an overview: Marianne Hirsch and Leo Spitzer, "The witness in the archive: Holocaust Studies/Memory Studies," in *Memory Studies* 2, 2 (2009): 151–170, 153.
7. Aleida Assmann, "Vier Grundtypen von Zeugenschaft," in *Zeugenschaft des Holocaust. Zwischen Trauma, Tradierung und Ermittlung*, ed. Fritz Bauer Institut, Michael Elm, and Gottfried Kößler (Frankf.a.M., New York: Campus Verlag, 2007), 33–51, 34f. [Four Basic Types of Testimony, in *Testifying the Holocaust. Between Trauma, Transmisson and Identification*].
8. Irmtrud Wojak, "'Die Mauer des Schweigens ist durchbrochen': Der erste Frankfurter Auschwitz–Prozess 1963–65," in *"Gerichtstag halten über uns selbst..." Geschichte und Wirkung des ersten Frankfurter Auschwitz-Prozesses*, ed. Irmtrud Wojak and Fritz–Bauer–Institut (Frankf.a.M.-New York: Campus Verlag, 2001), 21–42. ["'The Wall of Silence Has Been Broken': The First Auschwitz Trial in Frankfurt 1963–65," in *"Judgment Hold About Ourselves..." History and Impact of the First Auschwitz Trial in Frankfurt*].

9. Frank Bajohr, "'Arisierung' und Restitution: Eine Einschätzung," in *"Arisierung" und Restitution: Die Rückerstattung jüdischen Eigentums in Deutschland und Österreich nach 1945 und 1989*, ed. Constantin Goschler and Jürgen Lillteicher (Göttingen: Wallenstein, 2002), 39–59, 56 ["'Aryanization' and Restitution: An Assesment," in *"Aryanization" and Restitution: The Restitution of Jewish Property in Germany and Austria after 1945 and 1989*].
10. See Tobias Winstel, "Die 'Testamentsvollstrecker': Anwälte und Rechtshilfeorganisationen in der Wiedergutmachung," in *Die Praxis der Wiedergutmachung: Geschichte, Erfahrung und Wirkung in Deutschland und Israel*, ed. Norbert Frei, José Brunner, and Constantin Goschler (Göttingen: Wallstein Verlag, 2009), 533–553 ["The 'Executors': Lawyers and Legal Aid Organizations in the Wiedergutmachung," in *The Practice of the Wiedergutmachung: History, Experience, and Impact in Germany and Israel*].
11. Constantin Goschler, "Ghettorenten und Zwangsarbeiterentschädigung: Verfolgungsnarrative im Spannungsfeld von Lebenswelt und Recht," in *Ghettorenten: Entschädigungspolitik, Rechtsprechung und historische Forschung*, ed. Jürgen Zarusky (München: Oldenbourg Verlag, 2010), 101–111, 105f. ["Ghetto Pensions and Compensation for Forced Labor Workers: Narratives of Persecution between Experience and Law," in *Ghetto Pensions: Compensation Politics, Legal Practice, and Historical Research*].
12. Ibid., 108f.
13. Milton Kestenberg, "Diskriminierende Aspekte der deutschen Entschädigungspraxis: Eine Fortsetzung der Verfolgung," in *Kinder der Opfer, Kinder der Täter: Psychoanalyse und Holocaust*, ed. Martin Bergmann et al. (Frankf.a.M.: Fischer, 1995), 74–99, 79 ["Discriminating Aspects of the German Reparation Program: A Continued Persecution," in *Children of Victims, Children of Perpetrators: Psychoanalysis and the Holocaust*].
14. Wieviorka, "Die Entstehung des Zeugen."
15. Shoshana Felman, *The Juridical Unconsciousness: Trials and Traumas in the Twentieth Century* (Cambridge, MA: Harvard University Press, 2002), 148.
16. Irmtrud Wojak, "Die Mauer des Schweigens ist durchbrochen," 26. Here I cannot go into details of the differences between private and civil processes and national differences, but here one sees echoes of the tradition of German criminal law, where it is all about the evidence of complicity and guilt of the accused individual. Thus, to participate in a governmental legitimized mass crime is treated here as a single criminal offense, not as a crime against humanity, as at the Nuremberg trials, which were based upon American jurisdiction.
17. Judith Keilbach, *Geschichtsbilder und Zeugen: Zur Darstellung des Nationalsozialismus im Bundesdeutschen Fernsehen* [*Historical Images and Witnesses: Displaying National Socialism in German TV*] (Münster: LIT Verlag, 2008), 138–147.
18. See *Traumatic Stress: The Effects of Overwhelming Experience on Mind, Body, and Society*, ed. Bessel van der Kolk, Alexander McFarlane, and Lars Weisaeth (New York: Guilford Press, 1996); see also: Duncan Bell, *Memory, Trauma and World Politics: Reflections on the Relationship Between Past and Present* (London: Palgrave Macmillan, 2006).
19. Joanna Bourke, "When the torture becomes Humdrum," in *Times Higher Educational Supplement*, February 10, 2006, 19, cited in Bell, *Memory, Trauma and World Politics*, 9.
20. On the Austrian post-war reparations to victims of National Socialism, see, for an overview: *Schlussbericht der Historikerkommission der Republik Österreich: Vermögensentzug während der NS-Zeit sowie Rückstellungen und Entschädigungen*

seit 1945 in Österreich, ed. Clemens Jabloner et al. (Wien-München: Oldenbourg Verlag, 2003) [*Final Report of the Historical Commission of the Republic of Austria: Expropriation during the Nazi Period as well as Restitution and Compensation since 1945* (Publications of the Austrian Historical Commission)].

21. *Nationalfonds der Republik Österreich für Opfer des Nationalsozialismus: 15 Jahre Nationalfonds* (Vol.1: Entwicklung, Aufgaben, Perspektiven; Vol.2: Erinnerungen: Lebensgeschichten von Opfern des Nationalsozialismus) [*National Fund of the Republic of Austria for Victims of National Socialism* (Vol.1: Developments, Tasks, Perspectives; Vol.2: Memoirs: Life Stories of Victims of National Socialism)], Wien 2010. See also several public reports of the NF and GSF; the one from 2008/2009 is available on: http://www.en.nationalfonds.org/docs/Annual_Report_2008_09.pdf.

22. This interview with Ellis [anonymized] and her husband, conducted in German, is part of a larger project, called *The Afterlife of Restitution*, covering about ninety transgenerational interviews, conducted 2007–2009 in Austria, the Netherlands, the United Kingdom, and Argentina by the author, including interviews with ten employees of the NF and GSF.

23. According to the property declaration, the house was valued in July 1938 at 25,000 Reichsmark and was sold by Ellis's step-grandfather in November for 12,000 Reichsmark. After the war, in the 1950s, a restitution process was initiated by his daughters, and the city of Vienna estimated the value of the property around 54,000 Schilling, but the settlement (1953) was then only about 6,000 Schilling; whereas it should have been at least 30,500 Schilling, charged against the former selling price of 7,800 Schilling, which means the value mismatch was about 16,700 Schilling (Decision WA 2/2007 ad 46/2006, 43; brief: Decision 2007).

24. Here it must be noted that about seventy percent of the confiscated property in Vienna was restituted after the war. However, this was often performed under unfair conditions (Jabloner, Schlussbericht, 318f.).

25. Fiorentina Azizi and Günter Gößler, "Extreme Ungerechtigkeit und bewegliches System" ["Extreme Injustice and Dynamic System"], in *Juristische Blätter*, 7 (2006): 415–436.

26. Decision 2007, 5.

27. Ibid., 17.

28. Ibid., 44.

29. Since 1993 it has been possible to reclaim Austrian citizenship (without having to give up one's foreign citizenship), which until 2005 formed the requirement for receiving a pension. See Helga Embacher and Maria Ecker, "A Nation of Victims: How Austria dealt with the victims of the authoritarian Ständestaat and national socialism," in *The Politics of War Trauma: The Aftermath of World War II in Eleven European Countries*, ed. Jolande Withuis and Annet Mooij (Amsterdam: Aksant, 2010), 15–47, 32.

30. Nicole L.Immler, "Restitution and the Dynamics of Memory: A Neglected Trans-Generational Perspective," in *Mediation, Remediation, and the Dynamics of Cultural Memory*, ed. Astrid Erll and Ann Rigney (Berlin, New York: De Gruyter, 2009), 205–228, 220f.

31. Srila Roy, "Of testimony: The pain of speaking and the speaking of pain," present volume, 107. By Molly Andrews, "Beyond narrative: The shape of traumatic testimony," in *Beyond Narrative Coherence*, ed. Matti Hyvärinen, Lars-Christer Hydén, Marja Saarenheimo, and Maria Tamboukou (Amsterdam: John Benjamins Pub Co, 2010), 147–166, 150.

32. Emily Haslam, "Victim Participation at the International Criminal Court: A Triumph of Hope over Experience?" in *The Permanent International Criminal Court: Legal*

and Policy Issues, ed. Dominic McGoldrick, Peter Rowe, and Eric Donnelly (Oxford: Hart, 2004), 315–334.
33. Similarly Paul Gready argues, regarding the South African Truth and Reconciliation Commission, that processes matter as much as products. Paul Gready, "Telling Truth? The Methodological Challenges of Truth Commissions," in *Methods of Human Rights Research*, ed. Fons Coomans, Fred Grünfeld, and Menno T. Kamminga (Antwerp: Intersentia, 2009), 159–185, 175.
34. Luisa Passerini, "Women's Personal Narratives: Myths, Experiences, and Emotions," in *Interpreting Women's Lives: Feminist Theory and Personal Narratives*, ed. Personal Narratives Group (Bloomington, IN: Indiana University Press, 1989), 189–198, 197.

List of Contributors

Nanci Adler is division head of holocaust and genocide studies at the NIOD Institute for War, Holocaust and Genocide Studies (Royal Netherlands Academy of Arts and Sciences, University of Amstserdam), senior researcher, and one of the editors of *Memory and Narrative*. She has worked with oral histories and memoirs of Gulag survivors since the late eighties. She is the author of *Keeping Faith with the Party: Communist Believers Return from the Gulag* (2012), *The Gulag Survivor: Beyond the Soviet System* (2002), *Victims of Soviet Terror: The Story of the Memorial Movement* (1993), and numerous scholarly articles on the Gulag, political rehabilitations, and the consequences of Stalinism. Her current research focuses on transitional justice and the legacy of Communism.

Kelly Jean Butler is an honorary fellow in the School of Historical and Philosophical Studies, University of Melbourne, where she received her PhD in 2010. Her interdisciplinary work explores the place of testimony and memory in public culture, with a specific focus on the way that Australians witness the stories of Aboriginal peoples and asylum seekers. Her work has appeared in the *Journal of Australian Studies* and the collection *Frontier Skirmishes* (2010).

Christiaan Beyers is associate professor of international development studies at Trent University, and director of the Trent in Ecuador Program. His current research focuses on urban land restitution in South Africa, on which he is preparing a book manuscript. His broader interests include citizenship and rights-based struggles, forced displacement, law and justice in transitional states, and theories of narrative, memory, and collective identity.

María Valeria Galván is a sociologist, graduated from the School of Social Sciences of the Universidad Nacional de Buenos Aires (UBA). She holds a master's degree in sociology of culture from the Universidad

Nacional de San Martín (UNSAM) and a PhD in history from the Universidad Nacional de La Plata (UNLP). She is a post-doctoral fellowship holder of the CONICET grant (National Council for Scientific and Technological Research of Argentina), since 2012. She has published numerous articles in Argentina and Brazil on the cultural history of Argentine nationalism in the sixties.

Richard Haynes is senior lecturer and director of Stirling Media Research Institute and director of Graduate Studies for Arts and Humanities, University of Stirling, Scotland. He has published several books on media and sports, including *The Football Imagination: The Rise of Football Fanzine Culture* (1995), *Football in the New Media Age* (2003), *Media Rights and Intellectual Property* (2005), and *Power Play: Sport, The Media and Popular Culture* (2009). His next book will be a history of BBC Television Sport.

Gina Herrmann is associate professor of Spanish literature at the University of Oregon. She is an oral historian, currently completing a book, *Voices of the Vanquished: Spanish Republican Women in War and Prison*, based on two decades of collecting testimonies with survivors of the Franco regime. She is the author of *Written in Red: The Communist Memoir in Spain* (2009).

Nicole L. Immler holds a doctorate in history from the University of Graz and is a researcher at the University of Utrecht. After working at the General Settlement Fund for Victims of National Socialism in Vienna, she started a broad oral-history research project, examining (*The Afterlife of Restitution*) across the generations. Her main fields of interest are Austrian and European memory culture and politics, the historiography and memorialization of the Holocaust, and transitional justice mechanisms. Her publications include *Das Familiengedächtnis der Wittgensteins: Zu verführerischen Lesarten von (auto-)biographischen Texten* (2011) and "Restitution and the Dynamics of Memory: A Neglected Trans-Generational Perspective," in *Mediation, Remediation, and the Dynamics of Cultural Memory* (2009).

Sachiko Kawaura is professor of psychology in the Department of Psychology and Human Relations, School of Humanities, Nanzan University. She is the author of *Pilgrimage to Memories: An Exploration of the Historically Situated Ecological Self through Women's Narratives*

(2003). She combines field and interview research in order to understand people's connections to land. Her current research focuses on collective memories of Native American people whose land-based culture is the basis of their sovereignty.

Selma Leydesdorff is professor of oral history and culture at the University of Amsterdam, and one of the editors of *Memory and Narrative*. Over the last three decades she has worked with interviews of traumatized people and theories of how trauma affects the ability to narrate. Her dissertation, *We Lived with Dignity*, was a starting point for this book. Recently she published *Surviving the Bosnian Genocide: The Women of Srebrenica Speak* (2011). Her latest research has been the creation of a website with life stories of people involved in the Demjanjuk trial, and with the last survivors of Sobibor. Currently she is working on a biography of Sasha Pechersky, leader of the 1943 Sobibor uprising and victim of Nazism and Communism.

Anna Muller is lecturer at the Center for European Studies of the University of Florida. She received a PhD in history from Indiana University, Bloomington, and began working in 2010 as curator and coordinator for an exhibition on concentration camps, forced labor, and the Holocaust at the Museum of the Second World War, a Polish national museum set to open in 2014. Her research interests include twentieth-century Polish and East European history, gender, oral history, and memory studies. She is the author of a number of journal and book articles on Polish Stalinist prisons, oral history, and Polish opposition and resistance movements. She is currently compiling a (Polish-language) volume of interviews with women political prisoners from Eastern Europe.

Andrea Pető is associate professor at the Department of Gender Studies at Central European University. She has also been a Visiting Professor at the Universities of Toronto, Buenos Aires, Stockholm, and Frankfurt. Her books include *Women in Hungarian Politics, 1945–1951* (2003) and *Geschlecht, Politik und Stalinismus in Ungarn: Eine Biographie* (2007). Presently she is working on gendered memory of WWII and political extremisms. The president of the Hungarian Republic awarded her the Officer's Cross Order of Merit of the Republic of Hungary in 2005, and she received the Bolyai Prize from the Hungarian Academy of Sciences in 2006.

Srila Roy is a lecturer in sociology at the University of Nottingham. Her research and teaching focus on gender and feminist theory (especially postcolonial feminism), leftist and feminist social movements, violence and conflict, and memory, trauma, and emotions, with the contemporary political history of India and South Asia as a starting point. She is the author of *Remembering Revolution: Gender, Violence, and Subjectivity in India's Naxalbari Movement* (2012) and the edited volume *New South Asian Feminisms* (2012).

Helen Taylor employed narrative methods in her doctoral research that explored the meaning of home for Greek Cypriot and Turkish Cypriot refugees in London. She has taught a variety of refugee studies courses at the University of East London and has been involved in a number of research projects looking, for example, at education provision for refugee adolescents and the retraining of refugee health professionals. She has also worked as a journalist for many years.

Index

Abad, Irene, 79
Abdurahman (dispossessed South African man), 182–183
Aboriginal and Torres Strait Islander Commission (ATSIC) (Australia), 205
Aboriginal Legal Rights Movement (Australia), 216n60
Aboriginals Ordinance 1918 (Australia), 208
Abrahams, Harold, 167
Abrams, Lynn, xiv
Abu Ghraib, 91
Act VII (Hungary, 1946), 9
Adrienne (Greek Cypriot refugee in London), 42–47, 49
"Age of Testimony," xii
agency, collective, 186
agency, individual, 72, 101, 106–107, 178, 181–182
Agrupación Guerrillera de Levante y Aragón (AGLA), 79, 86
Aguilar, José de, 84
Ahmed, Sara, 5
Akerman, Piers, 199–200, 205, 206–207
Allison, George F., 153, 167, 171–172
Alliss, Peter, 165, 167, 172
Alston, Rex, 167, 169
Alterman, Raúl, 113, 123
American Indian Tribal History Project, 137, 151n21
Amnesty International, 99
Andrews, Molly, 48, 53n28, 102
anti-Communism: *Agrupación Guerrillera de Levante y Aragón* (AGLA), 79; Poland, 56, 58, 70; Tacuara Movement *(Movimiento Nacionalista Tacuara)* (MNT), 111, 112
anti-fascism, xix–xx
anti-liberalism, Tacuara Movement's, 112
anti-Semitism: false testimony, 204; Hungary, 4, 9; Restorative Nationalist Guard, 112; Soviet Union, 22–23, 32; Tacuara Movement, xxiii, 111, 112, 113, 125–126; Tacuara Nationalist Revolutionary Movement, 125
Apfelbaum, Erica, 45
Arapahoes, 134, 136, 151n26
Argentina: disappeared Jews, 115; human rights, 117–118, 120; Laws of Due Obedience and Full Stop *(Obediencia Debida and Punto Final)*, 117; "Liberating Revolution" *(Revolución Libertadora)*, 112; military dictatorship (1976-1983), 115; political violence, 115, 119, 128, 130n24 *(see also* Bank Labor Union's Hospital); state terrorism, 117–118
—political movements: General Confederation of Labour *(Confederación General del Trabajo)* (CGT), 113; Montoneros, 114, 116, 118; Mothers of Plaza de Mayo, 118; New Argentine Movement *(Movimiento Nueva Argentina)* (MNA), 112, 114; Restorative Nationalist Guard *(Guardia Restauradora Nacionalista)* (GRN), 112, 114
Argentine Israelite Mutual Association *(Asociación Mutual Israelita Argentina)* (AMIA), 115
Arlott, John, 162, 163, 166
Armfield, Jimmy, 165
Arrow Cross Party (Hungarian Nazi Party), 13, 14
Assmann, Aleida, xiii
asylum interviews, 41
Atherton, Mike, 165
Atkinson, Ron, 165
audience research, 160
Auschwitz, 12, 40, 220, 222
Australia: Aboriginal and Torres Strait Islander Commission (ATSIC), 205; *Aboriginals Ordinance 1918,* 208; *Bringing Them Home* (HREOC report), xxv, 199–202, 209, 308; Council for

Aboriginal Reconciliation, 202; *Cubillo v. Commonwealth* (2000), 200, 205, 208–210; Hindmarsh Island Affair, 210–211, 216n60; reconciliation and apology, need for, 201–202, 214n16; Reconciliation Convention (1997), 202
Australian indigenous people, 199–213; Aboriginal Legal Rights Movement, 216n60; *Bringing Them Home* (HREOC report), xxv, 199–202, 209, 308; burden of proof, 209; child removal as genocide, 201, 206, 213n6; compensation for, 203; conservative media responses to, 200, 204–208, 211–212; *Cubillo v. Commonwealth* "test case," 200, 205, 208–210; diversity among, 213n1; "false memory syndrome," accusations of, xxv–xxvi, 206; false testimonies, cases of, 203–204, 210, 212–213; Hindmarsh Island Bridge controversy, 200, 205, 210–211, 216n60; national apology to, 199, 202, 203, 214n16; Ngarrindjeri women, 210–211, 216n60; non-Indigenous disbelief, xxv; O'Donoghue controversy, Lowitja, 200; popular culture denial of their testimony, 211; restricted knowledge claims, 210–211; right to testify, denial of, xxv–xxvi; secondary witnesses, need for, 200, 201, 212; "stolen generation" of, 199
Australian non-indigenous people, 199–212; accusing indigenes of "false memory syndrome," xxv–xxvi, 206; affirming "white truth," 211; calling for "practical reconciliation," 202–203; charging indigenes with maligning national history, 211; demanding documentary evidence from indigenes, 209; refusing to witness indigenes' testimony, xxv, 203–204; secondary witnesses among, 202
—refuseniks: Akerman, Piers, 199–200, 205, 206; Bolt, Andrew, 199–200, 205–206, 207, 208, 210, 211; Devine, Frank, 205; Duffy, Michael, 205; Howard, John, 199–200, 202–203, 206, 211; McGuinness, P. P., 206; Pearson, Christopher, 205; Q'Loughlin, Maurice, 209; *Quadrant* (journal), 205, 206
Austrian compensation to victims of National Socialism, 223–231; "Washington Agreement," 224–225
autobiography of athletes, 154–164; ghost-writing, 161–162; male autobiographical tradition, 162; memory, 156, 159; sociology, 157–158; third person presentation, 163
Bajohr, Frank, 221
Bakhtin, Mikhail, xxv, 185–186
Balza, Martín, 117
Bank Labor Union's Hospital *(Policlinico bancario* of Buenos Aires), robbery of: Tacuara, 114, 122; television special about, 123–124
—participants: Nell, José Luis, 122; Rossi, Horacio, 116
Bardini, Roberto, 119–120
Barra, Rodolfo Carlos, 115
Basingstoke Boy (Arlott), 163
Battle of the Little Bighorn (1876), 136, 137
Battle of the Rosebud Creek (1876), 136
Baxter, Joe, 113, 120–121
Baxter, Peter, 165
BBC sports broadcasting, 153–173; audience research, 160; class, 158; commentary, first running, 167; commentary techniques, 156, 169–171; commentators, xxiv, 161, 164, 165, 166–169
Beckham, David, 161
Beckman, Karen, 91–92
Benaud, Richie, 165, 166, 167, 172
Bent's Fort (Colorado), 134
Berlant, Lauren, 104
Bibó, István, 7
biographical research in sociology, 157
Black, Roger, 165
Black Farce and Cue Ball Wizards (Everton), 162
Black Kettle (Cheyenne chief), 137
Bloch, Marc, 178
Blofeld, Henry, 165, 166
Bolt, Andrew, 199–200, 205–206, 207, 208, 210, 211
Born, Jorge, 130n20
Bourdieu, Pierre, 16
Brayton (dispossessed South African woman), 185, 192, 194
Brezhnev, Leonid, 29
Briggs, Asa, 157
Brison, Susan, 101
Brooks, Peter, 14, 15
Bugajski, Ryszard, 55, 72n2
Bureau of Indian Affairs, 139
Burns, Conrad, 151n21
Butler, Judith, 107

Caffatti, Jorge, 120–121
Campbell, Kristen, 14–15
Carmen, Leon, 204
Carpenter, Harry, 167
Carr, E. H., 48
Caruth, Cathy, 102
Cassirer, Ernst, 6
Chacón, Dulce, 82
Chapman, Tom, 211
Chapman, Wendy, 211
Charmaine (dispossessed South African woman), 185, 188–193, 194, 195
Cheyenne people: Executive Order (1884), 135, 138; Fort Laramie Treaty (1851), 136; General Allotment Act (1926), 139, 151n26; Sand Creek Massacre (1864), 137; separation between Northern and Southern, 134–135
—individual: Black Kettle, 137; Sweet Medicine, 135, 139; Two Moons, 138; White Bull, 138
Chivington, John M., 137
Chmielewska, Maria Walicka (Polish political prisoner), 61
Clarke, Jennifer, 209
Coe, Sebastian, 164
Cold War anti-fascist rhetoric, xix, 16
Coleman, David, 164–165, 167
collective agency, 186
collective memory, xvii–xviii, xxiii–xxiv, 72, 133–134, 136–139, 141–142, 144, 145–149
collectivizing intentionality, 194
Columbia Center for Oral History, xv, xvii
Commission for the Restitution of Land Rights (South Africa), 177
Communism: children of Gulag prisoners, xiv, xx, 19, 26, 28, 29–30; Soviet Communism, 34
Communist Party, Hungary, 5–6, 7, 8, 11
Communist Party, Soviet Union: banning, constitutionality of, 20; children of Gulag prisoners, xx, 20–24, 27–28; demise of, 19; "One Hundred Questions, One Hundred Answers" (manual), 28; released Gulag prisoners' continuing support for, 24, 26, 28, 32–33; XX Party Congress, 24, 28
Communist Party, Spain, 80
community, 189–197; as basis for restitution claims, xxv, 177; as a potentiality, 193, 197; as a way of speaking, 196

Contested Pasts (Radstone and Hodgkin), xvii
Corcuera, Javier, 81
Council for Aboriginal Reconciliation (Australia), 202
Crenzel, Emilio, 130n23
Crissel, Andrew, 153
Crow Indian Reservation, 138
Cuban Revolution, 112
Cubillo, Lorna, 208–210
Cubillo v. Commonwealth (Australia, 2000), 200, 205, 208–210
Cubitt, Geoffrey, 156
Cuevas, Tomasa (Spanish anti-fascist political prisoner), 81, 83, 84, 85, 87
Curthoys, Ann, 209
Custer, George A., 137
Cypriot refugees in London, 37–53; Greek refugees, xxi, 38, 42, 51, 52n2; Turkish refugees, xxi, 38, 42, 50–51, 52n2; weeping Panagia (Virgin Mary) icon, story about, xxi, 42–45
—individual: Adrienne (Greek woman), 42–47, 49; Dimitris (Greek man), 47–48, 50; Emine (Turkish woman), 51; Maroulla (Greek woman), 49–50; Salih (Turkish man), 47–48
Cyprus, 38, 44, 50
Czaplińska, Ruta (Polish political prisoner), 58, 61, 62, 65, 69–72

Dalby, W. Barrington, 167
Dandan, Alejandra, 121
Darlington Agency, 136
Das, Veena, 106, 110n45
Davies, Barry, 165, 167
Dawson, Carrie, 204
Demidenko/Darville, Helen, 204
Denzin, Norman, 47
Devine, Frank, 205
dialogism, 186
dialogue, xxv, 185–186, 194
Dimbleby, Jonathan, 161
Dimitris (Greek Cypriot refugee in London), 47–48, 50
Dirección General de Seguridad detention facility (Madrid), 83
District Six in Cape Town, South Africa, 177–193; Cape Flats, 178; community, past, xxv, 177, 189, 190; District Six Museum, 180; Guguletu townships compared to, 189–190; "white" District Sixers, 181

—dispossessed District Sixers: Abdurahman, 182–183; Brayton, 185, 192, 194; Charmaine, 185, 188–193, 194, 195; Fatima, 183; Jansen, Irene, 182; Nomsa, 185, 188–193, 194, 195; Nweti, 185, 187–193, 194, 195; Shamil, 182; Teresa, 185, 188–189, 191–193, 194
Dodson, Mick, 201
Duffy, Michael, 205
Duhalde, Eduardo Luis, 118
Dull Knife (Northern Cheyenne chief), 133, 136

Eichmann, Adolf, 113, 126
Eichmann trial (1961): Israeli identify, 6; victims' testimonies, xix, xxvi, 4, 6, 222
Ellis's restitution case (Austria), 225–232, 235n23
Emine (Turkish Cypriot refugee in London), 51
"emotional capital," 16
emotional communities, 5
emotionalism, 8
emotions: devaluing of, xix; expression in People's Tribunals (Hungary), 4, 5, 6, 10, 11, 12, 16; reliability of, 6
"encounter killings," 98
Endre, László, 3–4
Erect Horns (So'taeo'o prophet), 135
Everton, Clive, 162
evidence: autobiography as documentary evidence, xxiv; courts, xviii–xix; discrepancies in memories equated to lying, 205; evidence of ownership vs. evidence of belonging, 184–185; forced-migration researchers, 37–38; history, xi–xii; land restitution law, 194; of a moral kind, 179, 184, 187–188; as a product of dialogue, xxiv; spurious evidence, fabrication of, xix; truth, xi–xii; victims' testimonies, ix, xix
Evtushenko, Evgenii, 33
Exile and Identity (Jolluck), 57
Exodus from Indian Territory (1878), xxiii, 133, 138, 140, 147, 148

"false memory syndrome," xii, xxv–xxvi, 206
Fatima (dispossessed South African woman), 183
Federal Compensation Act (BEG, 1952) (Germany), 221–222

Felman, Shoshana, 4, 100, 201, 207
Fentress, James, 57
Feofanov, Iurii, 21
forced-migration researchers, 37–38
Fortunoff collection (Yale University), xvi
Fragments (Wilkomirski), 207–208
Franco dictatorship (1939-1975), survivors of. *See* Martínez, Esperanza; Montero, Remedios
Freeman, Cathy, 210
Freeman, Mark, 39
Fry, C. B., 168–169

Galimberti, Rodolfo, 116–117, 130n20
Galtieri, Leopoldo F., 18
Gasparini, Juan, 121
Gauri (Naxalbari movement member), 99, 108n14
General Allotment Act (1926), 139, 151n26
Genovese, Ann, 209
German Forced Labour Project, xvi
Germany: compensation for victims of Nazism, 221; criminal law, 234n16; media interest in victims' testimonies, 222–223; Nuremberg trials (1945-1946), 4, 220, 234n16
Glendenning, Raymond, 167, 171–172
Goot, Murray, 214n16
Gorbachev, Mikhail, xx, 23, 29, 31
Goschler, Constantin, 221–222
Gourevitch, Phillip, 207
Goya, Jorge Guillermo, 118
Gray, Andy, 165
Green, Alan, 165, 166
Grele, Ronald J., xv, 60
Gross, Andrew, 208
Gross, Jan, xiv
Gudmunsdottir, Gunnthorunn, 159
Guerrilleras, memoria de una esperanza (Martínez), 85
Guguletu township, South Africa, 185, 187, 188–189, 192
Guha, Archana (Naxalbari movement member), 99, 104, 105–106, 108n14
Guha, Lakita (Naxalbari movement member), 99–107; legal battle against custodial violence ("Archana Guha case"), 99, 108n14, 109n34; performative speech acts, xxii–xxiii, 101, 104; social recognition, 106, 108n14; torture, 99, 100; traumatization, xxii

Guha, Saumen (Naxalbari movement member), 99–100, 103, 104, 108n14, 109n34, 109n35
Gulag prisoners, 22–29; "conveyor-belt" interrogations, 23; "Doctors' Plot," 22–23; perestroika, 25, 31; Polish females, xxi–xxii; wives of "enemies of the people," 28
—individual: Il'in, Il'ia L'vivich, 27; Il'ina, Mariia Markovna, 27; Ioffe, Adolf, 22; Ioffe, Nadezhda, 22, 32; Markovich, Vladimir Solomonovich, 23; Rappaport, Iakov, 22–23; Shtern, Evgeniia Aleksandrovna, 23–24
Gulag prisoners, children of, xiv, xx, 19–35; indoctrination of, xx, 19, 21; Komsomol, membership in, 22, 24, 27; Memorial, membership in, 25; perestroika, 25
—individual: Ioffe, Natasha, 22, 32; Kuznetsova, Mariia Il'inichna, 26–27; Medvedev, Roy, 21–22, 32; Rappaport, Nataliia, 22–23; Smirnova, Evgeniia Vladimirovna, 23–26; Stepanov, D., 20–21, 32
Gunner, Peter, 208–209
Gutman, Daniel, 119, 126

"hackiography," 162
Halbmayer, Brigitte, 93n2
Halbwach, Maurice, xvii, 133–134
Half-Time: The Mike and Me (Wakelam), 167
Hand that Signed the Paper, The (Demidenko/Darville), 204
Hansen, Alan, 165
Hartman, Geoffrey, 49
Hedgepeth, Sonja, 78
Heguy, Silvina, 121
"Heirs to Stalin" (Evtushenko), 33
Historia de Celia (Montero), 87
Historical Commission (Austria), 224, 225
history: autobiography, xxiv, 156–160, 164, 170–171; changing vocabularies in interpreting, x–xi; evidence, xi–xii; individual perspective on, 158–159; jurisprudence, xviii; media history, 155; memory, xi–xii, 148, 156; oral sources, xvi; "recovery history," xiv; sociology, xv; of sports, 165; truth, xi–xii
Hitchens, Christopher, 91
Hitler, Adolf, 126
Hodgkin, Kate, xvii

Hoffman, Michael, 208
Holocaust: desire to bear witness *vs.* desire to forget, 49; false testimonies, 207–208; legal language for remembering, 8; testimonial evidence of gender violence, 78
Holocaust (German television series), 222
Howard, John, 199–200, 202–203, 206, 211
human rights, 117–118, 120, 203, 232
Hungary, 3–11; anti-Semitism, 4, 9; Arrow Cross Party (Hungarian Nazi Party), 13, 14; Communist Party, 5–6, 7, 8, 11; Criminal Code, 11; impermissibility of speaking about wartime events, 4; reconciliation in post-war, 15; transitional justice, 9–10; during World War II, 7
Hurricane Katrina, xiii
Hussain, Nasser, 165

Il'ina, Mariia Markovna, 27
India, 98–101; custodial violence, legal battle against ("Archana Guha case"), 99, 100–101 (*see also entries beginning with* "Guha,"); land issues, 98; political violence, 98–99
Infant of Prague, 88
International Criminal Court (ICC), 219, 232
international justice, typology of, 7–8
Interrogation (film), 55–56, 57, 72n2
Into the Wind (Reith), 157
Ioffe, Adolf, 22
Ioffe, Nadezhda, 22, 32
Ioffe, Natasha, 22, 32

Jackson, Colin, 168, 169
Jackson, Michael, 46
James, Daniel, 66
Janet, Pierre, 108n4
Jankó, Péter, 14
Jewish victims of Nazi persecution, xxvi
Johnston, Brian, 165, 166, 167
Jolluck, Katherine, xxi, 57, 63
Joly, Maud, 77, 79
Journey from the Fall (film), xii
justice, international, typology of, 7–8
justice, street, 7
Juventud Peronista (JP, Peronist Youth), 118, 130n20

Kartinyeri, Doreen, 210–211
Keilbach, Judith, 223
Khouri, Norma, 204

Khruschev, Nikita, 24
Kirchner, Néstor, 111, 117–118
Knudsen, John Chr., 41
Koolmatrie, Wanda, 204
Krysia (Polish political prisoner), 62
Kuznetsova, Mariia Il'inichna, 26–31, 33

La guerrilla de la memoria (film), 81
La Nacion (newspaper), 116
La voz dormida (Chacón), 82
LaCapra, Dominick, 12
Lakita. *See* Guha, Lakita
Laub, Dori: empathic listeners, xxv, 200; Fortunoff collection (Yale University), xvi
Laws of Due Obedience and Full Stop *(Obediencia Debida and Punto Final)* (Argentina), 117
Lejeune, Philippe, 203
Lenin, V. I., 29, 30, 31
Let History Judge (Medvedev), 21
"Liberating Revolution" *(Revolución Libertadora)* (Argentina), 112
Life's New Hurdles (Jackson), 168
Little Bighorn Battlefield National Monument, 137
Little Wolf (Northern Cheyenne chief), 133, 136
Longhurst, Henry, 170–171
Los malditos caminos (documentary film), 121–123
Lowe, Ted, 167
Ludkiewicz, Ewa (Polish political prisoner), 58, 65, 67–69, 71
Lughod, Lila Abu-, 11
Luker, Trish, 209
Lynam, Des, 165

MacPherson, Archie, 165
Malta Cross, 127
Manne, Robert, 211–212
Marfleet, Philip, 41
"Maria Cristina me quiere dominar" (song), 83, 84–85, 92
Markovich, Vladimir Solomonovich, 23
Martínez, Esperanza (Spanish anti-fascist political prisoner), 79–85, 89, 90, 92–93
Maskell, Dan, 165
mass atrocity, memory in study of, xii
Mauthausen Documentation Project, xvi
McGrath, Ann, 209
McGuinness, P. P., 206

McLaren, Bill, 165, 166, 169
Medvedev, Roy, 21–22, 32
Memorias de una guerrillera (docudrama), 79, 87–92
memory, xi–xii, xvii–xviii, xxii–xxvi, 125, 148, 156, 159; personal memory, xvii–xviii, xxiii–xxiv, 156; reliability, xii; remembering through autobiography, 156; self-censorship, xi, xx; social memory, 57; warps and wefts of, ix
memory communities, xii–xiii
Menem, Carlos Saúl, 111, 115, 130n20, 130n25
Miles, Nelson A., 138
"Miles' promise," 138–139, 149
Miller, Nancy, 103
Mink, Louis, ix
MNA. *See* New Argentine Movement
MNRT. *See* Tacuara Nationalist Revolutionary Movement
MNT. *See* Tacuara Movement
Montero, Remedios (Spanish anti-fascist political prisoner), 79–82, 85–93
Montoneros, 114, 116, 118
Moore, Brian, 165
Morin, Edgar, 120
Mothers of Plaza de Mayo, 118
Motson, John, 165
Mujeres de las Resistencia (Cuevas), 81
My Own Sweet Time (Koolmatrie), 204

Narrating Our Pasts (Tonkin), xvii
Narrative and Genre (Chamberlin and Thompson), xvii
National Armed Union *(Narodowy Zwiqzek Wojskowy)* (Poland), 70
Naxalbari movement (India) supporters: Gauri, 99, 108n14; Guha, Archana, 99, 104, 105–106, 108n14; Guha, Lakita (*see* Guha, Lakita); Guha, Saumen, 99–100, 103, 104, 108n14, 109n34, 109n35
Nazism, victims of, accounts of, 220–223
Nell, José Luis, 113, 122, 124
Nellie (Northern Cheyenne Indian), 142–144, 147, 148
New Argentine Movement *(Movimiento Nueva Argentina)* (MNA), 112, 114
Ngarrindjeri women (Australia), 210–211, 216n60
Ngcelwane, Nomvuyo, 192, 193, 195
Nichols, Bill, 86

Nietzsche, Friedrich, 97
Nike (Polish periodical), 60–72; former female political prisoners, depiction of, 56–57, 59, 60–72, 74n27; mode of narration, 62, 72
Nolan, Maggie, 204
Nomsa (dispossessed South African woman), 185, 188–193, 194, 195
Nora, Pierre, xiii
North Australian Aboriginal Legal Aid Service, 208
North Woman (Northern Cheyenne woman), 136
Northern Cheyenne, 133–152; adoption system, 141; anti-Cheyenne movements, 138; Battle of the Little Bighorn (1876), 136; Battle of the Rosebud Creek (1876), 136; collective memory of ancestral sacrifice, xxiii, 133–134, 141–142, 144, 145–149; Darlington Agency, 136; Executive Order (1900), 135; General Allotment Act (1926), 139, 151n26; House Concurrent Resolution 108 (1953), 139; hunting, 145, 146–147; "Miles' promise" to, 138–139, 149; military societies, 135; non-Indians, attitudes toward, 140, 142, 143; Northern Arapahoes, treaty with, 136; original homeland, 134; Post Traumatic Stress Disorder (PTSD), 146–147; traditional ways of life, 141, 145, 148, 152n42; tribal identity, 133, 147, 149; Vietnam War, military service in, 146–147
—individual: Dull Knife, 133, 136; Erect Horns, 135; Frank, 140–142, 147, 148; Little Wolf, 133, 136; Nellie, 142–144, 147, 148; North Woman, 136; Stone, 144–147; Woodenlegs, 139
Northern Cheyenne Sand Creek Massacre Historic Site Project team, 137
Noticias (magazine), 114–115
Nunca Más (National Commission on the Disappearance of Persons), 118
Nuremberg trials (1945-1946), 4, 220, 234n16
Nweti (dispossessed South African woman), 185, 187–193, 194, 195

O'Donoghue, Lowitja, 200, 205–206, 210
O'Hehir, Michael, 165
Olick, Jeffrey K., 148–149
Oliver, Kelly, 213
On the Genealogy of Morals (Nietzsche), 97, 107
Operación Rosaura (Argentine television show), 123–124
oral history: early years of, xiv; generalization, doubts about, xiv, xv, 39; historical context, xii–xiii, xv; international projects, xvi–xvii; "recovery history," xiv; shared imagination, xvi; victims' testimonies, 219
Order Has Been Carried Out, The (Portelli), xvi
Orlandini, Juan Esteban, 121
O'Sullivan, Peter, 167
Otwinowska, Barbara, 74n27
Ovett, Steve, 164

pain: bearing witness to someone else's, 99, 102–103, 106; inexpressibility of, 97–98; mnemonics, 97; patriarchal categories of speech, 98
Passerini, Luisa, xv–xvi, 86, 90–91, 232–233
Passponti, Darwin, 126–127
Paxman, Jeremy, 161
Pearson, Christopher, 205
Penner, D'Ann R., xiii
People's Revolutionary Army *(Ejército Revolucionario del Pueblo)* (ERP), 118
People's Tribunals (Hungary), 3–18; as anti-fascist courts, xix–xx, 16; Communist Party, Hungary, 5–6, 8, 11; defense attorneys, 15; emotions, expression of, 4, 5, 6, 10, 11, 12, 16; Endre, László, trial of, 3–4; evidence, types of, 12–13; gender, 5; hegemonic memory of events, construction of, 13; initial trials, 15; investigative phase, 8; Jewish identity, obscuring of, 9; legal language for remembering the Holocaust, 8; "material truth" *vs.* "psychic truth," 14; meaning, construction of, 13, 15; Nuremberg trials (1945-1946) compared to, 4; objective truth, reconstruction of, 12; "Old Hungary," resistance to, 11–12; post-war normalization, xix, 5–6; press coverage, 13; reconciliation in postwar Hungary, 15; Szálasi, Ferenc, trial of, 14; victims' testimonies, 4–5, 13–14; witnesses, 15
Perkins, Charles, 210
Perón, Juan Domingo, 111, 130n20
Places of Memory (Nora), xiii
Poland, women in, 63–64, 72

Polish female political prisoners, 55–72; agency, individual, 72; anti-Communist groups, 56, 58, 70; anti-Nazi resistance, 58, 65; empowerment, search for, 64–65; gender issues, 57–58, 63–64, 65, 67, 72, 74n27; interrogations, 61–62, 68; life after release, 56, 59, 70; National Armed Union *(Narodowy Związek Wojskowy),* 70; *Nike* periodical, depiction in, 56–57, 59, 60–72, 74n27; pride and dignity, maintenance of, xxi–xxii, 56, 60, 63; regrets, 68, 70–71; sexual violence in prison, 63–64, 74n27; Tonia (character in *Interrogation*), disapproval of, 55–56, 60, 62–63, 72; women deported to Siberia, 57, 63; women soldiers, rights of, 66–67
—individual: Chmielewska, Maria Walicka, 61; Czaplińska, Ruta, 58, 61, 62, 65, 69–72; Krysia, 62; Ludkiewicz, Ewa, 58, 65, 67–69, 71; Tomalakowa, Irena, 74n27; Zawacka, Elżbieta, 58, 65–67, 70–71; Żurowska, Halina, 61
Portelli, Alessandro, xv–xvi, 40, 44, 59–60
Post Traumatic Stress Disorder (PTSD), 146–147, 223
Powder River Expedition (1865), 135
Powles, Julia, 38
pragmatism, 8
Preston, Paul, 78, 79, 82
Putin, Vladimir, 31

Q'Loughlin, Maurice, 209
Quadrant (Australian journal), 205, 206

Radstone, Susannah, xvii
Rajan, Sunder, 105
Rappaport, Iakov, 22–23
Rappaport, Nataliia, 22–23, 32
Reconciliation Convention (Australia, 1997), 202
reenactments, 86–92
refugees, xx, 41, 46, 49–50, 51; personal narratives in researching, 38–39; political opinions, 48, 52n2; researchers, 41–42, 47–49, 51
Regimes of Memory (Radstone and Hodgkin), xvii
Reilly, Alexander, 209
Reith, John, 157
Restorative Nationalist Guard *(Guardia Restauradora Nacionalista)* (GRN) (Argentina), 112, 114

Ricoeur, Paul, 180–181
Ridd, Rosemary, 183
Riessman, Catherine, 40
Roberts, Brian, 157, 158
Robertson, Max, 167
Rome Statute (1998), 219
Rooney, Wayne, 161, 162
Rosaldo, Renate, 16
Rose, Deborah Bird, 212
Rossi, Horacio, 116
Rowse, Tim, 214n16
Roy, Srila, 231
Rudd, Kevin, 199, 202, 203
Runu Guha Neogi, 99, 100

Saidel, Rochelle, 78
Salgari, Emilio, 127
Salón de Cerveceros (Beer Workers Union Hall) confrontation, 123
Sanctuary movement, 46
Saquito, Nico, 84
Schrager, Samuel, 48
Scilingo, Adolfo, 117
Second World War, xvi
sexual violence: from Holocaust to Franco, 77–79; Jewish women during the *Shoah,* 78; Polish female political prisoners, 63–64, 74n27; prohibition against communicating cases of, 77–78; South African townships, 190, 192; Spanish Civil War, 77, 78; Spanish female anti-fascist political prisoners, xxii, 81, 82, 83–85, 89; testimonial evidence, 78–79
Sexual Violence against Jewish Women during the Holocaust (Hedgepeth and Saidel), 78, 85
Shamil (dispossessed South African man), 182
Shoah Visual Foundation, xvi
Shtern, Evgeniia Aleksandrovna, 23–24
Sieveking Lance, 167, 170
Sirota, Graciela Narcisa, 113
Śliwiński, Władysław, 67
Smirnova, Evgeniia Vladimirovna, 23–26, 33
Snyder, Jack, 7–8
Sobibor, survivors of, xiv
social memory, 57
sociology, xv, 48, 157–158
Sommer, Doris, 86
So'taeo'o people, 134, 135
South Africa: Commission for the Restitution of Land Rights, 177; Guguletu

Index 249

township, 185, 187, 188–189, 192; Mixed Marriages Act, 189; race-consciousness, 189; sexual violence in townships, 190, 192; Truth and Reconciliation Commission (TRC), xxiv–xxv, 102, 236n33

Southern Cheyenne people, 134–135, 136, 151n26

Soviet Communism, 34

Soviet Union: anti-Semitism, 22–23, 32; Communist Party, xx, 19, 20; dissident movement (1960s–1980s), 29; "Doctors' Plot," 22–23; perestroika, 25, 31; Stalinist past, view of, 33

Spain: anti-Communism, 79–80; Franco dictatorship, 78

Spanish Civil War (1936-1939), 77, 78

Spanish female anti-fascist political prisoners, 77–95; baby Jesus figurine, refusal to kiss, 81–82, 85–93; competing discourses, 92; *La guerrilla de la memoria* (film), 81; *La voz dormida* (Chacón), 82; life after release, 80–81; *Memorias de una guerrillera* (docudrama), 79, 87–92; *Mujeres de las Resistencia* (Cuevas), 81; torture, 81, 83–85, 89, 92; Valencia's prison for women, 85–86

—individual: Cuevas, Tomasa, 81, 83, 84, 85; Martínez, Esperanza, 79–85, 89, 90, 92–93; Montero, Remedios, 79–82, 85–93

Spanish Holocaust, The (Preston), 78, 82

speech acts: Bakhtin, Mikhail, 185–186; Guha, Lakita (Naxalbari movement member), xxii–xxiii, 101, 104; victims' testimonies, 231

Spielberg, Steven, xvi

sports television, studies of, 153–154. See also BBC sports broadcasting

Srebrenica, survivors of, xiv

Stalin, Josef, 21, 29, 33

Stepanov, D. (son of executed Gulag prisoner), 20–21, 32

Stone (Northern Cheyenne Indian), 144–147, 148

Svasek, Maruska, 9

"Swiss Nazi Gold Bank" affair, 223

Szálasi, Ferenc, 14

Tacuara Movement *(Movimiento Nacionalista Tacuara)* (MNT) (Argentina), 111–128; activists' memories, 125–128; changes in memory regimes, 117–121; contemporaries' view of, 113–114; films about, 121–125; former activists' memories, 125–128; Hitler, admiration for, 126; kidnapping by, 113; leftist militants of the seventies, 128; Malta Cross, 127; Nazi iconography/ideology, 124, 127; *Noticias* weekly magazine, 114–115; *Ofensiva* (Offensive) publication, 124; symbols, 113, 124; torture by, 113

—members: Bardini, Roberto, 119, 120; Baxter, Joe, 120; Caffatti, Jorge, 120; Galimberti, Rodolfo, 116–117; Gasparini, Juan, 121; Orlandini, Juan Esteban, 121; Rossi, Horacio, 116

Tacuara Nationalist Revolutionary Movement *(Movimiento Nacionalista Revolucionario Tacuara)* (MNRT) (Argentina): Bank Labor Union's Hospital *(Policlinico bancario* of Buenas Aires), robbery of, 114, 122; Cuban Revolution, 112, 113–114; Peronist left, 125

—members: Bardini, Roberto, 119; Baxter, Joe, 120; Caffatti, Jorge, 120; Gasparini, Juan, 121; Nell, José Luis, 122; Rossi, Horacio, 116

testimony: human rights campaigns, 203; individual healing, 101–102, 105; performative aspects, xxii–xxiii, xxvi, 87, 101, 104; sharing pain through, 106–107; tribal testimony, 133; of victims (*see* victims' testimonies)

Thompson, Paul, xv

Tolson, Andrew, 153, 170

Tomalakowa, Irena (Polish political prisoner), 74n27

Tonia (character in *Interrogation*), 55–56, 60, 62–63, 72

Tonkin, Elisabeth, xvii

torture: Guha, Lakita (Naxalbari movement member), 99, 100; Spanish female anti-fascist political prisoners, 81, 83–85, 89, 92; Tacuara Movement *(Movimiento Nacionalista Tacuara)* (MNT), 113; traumatization by, xxii

Tougaw, Jason, 103

transitional justice: collective and individual memories, xvii–xviii; Memory of WWII and Transitional Justice (project), 6; truth commissions, 219; victims' testimonies, xxvi, 203, 232

Trastulli, Luigi, death of, 40, 44

trauma: Post Traumatic Stress Disorder (PTSD), 146–147, 223; re-victimization

of victims, 223; stories of, 97, 102, 104, 105; victims' testimonies as expression of trauma rather than events, 207
truth: evidence, xi–xii; historical context, x; history, xi–xii; "material truth" vs. "psychic truth," 14; memory, x–xi, 212; personal narratives, 39–41; secondary witnesses, need for, 203, 212; victims' testimonies, ix–xi, xxvii
Truth and Reconciliation Commission (TRC) (South Africa), xvii, xxiv–xxv, 102, 236n33
Tsetséhestáhase people, 134, 135
Turner, Victor, 10
Two Moons (Cheyenne chief), 138

Vergara, Pau, 79, 82, 87
victims' rights, 219
victims' testimonies: about the Holocaust, 40, 49, 222; agency, individual, 46, 72, 101–102; bearing witness to someone else's pain, 99, 102–103, 106; co-testimony, 178, 179, 180–181, 186; desire to bear witness vs. desire to forget, xxi, 49–50; Eichmann trial (1961), xix, xxvi, 4, 6, 222; emotional content, xix, 6; factual inaccuracies, 40, 45–46; false testimonies, 203–204, 207–208, 211, 212–213; human rights regimes, 232; legal use of, xiii–xiv; official history vs., xxiv–xxvii, 136–138; power of a system to control individual's appraisals of events, 32; secondary witnesses' acknowledgment of, 200, 201, 203, 212; Truth and Reconciliation Commission (TRC) (South Africa), xxiv–xxv; truth value, ix–xi, 39–41; variability over time, 39–40, 49
Vidal Castaño, José Antonio, 84, 86, 87

Videla, Jorge Rafael, 118
Vietnamese refugees, xii
Vinjamuri, Leslie, 7–8

Waddell, Sid, 165
Wakelam, H. B. T., 167, 169, 170, 171–172
Walker, Murray, 165, 166, 172
Waring, Eddie, 161
"Washington Agreement" (Austria and United States), 224–225
Watson, Irene, 211
West, Peter, 168–169
Westerman, William, 46
Whannel, Garry, 165
White Bull (Cheyenne chief), 138
Whitlock, Gillian, 201, 204
Wickham, Chris, 57
Wiedergutmachung, 223
Wiesel, Elie, xii
Wilkomirski, Binjamin, 207–208
Wilson, Richard, xviii
Wilson, Ronald, 201
Wiśniewska, Maria, 64
Wolstenholme, Kenneth, 164–165, 167, 168
Woodenlegs (Northern Cheyenne President), 139
World War II, xvi, 6, 7

Yaeger, Patricia, 90
Yellowstone Western Heritage Center, 137, 151n21
Yugoslavia Tribunal, xviii–xix

Zawacka, Elżbieta (Polish political prisoner), 58, 65–67, 70–71
Zeitzeuge, 222–223
Zeuge, 222–223
Żurowska, Halina (Polish political prisoner), 61